Acquiring, Using, And Protecting Water In Colorado

Trout, Witwer & Freeman, P.C.
1120 Lincoln Street, Suite 1600
Denver, Colorado 80203
(303) 861-1963
(303) 832-4465 (fax)
www.troutlaw.com

BRADFORD PUBLISHING COMPANY
Denver, Colorado

DISCLAIMER

This book is intended to provide general information with regard to the subject matter covered. It is not meant to provide legal opinions or to offer advice, nor to serve as a substitute for advice by licensed, legal, or other professionals. This book is sold with the understanding that Bradford Publishing Company and the author(s), by virtue of its publication, are not engaged in rendering legal or other professional services to the reader.

Bradford Publishing Company and the author(s) do not warrant that the information contained in this book is complete or accurate, and do not assume and hereby disclaim any liability to any person for any loss or damage caused by errors, inaccuracies, omissions, or usage of this book.

Laws, and interpretations of those laws, change frequently, and the subject matter of this book can have important legal consequences that may vary from one individual to the next. It is therefore the responsibility of the reader to know whether, and to what extent, this information is applicable to his or her situation, and if necessary, to consult legal, tax, or other counsel.

Library of Congress Cataloging-in-Publication Data

Acquiring, using, and protecting water in Colorado / Trout, Witwer & Freeman, P.C.
    p. cm.
  ISBN 1-883726-98-0
  1. Water--Law and legislation--Colorado. 2. Water rights--Colorado. I. Trout, Witwer & Freeman. II. Title.

  KFC2246.A937 2004
  346.78804'32--dc22

                    2004016454

Cover design by Brent Beltrone
Acquiring, Using, and Protecting Water in Colorado
ISBN: 1-883726-98-0

Published 2004 by Bradford Publishing Company
1743 Wazee Street, Denver, Colorado 80202
www.bradfordpublishing.com

ABOUT THE AUTHORS

Trout, Witwer & Freeman, P.C.

Robert V. Trout is a shareholder, director, and officer of Trout, Witwer & Freeman, P.C., a Denver, Colorado law firm specializing in water rights, environmental law, and related matters. He received his undergraduate degree in mathematics and computer science from Dartmouth College, graduating *magna cum laude* in 1971, and received his J.D. degree from the University of Pennsylvania Law School, also graduating *magna cum laude*, in 1974. He was a Comment Editor of the *University of Pennsylvania Law Review* from 1972 to 1974 and a law clerk to Judge Walter R. Mansfield of the U.S. Court of Appeals for the Second Circuit in New York City from 1974 to 1975. He moved to Denver, Colorado in 1975 and joined Davis, Graham & Stubbs, where he became a partner in 1981. In 1992, along with two former partners, he founded his present law firm. He has more than 28 years of experience practicing water rights and related environmental law. He has taught water rights law at the University of Denver Law School and has been a lecturer and author on water rights and environmental law topics for many years. His publications include "Can and Will: The New Water Rights Battleground," 20 *Colo. Lawyer* 727 (1991); and "Water Law Requirements Affecting Environmental Compliance and Remediation Activities," 22 *Colo. Lawyer* 299 (1993). He is a member of the Colorado Supreme Court Civil Rules Committee; is a member of the Denver, Colorado, and American Bar Associations; and is licensed to practice law in Colorado and New York.

James S. Witwer is a director and shareholder of Trout, Witwer & Freeman, P.C. in Denver, Colorado, where he has worked since 1993. Mr. Witwer graduated *magna cum laude* from Yale College with a degree in political science in 1984, and received his J.D. degree, Order of the Coif, from the University of Colorado School of Law in 1989, where he served as Articles Editor of the *University of Colorado Law Review*. Prior to joining his current firm, he was an associate in the Denver office of Holme Roberts & Owen. Mr. Witwer represents municipal, business, and agricultural clients in the areas of water rights, eminent domain, public lands, and environmental law. He is author of "The Renewal of Authorizations to Divert Water on National Forests," 24 *Colo. Lawyer* 2363 (1995). He is also co-author of the forthcoming article, "Whose Water? Meeting New Federal Water Demands in Prior Appropriation States," to be published as part of the proceedings of the 50th Annual Rocky Mountain Mineral Law Institute. He is Chair of the Agricultural and Rural Law Section of the Colorado Bar Association.

Deborah L. Freeman is a shareholder with the law firm of Trout, Witwer & Freeman, P.C. in Denver, Colorado. She received her undergraduate degree from Stanford University with distinction in 1976 and her law degree from the University of Denver in 1982, where she was awarded Order of St. Ives and served on the *Denver Law Journal and Administrative Law Review*. Ms. Freeman is a past Chair of the Colorado Bar Association's Environmental Law Section.

Ms. Freeman's practice concentrates in the area of natural resources and environmental law, with particular emphasis on the federal Endangered Species Act, Clean Water Act, and NEPA compliance. She is a frequent speaker and writer on resource issues. Publications on endangered species include her paper entitled, "Against the Flow: Emerging Conflicts Between Endangered Species Protection and Water Use," published in the 1994 *Proceedings of the Rocky Mountain Mineral Law Foundation*, and her article on "Reinitiation of Endangered Species Act: § 7 Consultation Over Existing Projects," which appears in the ABA *Endangered Species Act: Law, Policy and Perspectives Deskbook* published in 2002. Ms. Freeman lives in Steamboat Springs, Colorado, with her husband and three sons, Ramsey, Jordan and Connor. They all share a love of skiing and the outdoors.

Peggy E. Montaño was born in Farmington, New Mexico. She received her B.A. from Colorado Women's College in 1977 and her J.D. from the University of Colorado in 1980. Ms. Montaño is admitted to the following courts: Colorado and U.S. District Court, District of Colorado (1981); U.S. Court of Appeals, 10th Circuit (1989). She is the author of "Non-Indian Federal Reserved Rights Since the Rio Mimbres Decision," 37th Annual Rocky Mountain Mineral Law Institute (1991). Ms. Montaño was a First Assistant Attorney General, Colorado, 1988; Chairman of the Colorado State Parks Board, 1996-1998; Member, 1994-1999; Federal Representative, Presidential Appointment, Louisiana/Texas Sabine River Commission; and Advisor, University of Colorado Natural Resources Law Center. She is a member of the Denver (Trustee, 1997-1999), Colorado, and American Bar Associations; Colorado Hispanic Bar Association (Past President, 1995); and American Inns of Court, Doyle's Inn. Her practice areas include real property, natural resources, water law, and municipal corporations

Paul L. Benington was admitted to the bar in Colorado in 2001. He graduated from the University of Michigan Law School, Ann Arbor, J.D., *cum laude*, in 2001 and Michigan State University, B.S., *cum laude*, in 1981. Mr. Benington is a member of the Colorado Bar Association. He was Executive Director of the Leelanau Trails Association from 1995 to 1998, and Associate Director of the Grand Traverse Regional Land Conservancy from 1992 to 1995. Prior to that he was the Director of the Mort Neff Outdoor Education Center from 1989 to 1992. His practice areas include water law, endangered species, natural resources, and municipal law.

Peter D. Nichols practices water, water quality, and related law. He recently drafted the *amicus curiae* briefs filed by Colorado, New Mexico, and other western states and by a coalition of western water users with the U.S. Supreme Court in *Miccosukee Tribe of Indians v. So. Florida Water Mgmt. Dist.*, 124 S. Ct. 1537 (2004). Nichols was the principal author of "Water and Growth in Colorado—A Review of Legal and Policy Issues," published by the Natural Resources Law Center of the University of Colorado School of Law. Recent scholarship includes "Conservation Easements and Water Rights," Agriculture and Rural Law Roundup, Colorado Bar Association, Steamboat Springs, Colo. (June 26, 2003); "Watering Growth in Colorado: Swept Along by the Current or Choosing a Better Line?" 6 *U. Den. Water L. Rev.* 411(2003); and "Do Conservation Easements and Water Mix (in Colorado)," 5 *U. Den. Water L. Rev.* 504 (2002). A former legislative staffer, he has been active on the local and state political scenes. He has served on numerous governmental panels, including the Water Quality Control Commission from 1993 to 1999 (chair, 1997-1998), the Garfield County (Colo.) Planning and Zoning Commission, and Colorado Governor Romer's "Smart Growth" and "Environment 2000" projects. Nichols is also Past President of the Colorado Water Congress Board of Directors. A member of the Colorado Bar who earned a J.D. from the University of Colorado Law School in 2001, he also holds an M.P.A. from CU and a B.A. from The Colorado College.

Gabriel Racz is an associate with Trout, Witwer & Freeman, P.C. He holds a B.M. in Piano Performance from Ithaca College (1994) and a J.D. from the University of Illinois College of Law (2000), where he was made a member of the Order of the Coif and was an Articles Editor for the *University of Illinois Law Review*. During his studies, Mr. Racz researched such diverse topics as controlled choice school desegregation programs, legal and social responses to unsolicited commercial e-mail, and late medieval plainchant. Prior to joining Trout, Witwer & Freeman in June 2001, he was a law clerk to Judge Lawrence Manzanares, Denver District Court. Mr. Racz's practice focuses on eminent domain law, representing both landowners and condemnors, water rights, municipal law, and environmental law including the Endangered Species Act. He lives in Denver, Colorado, with his wife, Melanie Walker.

Douglas M. Sinor was admitted to the Colorado bar in 1999. He received his J.D. from the University of Denver College of Law in 1999 and his B.S. from the Colorado State University in 1987. Mr. Sinor is a member of the Denver Bar Association, the Colorado Bar Association, and the Order of St. Ives. He is also a recipient of the American Jurisprudence Award. Mr. Sinor is the author of "Tenth Circuit Survey of Environmental Law," 75 *D.U.L. Rev.* 859 (1998). He lives in Lakewood, Colorado with his wife, Jenni, and his one-year old son, Carson. His practice focuses primarily on water law.

Pauline R. Wilber is a paralegal with Trout, Witwer & Freeman, P.C. She has a B.A. from Fort Lewis College and a certificate from Denver Paralegal Institute. From 1984 to 1995 she was a senior legal assistant with Gold Fields Mining Corporation. At Trout, Witwer & Freeman she assists counsel with litigation support, legal research, and research with various governmental agencies regarding land status and environmental and natural resource issues. Ms. Wilber and her sisters own and operate a cattle ranch near Meeker, Colorado. She lives in Denver, Colorado with her daughter, Anna Marie Stehle.

TABLE OF CONTENTS

SECTION THREE: USING WATER

SECTION FOUR: PROTECTING WATER

SECTION FIVE: LOOKING TO THE FUTURE

Working with Water
By Justice Greg Hobbs

Working with water is fun, and can often be a lot of hard work.

Consider the farmer who cleans out the irrigation ditch, straightens the furrow rows, sets the siphon tubes, and carefully changes them from row to row until the water's duty to the corn or garlic is done.

Consider the dedicated people of a city's public works department. They worry about storing, treating, and delivering the water for homes and businesses when it's needed, and returning the unused water to the stream clean enough for fish, swimmers, boaters, towns, and farmer's fields.

Consider the businesses that make consumer drinks or pour the water through the turning turbines for electricity or grow the greenhouse plants that grace the homes of citizens with flowers.

Consider the homeowners building in a rural subdivision. Each bought an open tract with plenty of vista, or forest canopy, to escape the city's forbidding din on weekends or to relocate their plugged-in business among the grace and glory of Colorado's splendid solitude.

Consider the out-of-state skier who has booked for her family a long-anticipated Thanksgiving vacation on the ski slopes, or the rafter in the summer sun riding the flowing current through a slotted red-walled canyon, or the urban kayaker scooting off a wave top crashing down an in-channel whitewater course.

Consider a greenway walk along the fisher heron's refuge path, where once a dumping ground for industrial refuse stunk with muck.

Consider the 18 downstream states that depend on water leached from melting snows high along both sides of the Great Divide.

Consider the native greenback cutthroat trout.

Now consider the ravages of a sustained drought.

That's what *Acquiring, Using, and Protecting Water in Colorado* is all about: conservation, distribution, and the beneficial use of scarce water in community.

Colorado has been about this task since the Puebloans of Mesa Verde built and operated their reservoirs between 750 and 1180 A.D.; since the establishment of Bent's Fort in American Territory on the north bank of the Arkansas River in the 1830s; since the migration of Northern New Mexico Hispanos onto a former Mexican land grant where the oldest continuous water right in Colorado, the San Luis People's Ditch of 1852, continues to perpetuate the Spanish acequia tradition; since the cry "Eureka!" sounded at the confluence of the Platte and Cherry Creek and Pikes Peak Region in the seminal Colorado year of 1858; since the first ditch to grow vegetables for the Front Range miners was cut into the banks of Clear Creek; since the First Territorial Legislature passed its first water law in 1861; and so along the current of Colorado's water use ever since into the future.

Laws express the customs and values of the people. The water law reflects how Colorado citizens choose to survive, and—hopefully—thrive in a vast and beautiful land that's dry and full of amazing creatures, mountains, mesas, plains, streams, and intermittent arroyos.

Water is a public resource. That's the fundamental precept of Colorado water law. Wherever it comes from—surface or groundwater, no matter what elevation, no matter what depth one must go to find it—water serves the people and the environment.

Water in our state operates under a set of firm and changing principles, adopted with the intent of being principled and the expectation of being applied justly. Accordingly, all three branches of Colorado government are involved in water and always have been. The people of Colorado etched the basic principles into the marble of the Colorado Constitution.

The Colorado General Assembly codifies the water law in a constant process to reflect the changing economy and desires of Coloradans, consistent with the constitution.

The water courts, to whom the legislature assigned this job, determine the priorities of each water right that shares the supply of the surface stream, or the tributary groundwater aquifers that feed the surface streams.

The State Engineer, the seven Water Division Engineers, and the local Water Commissioners administer the relative priorities of the water rights, according to the Water Court decrees, senior to junior to the limit of the available water.

The Ground Water Commission and the State Engineer control the issuance of well permits for the use of deep groundwater that heavy pumping might exhaust quickly because it's not recharged naturally.

And everywhere one goes in the throes of the early twenty-first century drought, Coloradans want to learn about and care for the water they love in their neighboring watershed backyard.

That's why this handbook about our water law is so important now. It's written for people who want to understand, in a common-sense fashion, what the relative few—the water engineers, attorneys, and managers—almost solely commanded until recently, not because they were greedy and tried to keep everyone else ignorant, but because we trusted them to get the job done and stayed out of their way.

Now getting the job done, because of many changes in state and federal law, requires the participation of the many among us whose full-time work does not involve the complexities of law, policy, natural science, engineering, and administration, which undergird the water law.

This book reveals straightforwardly 143 years of Colorado water law in terms of today's understanding and practices. You will visit a working piece of Colorado's history and culture in each page.

You will learn just how strapped Colorado is in meeting its water needs, and how relatively easy or terribly complex getting water for a new or changed use you might want to make can be.

You will see how the federal water quality, endangered species, and forest protection laws shape each major water development decision in our state. You will come to know how we are living on the water lines and the reservoirs that generations of the past built and handed over to us, and that conservation is a necessity.

You will gain insight into how Colorado's many water organizations function, and how existing water rights can be bought, sold, and leased. For over 100 years, Colorado water law has established a market for transferring water rights to new and different uses from their prior uses and points of diversion. Because beneficial use is the basis, measure, and limit of prior appropriation water rights, historic use of water rights must be defined and quantified before they can be changed to different uses, or the water taken out of the streams or aquifers at different points of diversion. The protection of other water rights is an essential feature of water court change-of-water-rights proceedings. Conditions designed to prevent an enlargement of the historic consumptive use made of the water right is typically a feature of any contemporary change decree. Often crucial to approval of the change is maintenance of historic return flow patterns upon which other water rights depend in whole or part for their supply.

You will grasp how an augmentation plan works to allow out-of-priority diversions and uses that could not otherwise occur under priority administration. This is possible through State Engineer-approved, temporary substitute water supply plans and water court-approved augmentation plans. These plans replace water to the stream in sufficient quantity and quality to satisfy the priorities of other water rights.

You will appreciate the difficult and essential job of the state and division engineers and the local water commissioners. They enforce the final decrees of the water courts, in accordance with Colorado's constitution, statutes, and case law precedent. Without enforcement, water rights lose the security and reliability to serve the needs of all who depend on them. Whether for a farm, city, business, recreation, or the environment, the value of a prior appropriation water right resides in the enforcement of its decreed priority in time of scarcity. The water officials also have the crucial job of delivering water out of state to comply with the nine interstate compacts and three equitable apportionment decrees that affect Colorado's right to use water.

You will discover, how in its 2003 session, the General Assembly adopted legislation for stored water banks in all seven water divisions, prohibited new residential covenants that restrict use of drought-tolerant landscape, authorized conservation easements for water rights, required financial mitigation to a county when transferring agricultural water permanently out of the county, and provided for interruptible water leasing from farms to cities and for instream flows during drought emergencies.

You will realize that many important questions await answers. Because water law tracks the customs and values of the people, new statutes and court decisions will continue to speak about how the basic principles of Colorado water law continue to adapt to changing times and changing uses.

At its core, this book explains how Colorado has responded to one of its most important public priorities: how to deliver water to humans for use while also protecting the environment. So, this book is necessarily about water scarcity and smart practices. Ultimately, of course, this practical handbook is a guide to those who need or want to understand the water law better. As the authors point out, this or any other guide does not substitute for good legal and engineering advice about a particular problem or case.

The authors conscientiously explore their understanding of Colorado water law. In doing so, they underscore how water is Colorado's most basic and important resource. In the drought year 2002, for example, Colorado citizens and the riparian environment lived principally on six million acre-feet of water released from stored reservoir water collected in the good years. Our mountain snow and infrequent rains normally produce an average of 16 million acre-feet of water per year. Up to two-thirds of that goes out to downstream states under the interstate water law. In 2002, Colorado produced only four million acre-feet, and much of that went to the other needy states.

Let's talk reality. Colorado is close to developing all the water to which it is entitled under interstate law. We are now up against our water limits, and conservation in all its forms will be required, including more efficient use and additional above-ground and underground storage projects.

Our inclusion of all points of view in contemporary water decision making is a great source of strength and a cause for great concern. Surely, in each and every generation, we have learned from cyclical drought that in scarcity is the opportunity for community. We must store wisely for the time and place of want.

We must realize much more carefully the basic maxim of Colorado water law, that the water is a public resource to be used beneficially, without waste. Let the hallmark of our generation be civilized action, not neglect.

ACKNOWLEDGMENTS

When Greg Smith at Bradford first approached us about writing this book, we were all a bit skeptical. Our perspective quickly changed as we talked to clients, water users, water organization board members and officials, and non-water lawyers who find themselves thrust—often kicking and screaming—into a position where they need to understand Colorado water law. It is our hope that this book will be a useful starting point for them, who truly became the inspiration to pursue this project to completion.

This book represents our best collective view of the state of Colorado water law today, including what it is not, and what it may not be. Our pride of authorship is, of course, tempered by the sure knowledge that our colleagues in the water bar won't hesitate to quote our work back to us when it serves their clients' interest, or to rib us for inevitable mistakes or ambiguities. Naturally, we are equally sure that any mistakes and ambiguities occur only in those sections that will be quoted back to us, uncomfortably, in the future. With only mild trepidation, we welcome any comments, suggestions, and different points of view.

This project would not have been possible without the commitment of every attorney in the firm—each of whom chose to contribute—to produce the same high quality work we strive to deliver to our clients. Each contributed substantial research, knowledge, time, and writing expertise, although Peter Nichols, Doug Sinor, and Bob Trout deserve particular recognition.

This project also would not have been possible without our exceptionally competent support staff, including Lynn Cohen, Vickie Butler, and Rosalie Martinez. Most importantly, special thanks to Glenice Martinez, legal secretary extraordinaire, who cheerfully, proficiently, and steadfastly put together countless drafts from eight different attorneys with unique work and writing styles, while somehow staying on top of her usual heavy workload.

And thanks of course to poet and jurist Greg Hobbs, who graciously agreed to write an inviting foreword.

—Trout, Witwer & Freeman, P.C.
May 2004

INTRODUCTION

This book is intended to be consulted and used by people who are not water professionals, but must use, manage, or otherwise deal with Colorado water rights—people such as landowners, water users, purchasers, or sellers of land or water rights, employees of organizations that use or manage water rights, attorneys who are not specialists in water law, public officials, and citizens interested in the details of water law. It is not a legal treatise on Colorado water law. It is intended to provide the user with a relatively simple and clear explanation of Colorado water law without extensive legal citation or analysis. It is also intended to provide the reader with a description of all of the important aspects of Colorado water law, guidance for dealing with routine matters, descriptions of particularly difficult or unsettled issues, and sufficient information to know when additional help should be obtained.

Colorado is an arid state. Water is generally scarce and is often not located in places where it is needed for use. Most crops cannot be grown in Colorado without artificial irrigation. For these and similar reasons, the right to use water has been critically important in Colorado since before statehood. It is so important, that several sections of the Colorado Constitution are devoted to water and its use.[1]

Water use in Colorado is governed by the doctrine of prior appropriation. Under this doctrine, the single most important characteristic of a water right is its priority. Every water right has a priority date, which historically was the date on which the water was first diverted and used in some fashion. Under the prior appropriation doctrine, water is allocated to water rights based exclusively on their priority dates. This means that water rights with the earliest priority dates carry the right to divert and use all of the water that they need (subject to the terms and conditions of the right) before water rights with more junior priorities can receive any water. In other words, under the doctrine of prior appropriation, shortages of water are not shared. Scarce water is allocated based on priorities. Senior priorities are entitled to receive all of the water to which they are entitled before junior priorities can receive any water.

The Colorado Supreme Court defines a water right as "a right to use beneficially a specified amount of water, from the available supply of surface water or tributary groundwater, that can be captured, possessed, and controlled in priority under a decree, to the exclusion of all others not then in priority under a decreed water right, which applies to surface streams and tributary ground water."[2] Water rights have many conditions and limitations that define and limit their use, including the source of the water, the rate of flow of possible diversions, the amount that may be diverted, the permissible uses of the water, the time when the water may be diverted, the place

---

[1]   COLO. CONST. art. XVI, §§ 5 to 8.

[2]   *Santa Fe Trail Ranches Prop. Owners Ass'n v. Simpson*, 990 P.2d 46, 53 (Colo. 1999).

where the water may be used, the place where the water may be stored, and other limitations depending on the circumstances.

Although water is usually used on land in some fashion, water rights in Colorado are separate and distinct from land. One can own the right to divert water from a natural stream and apply it to beneficial use at any location independent of land ownership. Water rights are conveyed like real estate, and can be conveyed separately from the land on which they may be used.

Water law is greatly influenced by what is known as the hydrologic cycle. The hydrologic cycle refers to the process in which water is removed from the oceans and land surfaces by evaporation, transported in the atmosphere as water vapor, deposited on the land and oceans as precipitation, and carried back to the oceans by rivers and streams. It includes the water contained in underground water-bearing formations that are hydrologically connected to the surface streams, called alluvial aquifers.

Measuring Water:	1 cfs	= 449 gallons per minute
	1 acre-foot	= 325,890 gallons

To understand water diversions in Colorado, one must understand specialized units of measure. Direct flow water rights from streams typically are decreed and measured in cubic feet per second (cfs), sometimes called second feet. One cubic foot per second is a rate of flow past a measurement point, and equals 449 gallons per minute. Water discharging at this rate of flow would completely fill the unfinished basement of a 1,000 square foot house in less than two and a half hours. Gallons per minute (gpm) is another common flow measurement, typically associated with wells. Water discharging at a seven to eight gpm rate is about the amount of water that typically exits a garden hose with the spigot opened all the way.

Water storage rights are typically decreed and measured in acre-feet, a measure of volume. One acre-foot is the amount of water that will cover one acre of land (slightly less than a football field without end zones) one foot deep. One acre-foot equals about 326,000 gallons. One cfs flowing for 24 hours equals about two acre-feet.

Archaic forms of water measurement still float to the surface. In Colorado, for example, 38.4 "miner's inches" equal one cfs. But beware of "inch" measurements; they vary in other states, and even in Colorado may represent different values in different places or contexts.

The statutes, court decisions, and administrative regulations that define and regulate the right to use water are called water law. It started to develop when Colorado first became a territory in 1861 and continues to evolve as the needs of Colorado society change. It is not static. It can and must change as society changes.

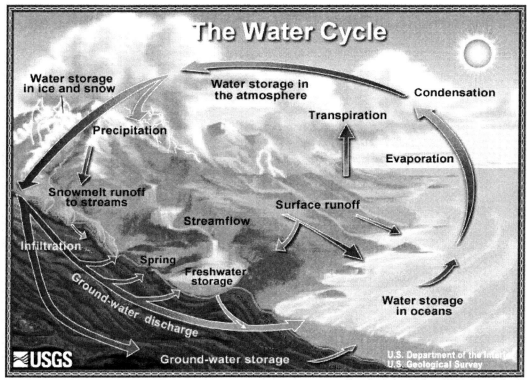

Illustration by John M. Evans USGS, Colorado District

Thus, the substance and practice of water law cannot be gleaned from simply reading the statutes and case law. Some practices and policies have evolved over time and are not codified. Where this is the case, we have attempted to describe the practice or policy and alert the reader. If the information contained in this book is not adequate or detailed enough for the user's needs, the user should consult an attorney or other professional specializing in Colorado water law.

This book is divided into chapters and sections addressing different aspects of water law. It also contains a glossary and contact information. It is intended to be used primarily as a resource when the user has a specific question or problem, so that the user can consult the specific sections that address the problem at hand.

The reader may notice some redundancy in this book. This is intentional. Since a book of this nature is likely to be consulted for specific issues, and the reader is not likely to read the book from front to back, the authors have attempted to limit the amount of page flipping by addressing the relevant issues in more than one place when they are particularly important. In other instances, the authors have attempted to provide useful cross-references among the sections of the book to alert the reader to other topics that should be reviewed when a particular issue is of interest.

MEASURING WATER:
SECOND FEET, ACRE-FEET, AND MINER'S INCHES

To understand water diversions in Colorado, one must understand specialized units of measure. Direct flow water rights from streams typically are decreed and measured in cubic feet per second (cfs), sometimes called second feet. One cubic foot per second is a rate of flow past a measurement point, and equals 449 gallons per minute. Water discharging at this rate of flow would completely fill the unfinished basement of a 1,000 square foot house in less than two and a half hours. Gallons per minute (gpm) is another common flow measurement, typically associated with wells. Water discharging at a seven to eight gpm rate is about the amount of water that typically exits a ¾-inch garden hose with the spigot opened all the way.

Water storage rights are typically decreed and measured in acre-feet, a measure of volume. One acre-foot is the amount of water that will cover one acre of land (slightly less than a football field without end zones) one foot deep. One acre-foot equals about 326,000 gallons. One cfs flowing for 24 hours equals about two acre-feet.

Archaic forms of water measurement still float to the surface. In Colorado, for example, 38.4 "miner's inches" equal one cfs. But beware of "inch" measurements; they vary in other states, and even in Colorado may represent different values in different places and contexts.

SECTION ONE: OVERVIEW

CHAPTER 1 BASIC WATER LAW

---

§ 1.1   WATER ALLOCATION SYSTEMS

The primary function of water rights law is to resolve disputes between water users by providing a principled means to allocate the resource. In states where water is scarce, more disputes generally arise and, consequently, the water law in arid states is usually more developed and complex than in states where water is plentiful. Therefore, it is not surprising that Colorado, which is mostly arid yet has the headwaters of seven major rivers within its borders, has some of the most complex and highly developed water law in the United States.

Many states have different systems for allocating surface water and ground water. For surface water, there are two general forms of allocation systems in the United States, the prior appropriation system and the riparian system. Ground water allocation systems vary from state to state and depend on the type of ground water involved. See Chapter 4 for a complete discussion of ground water allocation systems in Colorado.

Except for Hawaii and Louisiana, all states generally follow either the prior appropriation, the riparian system, or a hybrid of the two systems. Colorado follows the doctrine of prior appropriation, and 18 other western states also follow the prior appropriation system in one form or another. Before considering the many intricacies of the prior appropriation system in Colorado, however, it is helpful to understand the riparian system, how it is different from the prior appropriation system, and why the two systems developed.

§ 1.1.1   The Eastern Riparian System

The Eastern United States, where water is typically more plentiful, generally uses the riparian system of water law. The basic principle of the riparian system is that a landowner whose land borders a water body has the right to make reasonable use of the water on the land if it does not interfere with the reasonable uses of other riparian land owners.

The riparian system has its roots in English common law; however, it was further developed in the early nineteenth century in the United States when the industrial revolution led many water-powered mills to compete for the natural flow of rivers. As industrial mills began to proliferate along the rivers of the Northeast, disputes arose when upstream mills dammed or diverted the flow of the river in order to harness the power of the water, but interfered with a downstream mill's ability to use the water for power. In response, the courts developed the law of "reasonable use." All riparian land owners were held to have equal rights to use the water flowing in the stream, but that use could not interfere with the reasonable use of others.

The riparian doctrine was suitable for allocating water during the 1800s in the Northeast where water is generally plentiful and the predominant uses were industrial mills using water for power. The basic riparian system, however, has many limitations. For example, the riparian system does not allow for water use on non-riparian land or consumptive uses that would diminish the flow of the river to the extent that it would unreasonably interfere with downstream users' riparian rights. For these reasons, the riparian doctrine has been modified by statutes in most states to allow for consumptive uses, such as irrigation, uses by non-riparian land owners, and uses by municipalities. The major limitation of the riparian system, however, is that, in times of water shortage, all water users share the burden of the shortage equally. If shortages are common, there is little incentive for investment under this system because there is no guarantee that sufficient water will be available for a particular use.

§ 1.1.2 The Western Prior Appropriation System

The riparian system of water law was generally not adopted in the western United States, where irrigation and mining, rather than industry, were the predominant early uses, and water was often scarce. In the West, irrigation and mining often occurred on public, non-riparian lands, requiring diversion and transportation of the water by means such as a ditch. The early gold miners required water for placer mining and developed a method of water allocation based on first in time, first in right. This became known as the prior appropriation system, and was extended to irrigation and other uses. As the western United States began to be settled, the federal government acquiesced to the local custom of water allocation under the prior appropriation system and acknowledged the creation of private water rights on public land through appropriation. Congress further provided that all patented lands transferred to private ownership would be conveyed subject to any prior appropriative rights to use water.

The hallmark of the prior appropriation system is that the first user to divert and put water to beneficial use has a prior right to that source of water as compared to later users. Under this system, the riparian landowner has no rights based on simply being next to the stream. Under the prior appropriation system, water users do not share the burden of shortages. The prior user is entitled to divert the full amount of water to meet his or her entire water right before the next junior user is allowed to divert any water. Thus, senior appropriators are rewarded for their efforts to put water to beneficial use by being assured that their needs will be fulfilled in times of shortage, while later appropriators have the knowledge that their needs may not be met, and can plan their investments and efforts accordingly. The prior appropriation system generally promotes stability and development of the water resource. No comparison of the reasonableness or relative value of competing uses is made as long as water is put to beneficial use. Therefore, the prior appropriation system is conceptually a relatively simple system to administer.

Limitations of the Prior Appropriation System

While the prior appropriation system was well-suited for promoting development and allocating water among traditional uses, such as irrigation, mining, and domestic that developed in the West in the nineteenth and early twentieth centuries, some people believe the prior appropriation system is not adequate to provide for recreation and environmental uses that have developed more recently. Some western states have adopted public interest doctrines or policies to address environmental uses of water and preservation concerns.[1] To the extent these doctrines or policies attempt to limit appropriations or provide equal footing for newly evolving environmental uses, however, they depart from a pure prior appropriation system. Colorado has not adopted a public trust or interest doctrine, but has enacted certain statutory changes to accommodate these new values to an extent. See Sections 3.4.1 and 3.4.2. Other doctrines, such as the federal reserved water rights doctrine, and federal statutes, such as the Endangered Species Act, have brought other public interests to bear on Colorado's pure prior appropriation system. These doctrines and statutes are discussed in more detail in later chapters of this book.

§ 1.1.3   Prior Appropriation in Colorado

The doctrine of prior appropriation is adopted in Colorado's Constitution. Section 5 of Article XVI of the Colorado Constitution provides that the water of every natural stream in Colorado is public property, which shall be dedicated to the use of the people by diversion and application to beneficial use, subject to the rights of prior appropriators.[2] Section 6 of Article XVI of the Colorado Constitution further provides that "[t]he right to divert the unappropriated waters of any natural stream to beneficial uses shall never be denied."[3] Thus, under the Colorado Constitution, nothing more than diversion and application of water to beneficial use is necessary to create a water right. No judicial or administrative approval is required. Because the water of every natural stream in Colorado is public property, however, a person may only acquire the right to use water, rather than ownership of the water itself. All water that is not consumed after a beneficial use must be returned to the stream. Therefore, a water right is sometimes referred to as a usufructuary right.

In 1882, the Colorado Supreme Court ruled that the doctrine of prior appropriation has always existed in Colorado, even before legislation on the subject of irrigation was developed, due to the necessity of artificial irrigation for agriculture.[4] This case involved a riparian landowner along the St. Vrain Creek who challenged a prior appropriator's right to divert water from the creek. In ruling against the riparian

---

1   *National Audubon Soc'y v. Superior Court of Alpine County*, 658 P.2d 709 (Cal. 1983).
2   COLO. CONST. art. XVI, § 5.
3   COLO. CONST. art. XVI, § 6.
4   *Coffin v. Left Hand Ditch Co.*, 6 Colo. 443 (1882).

landowner, the Court held that "the first appropriator of water from a natural stream for a beneficial purpose has, with the qualifications contained in the constitution, a prior right thereto, to the extent of such appropriation."[5]

While Section 5 and the first part of Section 6 of Article XVI of the Colorado Constitution seem to clearly adopt the prior appropriation system, later parts of Section 6 appear to soften that doctrine by providing for a preferential ranking of water uses:

> Priority of appropriation shall give the better right as between those using the water for the same purpose; but when the waters of any natural stream are not sufficient for the service of all those desiring the use of the same, those using the water for domestic purposes shall have the preference over those claiming for any other purpose, and those using the water for agricultural purposes shall have preference over those using the same for manufacturing purposes.

Colorado courts, however, have held that Colorado's system is one of "pure" prior appropriation, and have interpreted this part of Section 6 to simply mean that preferred uses may condemn water rights used for less preferred uses.[6]

§ 1.2   WATER RIGHT ADJUDICATION

§ 1.2.1 Water Courts

Under the prior appropriation system, the value and reliability of a water right is a function of its priority with respect to other water rights on the stream system. In order to prioritize water rights, Colorado early on developed a system of water right adjudication to determine the date of appropriation and the priority of a water right with respect to other water rights. Although a water right is created upon application of water to beneficial use, a water right owner is not entitled to have his or her water right administered within the priority system until he or she obtains a decree confirming the water right priority. Water courts do not grant water rights, but merely confirm and establish the priority of water rights. Water courts also do not usually determine ownership of a water right. Colorado is the only prior appropriation state that has not delegated the prioritization of water rights to an administrative agency.

---

5   *Coffin*, 6 Colo. at 447.
6   *Black v. Taylor*, 128 Colo. 449, 264 P.2d 502 (1953).

§ 1.2.2 Early Water Right Adjudications

Prior to 1969, the water rights statutes in Colorado provided for a system of "general adjudications." The state was divided into 80 water districts. An appropriator initiated an adjudication by filing a claim in the district court of the county where the water district was situated. If there had been no previous adjudication of water rights in the district, an "original adjudication" was initiated and all potential water rights claimants were notified and joined in the case. The respective rights of each party would then be adjudicated in one decree. The priority of the water rights decreed in the general adjudication was determined based on the date of initiation of the appropriation, with the earliest date being the most senior. Subsequent water rights in the district would be adjudicated in "supplemental adjudications," in which all claimants of unadjudicated water rights were joined. Priorities decreed in supplemental decrees were junior to all priorities determined in a previous supplemental or original adjudication, regardless of the date on which the appropriation was initiated. Thus, the water right priority was determined by the date of the decree and, within the same decree, by date of initiation of the appropriation.

Under this system, the water districts did not follow watershed boundaries, and water rights owners were not always notified or aware of a general adjudication proceeding in the same or another district that might affect their water rights. The statutes compensated by allowing decrees to be challenged within a certain time period after they were entered. Consequently, decrees were reopened frequently. Also, because water districts did not include entire river basins, it was difficult or impossible for a water right owner to determine his water right priority with respect to other water rights on the same stream system in another district.

§ 1.2.3 Water Right Determination and Administration Act of 1969

The Colorado legislature responded to these and other problems in 1969 by enacting the Water Right Determination and Administration Act of 1969 (1969 Act).[7] The 1969 Act divided the state into seven water divisions following the state's seven major river basins and provided for tabulation of water right priorities within each division. The seven major river basins and divisions are the South Platte River (including Laramie River) (Division 1); Arkansas River (Division 2); Rio Grande (Division 3); Gunnison River (Division 4); Colorado River (Division 5); Yampa River (including North Platte River) (Division 6); and San Juan/Animas Rivers

---

7   C.R.S. §§ 37-92-101 to 37-92-602.
8   C.R.S. § 37-92-201.

(Division 7).[8] In each division, one district court is assigned to be the water court and has exclusive jurisdiction over water matters within the division. One district court judge is also appointed to be a water judge for the division, and a water referee is usually appointed to investigate and make rulings.

§ 1.2.4 Filing a Water Court Application

Under the 1969 Act, a person may now obtain a decree for his or her water right on an individual basis by filing an application in the appropriate water court without joining other water users in a general adjudication. Thus, water rights are now decreed and assigned priorities on a continuous basis. The water court application must be verified and filed in quadruplicate together with a filing fee. Filing fees vary based on the kind of water right and number of water rights being sought. Along with information regarding the amount and source of water claimed, the applicant must also identify the name and address of any landowner on which diversion or storage structures are or will be located. Once decreed, the water right will be incorporated into the tabulation of other priorities within each division, based on the date of the decree and the date of initiation of appropriation.

> Standardized water court applications for various kinds of water rights should be used and are available from the water court or the Colorado courts Web site:
> http://www.courts.state.co.us/chs/court/forms/waterforms/water.htm

§ 1.2.5 Notice

To provide notice to other water users of an application filed in water court, the 1969 Act set up a system of publication notice, whereby every application filed in water court is published in a local newspaper and in a monthly water court "résumé" for each water division. Newspaper publication is necessary to comply with federal constitutional due process requirements; however, it is often easier for water users to review the monthly water court résumé to determine if there are any applications that might affect their water rights. Water attorneys typically review the résumé each month to determine if there are any applications of interest to their clients; however, any person may subscribe to the water court résumé for each division for a nominal fee. The water court résumé for each water division is published by the middle of each month and contains a description of all water right applications filed in the previous month. The water court is also required to send a copy of the application to any person whom the referee has a reason to believe might be affected, including at a minimum the persons identified as owning land on which any structure identified in the application is located. Additional notice requirements apply to an application for a change of irrigation water rights that constitutes a "significant water development activity," which is defined as the removal of water that results in the transfer of more than 1,000 acre-feet of consumptive use per year.[9] See Section 10.1.2 for detailed discussion of this type of application.

> The résumés for each water court can be downloaded free from the Colorado courts Web site:
> http://www.courts.state.co.us/supct/supctwaterctindex.htm

§ 1.2.6 Opposing an Application

Any person may file a statement of opposition to a water right application and hold the applicant to strict proof of all elements of the claimed appropriation. A person may also oppose an application for change of water rights or plan for augmentation on the ground that granting of the application may cause injury to the opposer's water rights. Statements of opposition may be filed up to the last day of the second month after the month in which the application is filed. After the statement of opposition deadline has expired, a person may move to intervene in a water court proceeding upon a showing of "mistake, inadvertence, surprise, or excusable neglect."[10]

> A standardized statement of opposition form is available from the water court or the Colorado courts Web site:
> http://www.courts.state.co.us/chs/court/forms/waterforms/jdf303w.pdf

§ 1.2.7 Referee's Ruling

All water court applications are initially referred by the water judge to the water referee. The referee, without conducting a formal hearing, makes such investigations as are necessary to determine the veracity of the statements in the application and whether the application should be granted or denied in whole or in part. The referee consults with the Division Engineer regarding the application and the Division Engineer files a report summarizing the consultation. If the referee makes a ruling, it is subject to review by the water judge. Any person may file a protest to a referee's ruling within 20 days of the mailing of the ruling. If no protest to a ruling is filed

---

9   C.R.S. § 37-92-302(3.5).
10   C.R.S. § 37-92-304(3).

within 20 days, the ruling will be made a judgment and decree of the water court, unless the water judge finds the ruling to be contrary to law. If the ruling is protested, the court will consider the application *de novo*, meaning that the findings of the referee carry no presumptive validity and are not binding on the court. If an application is heavily contested, the referee may decide to avoid duplicative proceedings and re-refer the application back to the water court for determination by the water judge. Also, any party may require the application to be re-referred to the water judge by certifying his or her intent to protest an adverse ruling of the referee.[11]

§ 1.2.8 Proceedings Before the Water Judge

If an application is re-referred to the water court or a referee's ruling is protested, and if the case is not settled, the water judge will hold a hearing or trial to determine the merits of the application. The Division Engineer must appear to furnish pertinent information and may be examined by any party. The Division Engineer may also be a party to the proceeding as an opposer and be represented by counsel from the Attorney General's office. Water court proceedings are generally governed by the Colorado Rules of Civil Procedure; however, the water courts have established Uniform Local Rules for all State Water Court Divisions, which also must be consulted. Upon entry of a judgment and decree confirming a water right, a copy of the decree is sent to the State and Division Engineers' offices, and the State and Division Engineers are required to enter the priority, location, and use of the water right in the state's tabulations, and administer the water right in accordance with the decree.

The water judge may correct clerical mistakes in a decree on his own initiative or in response to a petition if such petition is filed within three years. During the same three-year period, the water judge may also correct substantive errors in the decree on the petition of any person whose rights have been adversely affected by the decree, and upon a showing that the person failed to file a protest to the ruling of the referee due to "mistake, inadvertence, or excusable neglect."[12] This provision is intended to protect the due process rights of a water right owner who, despite the publication requirement, was not made aware of a water right adjudication that could affect his or her water right. As a practical matter, this means that no water right decree is truly final until three years after its entry. The water court is also required to retain jurisdiction over decrees for changes of water rights and augmentation plans, as explained in Section 10.3.[13]

---

11 C.R.S. § 37-92-303(2).
12 C.R.S. § 37-92-304(10).
13 C.R.S. § 37-92-304(6).

Water court decisions may be appealed in the same way as any other civil matter. Due to the importance of water matters, appeals of water court decisions are made directly to the Colorado Supreme Court.

§ 1.3   TYPES OF WATER RIGHTS

Water rights for new appropriations may be either "absolute" or "conditional." An appropriator may claim an absolute (perfected) water right if he or she has put water to beneficial use, or may claim a "conditional" (unperfected) water right if he or she has taken a substantial first step toward completion of, but has not yet completed, an appropriation of water for a beneficial use. If a conditional appropriation is completed with reasonable diligence, the appropriation date will relate back to the date the first step toward appropriation was completed. This provides planning security for large projects that may take considerable time to complete. Conditional water rights are discussed in more detail in Section 3.3.

Water rights are also differentiated on the basis of whether the use will be made by direct flow diversion, by storage, or by exchange. Different applications and elements of proof are required for each kind of water right. Direct flow water rights are defined in terms of a flow rate, usually cubic feet per second (cfs). Water rights that are decreed only for direct flow use only may not be stored (except temporarily for regulation purposes) unless changed to allow storage in a subsequent water court proceeding. As discussed in Section 16.1, storage water rights are defined in terms of a volume, usually acre-feet. Storage water rights may be for one fill per season or for multiple fills. Rights of substitution or exchange are usually defined in terms of a maximum flow rate, but may also be defined in terms of a total volume. Water rights are also differentiated based on whether the water being appropriated is surface water or ground water.

In addition to confirming the priority of new water rights, water courts also adjudicate changes in use of existing water rights and plans for augmentation to replace depletions from new uses with water from other sources. Changed water rights retain their original priority, but may be subject to new restrictions on use. No priority is determined for plans for augmentation. Both changes of water rights and plans for augmentation are approved for operation upon a showing that no injury will occur to other water rights. Plans for augmentation may also involve exchanges of water. Changes of water rights, plans for augmentation, and exchanges are discussed in more detail in Chapter 10.

§ 1.4   WATER RIGHTS ADMINISTRATION (STATE ENGINEER)

The State Engineer's office, which is an administrative agency under the Colorado Department of Natural Resources, has the duty of administrating water rights according to the priorities confirmed by the water courts. A Division Engineer is assigned to each water division. Each water division is further divided into water districts, which are managed by Water Commissioners. The Water Commissioners, under the supervision of the Division Engineers and the State Engineer, are charged with the day-to-day regulation and administration of headgates and other diversion structures in the river system in accordance with the priorities set forth in decrees. Water rights administration is discussed in more detail in Chapter 8.

§ 1.5   POSTPONEMENT DOCTRINE

§ 1.5.1   In General

The postponement doctrine is a modification of the "first in time, first in right" principle of the prior appropriation system that is intended to encourage the prompt adjudication of a water right. Under the postponement doctrine, a water right that is first in time relative to other water rights may have its priority postponed, as illustrated below, depending upon when it was adjudicated.

As to water rights adjudicated under the law in effect before the 1969 Act, the postponement doctrine provides that a water right is junior to all water rights adjudicated in proceedings that occurred prior to the proceeding in which the subject water right was adjudicated (either original or supplemental, see Section 1.2.2). As to water rights adjudicated in the same proceeding, the water rights are given priority based upon their appropriation date. Thus, a water right with a July 1, 1880 appropriation date adjudicated in the first supplemental adjudication in a given water district would be junior to a water right with a July 1, 1882 appropriation date adjudicated in the original adjudication in that water district. For this reason, in order to properly evaluate the relative priority of an old water right, one must know the appropriation date of the water right, the date of the decree in which the water right was adjudicated, and the dates of all prior decrees entered in the same water district.

As to the water rights adjudicated under the 1969 Act, things are simpler. First, all water rights adjudicated under the 1969 Act are junior to water rights adjudicated under prior law, regardless of priority date.[14]

---

[14]   C.R.S. § 37-92-306.

Under the 1969 Act, the decreed appropriation date is used only to determine the relative sequence of priorities among water rights based on applications filed in the same calendar year. As between water rights based on applications filed in different years, the priorities for all water rights filed in a particular year are junior to all priorities awarded upon applications filed in previous years, regardless of the respective appropriation dates.[15]

Consider the following example:

Water Rights	Appropriation Date	Application Filing Date
A	July 4, 1903	December 30, 2004
B	January 1, 2003	January 2, 2004
C	December 29, 2003	December 30, 2003

Water Right C's one-day old water right would have a 2003 priority that is senior to the 2004 priorities of both Water Right A and B, even though both A and B appropriated water before C. Water Right A, the 100-year-old right, would be senior to the one-year-old Water Right B, even though B filed its application before A. Among water rights filed upon in the same year, the earlier appropriation date takes priority. In a pure prior appropriation system, the order of priorities would be A, B, C, but under the postponement doctrine, the order of priorities is C, A, B.

§ 1.5.2   Federal Water Right Claims Under the McCarran Amendment

The legal doctrine of sovereign immunity prevents the United States from being sued without its consent. Thus, in the many western states that had adopted prior appropriation systems, the extent and priority of federal water rights were not known and could not be determined in state water court adjudications because the United States had not consented to be joined in the water right proceedings. To remedy this situation, Congress enacted the McCarran Amendment in 1952,[16] which provides that the United States can be involuntarily joined as a party in state general adjudications, and, once joined, state courts have jurisdiction to determine federal water rights.

Once the United States is properly joined under the McCarran Amendment, all water rights initially claimed by the United States are not subject to Colorado's postponement doctrine and may be decreed priorities that antedate other adjudicated water rights.[17] The United States must, however, assert all of its claims once it is

---

15   C.R.S. § 37-92-306.

16   43 U.S.C. § 666.

17   *United States v. Bell*, 724 P.2d 631 (Colo. 1986).

joined in order to avoid postponement. Any new claims asserted later will be subject to the postponement doctrine.[18] As a practical matter, the United States has now been joined as a party in water court proceedings in all seven water divisions in Colorado, although some claims had not yet been resolved at the time of this publication. Future federal water right claims are subject to the postponement doctrine.

§ 1.5.3 Other Exceptions

The 1969 Act provides for three exceptions to the postponement doctrine. First, because of the early lack of understanding of the connection between tributary ground water and surface water, wells were often not adjudicated prior to 1969. To encourage wells to be adjudicated and provide some protection for owners of existing wells, the 1969 Act provides that a tributary ground water right for which an application was filed before July 1, 1972 would be given a priority date as of the date of appropriation without postponement.[19] Second, the priorities of existing exchanges are not subject to postponement when adjudicated.[20] Finally, if a ground water right for an "exempt" well is adjudicated, it will be given a priority date as of the date of appropriation, regardless of the water court filing date.[21]

§ 1.6   LEGAL CLASSIFICATIONS OF WATER

Although Colorado generally follows the prior appropriation system for allocating water, there are several exceptions to this rule and different rules apply in some cases. The different rules are discussed in detail later in this book; however, it is important to first have a general understanding of the various types of water in Colorado and the legal distinctions that apply to each.

§ 1.6.1 Surface Water

Surface water includes all water in rivers, streams, lakes, wetlands or other natural waterways, and diffuse runoff. Although Colorado does not have many large lakes, Colorado has seven major rivers that originate within the borders of the state. The headwaters of these major rivers are high in the Rocky Mountains, and are fed largely by melting snow. Water on the earth's surface is replenished every year by precipitation in the form of rain and snow. Surface water is allocated according to the prior

---

18   *Bell*, 724 P.2d at 637-40.
19   C.R.S. § 37-92-306.
20   C.R.S. § 37-92-305(10).
21   C.R.S. § 37-92-602(4).

appropriation system, as modified by the postponement doctrine. As discussed above, no administrative approval is required to create a water right; however, adjudication is necessary to allow the water right to be administered within the prior appropriation system.

§ 1.6.2 Ground Water

Ground water is water that is trapped in the interstices of soil and rock particles below the surface of the earth. Saturated water-bearing formations of the earth are often referred to as aquifers. Unlike surface water, the diversion of ground water requires administrative approval in the form of a well permit from the Colorado State Engineer's Office. There are three major kinds of ground water for purposes of understanding Colorado water law.

Tributary Ground Water

Ground water that is hydraulically connected to surface water so as to influence the rate of flow of surface water is known as tributary ground water. Because tributary ground water is hydraulically connected to surface water, it is also replenished by surface water percolating into the ground. A familiar example of tributary ground water is water that is found in the alluvial aquifer underneath and surrounding a river or stream. Water from the stream seeps into the porous alluvial soils around the stream until the soils are saturated. The pumping of such ground water will eventually reduce the surface water in the stream to some degree because surface water will percolate into the aquifer to fill the void left by the pumping. The impact of tributary ground water pumping on the surface water, however, may be greatly delayed or attenuated, depending on the location of the well and the characteristics of the aquifer, because ground water flows slowly. Because tributary ground water is linked with surface water, it also allocated under the prior appropriation system in concert with surface water rights. In addition to a well permit, the tributary ground water user must obtain a water court decree in order to have his or her ground water right administered in the prior appropriation system.

Today, ground water is presumed to be tributary in Colorado until proven otherwise,[22] except in "designated" ground water basins and within certain deep aquifers. For this reason, a landowner does not own, or have any prior rights to, tributary ground water underlying his or her land. Colorado did not always recognize the hydraulic connection between tributary ground water and surface water, however. For

---

22   *Safranek v. Town of Limon*, 123 Colo. 330, 228 P.2d 975 (1951).

many years, wells in alluvial aquifers were not regulated under the prior appropriation system. When it became clear in the 1960s that wells were affecting older surface water rights on many of Colorado's rivers, tributary ground water began to be integrated into the priority system with the enactment of the 1969 Act. This process is still ongoing in Colorado. In some cases, the law in other western states has been even slower to recognize the relationship between surface water and tributary ground water.

Non-Tributary Ground Water

Ground water may be so physically separated from surface water by impermeable layers or great distances so as to have little or no hydraulic connection with surface water. If such ground water is located outside a designated ground water basin, and its withdrawal will not within 100 years deplete the flow of a natural stream at an annual rate greater than one-tenth of one percent of the annual rate of withdrawal, it is classified as non-tributary ground water.[23] The right to use non-tributary ground water is allocated based on the ownership of the overlying land, rather than the prior appropriation system. The owner of the overlying land may obtain a right to use non-tributary ground water by obtaining a well permit from the State Engineer or may seek to have the water court determine the non-tributary ground water rights before drilling a well. Ground water within the Dawson, Denver, Arapahoe, and Laramie-Fox Hills aquifers in the area known as the Denver Basin (a kidney shaped area along the Front Range of Colorado between Greeley and Colorado Springs) is presumed not to be tributary in nature.[24] Non-tributary ground water also occurs in other parts of the state. A complex set of statutes and rules and regulations promulgated by the State Engineer govern the allocation of non-tributary ground water. This topic is discussed in detail in Section 4.4.

Not Non-Tributary Ground Water

The Colorado legislature has also defined a unique category of ground water located outside the boundaries of a designated ground water basin within the Dawson, Denver, Arapahoe, and Laramie-Fox Hills aquifers in the Denver Basin. Water within this classification is water that would otherwise not meet the definition of non-tributary ground water, and is known as "not non-tributary" ground water.[25] The legislature has provided that not non-tributary ground water shall also be

---

23 C.R.S. § 37-90-103(10.5).
24 *Id.*
25 C.R.S. § 37-90-103(10.7).

allocated on the basis of land ownership; however, use of not non-tributary ground water is subject to certain augmentation or replacement requirements that are discussed in more detail in Section 4.4.3.

Designated Ground Water

Another type of ground water classification created by the legislature is ground water that is within areas known as designated ground water basins. Designated ground water, as it is called, is ground water within the geographic boundaries of a designated ground water basin that (1) in its natural course would not be available to and required for the fulfillment of decreed surface rights, or (2) is in areas not adjacent to a continuously flowing natural stream in which ground water withdrawals have constituted the principal water usage for at least 15 years prior to designation of the basin.[26] While designated ground water is not necessarily not tributary to surface streams, it is allocated based on a modified form of the prior appropriation system largely independent of the surface stream priority system. The Colorado Ground Water Commission, not the water court, has jurisdiction to determine rights to use ground water within designated basins. Colorado has eight designated ground water basins, which are generally located on the eastern plains. Again, a complex set of statutes and rules and regulations govern designated ground water basins, and these are discussed in detail in Section 4.3.

---

[26] C.R.S. § 37-90-103(6)(a).

SECTION TWO: ACQUIRING WATER

CHAPTER 2 HOW MUCH WATER DO YOU NEED?

§ 2.1   GENERAL CONSIDERATIONS

The question of how much water is needed for a particular use can be difficult to answer and, depending on the circumstances, may require the services of a water engineer. The question is often complicated by considerations of whether existing water rights will be used, whether existing rights will need to be changed to allow a new use or place of use, or, if new junior water rights will be used, whether such rights will be sufficiently reliable. If existing water rights will be changed to new uses, the user must obtain approval from the water court to change the use of the water right, and a historical use analysis will likely be required to obtain such approval. Changes of water rights are discussed in Section 10.1. If new water rights will be appropriated, the timing of demand and water availability must be analyzed to determine how much water will be required and to determine whether storage will be required to provide a firm yield for the intended use. "Firm yield" refers to the amount of water that a particular water right will provide every year over some time period (perhaps 50 years), including drought years. If storage is required, evaporation and seepage must be factored into the consideration of how much water will be needed. In addition, new water rights may need to be augmented and replacement supplies obtained. Augmentation plans are discussed in Section 10.3.

This chapter provides basic rules of thumb for different uses under simple water use scenarios; however, the reader should consult with a water engineer in cases involving large or complex projects, changes of water rights, or augmentation plans.

§ 2.2   SPECIFIC USES

§ 2.2.1   Irrigation

The amount of water required for irrigation depends on the type of crop and soil, the method of irrigation, and the natural precipitation and climate of the area. As a general rule, agricultural crops in Colorado consume 1.5 to 2.0 acre-feet of irrigation water per acre in addition to precipitation, depending on the location and type of crop. Turf irrigation may consume as much as 2.5 acre-feet of irrigation water per acre of grass. Vegetables and small grains may consume as little as 1.0 acre-foot of irrigation water, while alfalfa may consume 3.0 acre-feet per acre.

The amount of water that must be applied to meet the crop irrigation requirement varies with the type of irrigation method used. Conventional furrow irrigation methods are approximately 55 percent efficient, meaning that only 55 percent of the water applied may be used by the plants. Sprinkler irrigation is approximately 75 percent efficient, while drip irrigation may be as much as 90 percent efficient. These efficiencies do not factor in ditch seepage losses that typically occur if the water is transported to the land in unlined ditches. As a general rule, a direct flow diversion of one cfs is sufficient to irrigate 40 acres of agricultural crops in Colorado, although various water decrees throughout Colorado have found the water needed for agricultural irrigation to range from one cfs to ten acres, to one cfs to 80 acres. This rule of thumb assumes average soil type and ditch seepage. Sandy soils, leaky ditch systems, or water intensive crops may require more water.

Many municipalities are moving toward using separate non-potable systems for irrigation of parks, golf courses, and even for residential irrigation. Special consideration, however, should be given to use of mutual ditch company shares for these purposes. See Section 15.3 for discussion of mutual ditch companies. In many cases, it is desirable to irrigate lawns, parks, and golf courses for a greater portion of the year than agricultural crops; however, the company ditch may not run during the early and late seasons when other agricultural users are not irrigating. In this situation, a supplemental supply will be required for irrigation during the shoulder seasons. In some cases, however, the ditch companies have begun to divert earlier and later to accommodate these new needs.

If the reader is purchasing agricultural land that receives water through mutual ditch company stock or contract rights from a water conservancy district, the ditch company or district will likely be able to make recommendations or even have regulations concerning how much water is required for irrigation. When purchasing agricultural land together with water rights that were historically used on the land, it is frequently not safe to assume that the water supply is sufficient. In many cases, the land historically irrigated may have had supplemental water supplies from a water conservancy district or other water organization. However, these supplemental supplies may have been previously sold, leaving the remaining supply inadequate to meet the intended irrigation requirements. For more information on investigation of water rights purchases, see Section 5.1.

§ 2.2.2 Domestic or Household Use

A typical family uses approximately one-third of an acre-foot of water per year for in-house uses, excluding outside irrigation. In-house use means water used in the kitchen, for washing clothes, for baths and showers, and for sinks and toilets. Only ten percent or less of that amount is consumed, however. Ninety percent or more of the water that is used in-house is typically returned to the stream system through either underground percolation from a septic system or effluent discharged from a waste water treatment plant. In certain situations where service from a public water supplier is not available, it may be possible for a home owner to obtain a well permit for a small capacity "exempt" well that pumps up to 15 gallons per minute. Such a well often does not require an augmentation plan and, with a small pressure tank (approximately 40 gallons), is more than enough to satisfy most single family household needs. Small capacity "exempt" wells are discussed in Section 4.2.4.

In the case of a small subdivision to be served by one or more private wells, an augmentation plan may be required to replace the amount of water that is consumed and not returned to the stream system. (Augmentation plans are discussed in Section 10.3.) In that case, an augmentation water supply will be needed to replace the water that is consumed. If water use is restricted to in-house use only, the augmentation plan may only require replacement of the approximately ten percent of total diversions that is consumed. Outside irrigation or other uses, such as livestock watering, will substantially increase the amount of water that may need to be replaced. The city or county that has jurisdiction over the subdivision may also have land-use regulations concerning the minimum water supplies.

If water service is to be provided by a municipality or other public water provider, the water provider, as a condition to providing service to new developments, will likely require the developer to dedicate water rights to the water supplier that are sufficient to meet the projected demand of the development. The water rights dedication requirements are usually based on known or estimated yields of different types of water rights and the number of "single family equivalent" units that are planned to be built. In some cases, the water provider may also accept money in lieu of water rights dedication.

§ 2.2.3   Industrial and Commercial Uses

The amount of water needed for industrial and commercial uses depends on the specific use; therefore, it is not possible to give any general rules of thumb. The percentage of water consumed by industrial and commercial uses also depends on the use. In some cases, the use may be virtually non-consumptive and require very little replacement water if an augmentation plan is needed, or the use may be wholly consumptive and require 100 percent replacement of diversions in situations where an augmentation plan is needed.

§ 2.2.4   Evaporation and Seepage

When planning a water project involving water storage, the reader should keep in mind that water storage will incur evaporation losses. The owner of an on-channel reservoir will be required to account for evaporation that occurs when the water right is out of priority, and will be required to obtain a reliable supply to keep the reservoir full or will be required to lower the level of the reservoir to account for out-of-priority evaporation. See discussion of reservoir evaporation in Section 16.1. Off-channel reservoirs will require refilling to replace evaporative losses if the owner desires to keep a constant water level. Evaporation rates vary by location and season and from year to year. Evaporation is generally considered nominal in the winter months in most locations in Colorado. On average, evaporation rates range from 1.0 to 2.0 acre-feet per surface acre of water stored per year but can reach over 3.0 acre-feet per surface area in eastern Colorado and other non-mountainous areas of the state. Unless the reservoir is lined, it will also incur seepage losses. Seepage losses can be extremely high in sandy or other coarse soils, but are usually less in clay soils.

CHAPTER 3 SECURING NEW
SURFACE WATER RIGHTS

§ 3.1   INTRODUCTION

The Colorado Constitution guarantees the right to appropriate the water of any natural stream through the application of water to a beneficial use. Thus, a water right is created at the time water is put to beneficial use, but the owner is not entitled to administration of that water right under the prior appropriation system until the water right is confirmed by a water court decree. To obtain a decreed water right priority that is enforceable under the prior appropriation system, the appropriator must demonstrate that all the elements of an appropriation have been met. If the appropriator has put water to a beneficial use, he or she may seek a decree for an "absolute" water right. If, however, the would-be appropriator has not yet put water to beneficial use, but has the requisite intent to do so, he or she may still seek a decree for a "conditional" water right. If the conditional water right owner completes the appropriation with reasonable diligence, he or she may obtain an absolute priority that relates back to the date on which the appropriation was initiated. This chapter discusses the substantive elements of appropriation of surface water, and the requirements to obtain decrees for conditional and absolute water rights. This chapter also discusses several special kinds of water rights, such as those that have been recognized for instream uses and water rights associated with land reservations made by the federal government.

§ 3.2   ELEMENTS OF THE CONSTITUTIONAL RIGHT TO APPROPRIATE

§ 3.2.1   Right in General

The right to appropriate unappropriated water in natural streams within Colorado is guaranteed by Section 5, Article XVI of the Colorado Constitution, which provides:

> The water of every natural stream, not heretofore appropriated, within the state of Colorado, is hereby declared to be the property of the public, and the same is dedicated to the use of the people of the state, subject to appropriation as hereinafter provided.[1]

Section 6 of Article XVI of the Colorado Constitution further provides that "[t]he right to divert the unappropriated waters of any natural stream to beneficial uses shall never be denied."[2] Colorado courts have carefully interpreted these constitutional provisions to define the elements of an appropriation as well as limits on the kind and amount of water that may be appropriated. Each of the elements and limits of the constitutional right to appropriate are discussed in the following sections.

§ 3.2.2   Waters Subject to Appropriation

The constitutional right to appropriate water is limited to waters of any "natural stream" within Colorado. For purposes of defining the scope of the Constitution, waters of a "natural stream" include all surface water and ground water in or tributary to all natural streams within Colorado. Ground water is discussed in detail in Chapter

---

1   COLO. CONST. art. XVI, § 5.
2   COLO. CONST. art. XVI, § 6.

4. A natural stream also includes a surface stream that, as a natural or man-induced phenomenon, terminates within the state through naturally occurring evaporation or transpiration of its waters.[3]

Intermittent streams or drainages meet the definition of natural streams, even if they flow infrequently or only during periods of flood. All surface water is presumed to be tributary to a natural stream;[4] therefore, even diffused runoff water that has not collected in a defined channel is subject to the prior appropriation system unless it can be proven that the water is not tributary to any stream. As a practical matter, while a landowner may obtain the right to use surface water arising on or running through his land, such right may be subject to curtailment or administration for the benefit of other more senior water rights on the same stream system.

Water that is made available for use, which would not otherwise be available to a stream by natural means, may be appropriated independent of the priority system. This type of water is sometimes referred to as "developed" water. Developed water is discussed in Section 3.4.5.

§ 3.2.3 Water Available for Appropriation

The constitutional right to appropriate water is limited to unappropriated water. Determining beforehand whether there is unappropriated water in a stream has historically proved to be difficult given the fact that water users on a particular stream may have undecreed water rights or decreed—but conditional (unperfected)—water rights, or may not be using the full amount of a decreed water right. The variability of hydrologic conditions also means that unappropriated water may be available in some years, but not other years, or for only part of the year. When a shortage occurs, however, a senior water user can be protected under the priority system by requesting the state water officials to curtail diversion of junior priorities for the benefit of the senior priority. Consequently, Colorado courts historically have not carefully scrutinized whether unappropriated water is available before awarding an appropriator a conditional water right decree. More recently, however, Colorado courts have required the applicant for a conditional water right to show that unappropriated water is available as part of the statutory "can and will" requirement.[5] The can and will provision and its water availability component are discussed in more detail in Section 3.3.4.

---

3   C.R.S. § 37-82-101(2).
4   *Safranek v. Limon*, 123 Colo. 330, 228 P.2d 975 (1951).
5   C.R.S. § 37-92-305(9)(b).

§ 3.2.4   Beneficial Use

The Colorado Constitution provides for the right to divert the unappropriated waters of any natural stream for "beneficial uses."[6] Therefore, a water right may not be appropriated unless the water is put to a "beneficial" use. The beneficial use requirement encourages the actual use of water and discourages the holding of water rights for speculative purposes. Courts have interpreted beneficial use broadly, however. Almost any use of water that requires diversion or impoundment may be considered beneficial, including irrigation, mining, manufacturing, domestic, and impoundment for recreation and fish and wildlife purposes.

Environmental uses are somewhat unique, however. Only the Colorado Water Conservation Board may appropriate water to remain in a stream or a natural lake for preservation of the natural environment. Certain entities such as cities, municipalities, and water districts may also appropriate water to be used in the stream for recreational use by controlling it in the stream channel using structures that create features to provide a recreation experience in and on the water.[7] Such water rights are referred to as recreational in-channel diversion (RICD) water rights, and are discussed in Section 3.4.2.

Waste

The waste of water cannot be the basis of an appropriation. The limit of beneficial use is the amount of water that is reasonable and appropriate under reasonably efficient practices to accomplish the intended use without waste.[8] Waste is not specifically defined in the statute, but any amount of water beyond what would be reasonably needed to accomplish the intended purpose using reasonably efficient practices may be considered waste. The courts have not typically scrutinized the efficiency of a claimed use; however, where *no* showing of efficiency is made, the court may deny the water right claim. For example, in one early case, the court considered a claim by a resort for all of the water in a waterfall on the basis that mist from the waterfall was used to irrigate vegetation on the canyon walls, which was then enjoyed by the resort visitors.[9] The court ruled that such a claim for water in a waterfall for the purpose of irrigating the canyon vegetation by mist could not be granted because no comparison was made of the amount claimed to the amount of water that would be required to sustain the vegetation under usual irrigation practices. A claim of waste is sometimes

---

6   COLO. CONST. art. XVI, § 6.
7   C.R.S. § 37-92-103(4).
8   C.R.S. § 37-92-103(4).
9   *Empire Water & Power Co. v. Cascade Town Co.*, 205 F. 123 (8th Cir. 1913).

raised by objectors or the Division Engineer in a water court proceeding to reduce the amount of water decreed for an initial appropriation.

Duty of Water

One judicial response to the beneficial use requirement, and an early attempt to limit excessive irrigation water right claims, is the court-imposed "duty of water" limitation.[10] Simply put, the duty of water for irrigation use is the amount of water reasonably needed to be applied to a given tract of land to produce the maximum crop. Some early decrees contain limitations of one cfs of water for 40 acres of irrigated land.[11] Historically, however, courts have made little attempt to compare the efficiency of proposed uses or limit excessive claims. In some cases, irrigation water rights have even been decreed for flow rates greater than the capacity of the diversion ditch. The duty of water issue may be raised by the Division Engineer, however, in his required consultation with the water referee concerning water court applications. See Section 1.2.8 concerning the water adjudication process.

Reasonable Means of Diversion

Another tenet of Colorado water law related to the beneficial use limitation is the requirement that a diverter establish a reasonable means of effectuating his diversion. Colorado statute provides that a diverter may not "command the whole flow of the stream merely to facilitate his taking the fraction of the whole flow to which he is entitled."[12] This limitation stems from a famous case involving a senior irrigator, who used water wheels powered by current in the river to lift water out of the river for irrigation, and a junior dam builder whose dam backed water up to the water wheels and prevented their use. The irrigator sued and, on appeal, the United States Supreme Court ruled in favor of the dam builder, finding that the irrigator's means of diversion was not reasonable.[13] In a Colorado case involving a dispute between a junior well owner and a senior well owner, the Colorado Supreme Court held that the senior appropriator, whose well was so shallow that minor decreases in the water table caused it to fail, was not protected from junior appropriations because the means of diversion was not reasonable.[14] The Court also stated that the senior appropriator

---

[10]   *Farmers Highline Canal & Reservoir Co. v. City of Golden*, 129 Colo. 575, 272 P.2d 629 (1954).

[11]   J. Corbridge Jr. & T. Rice, VRANESH'S COLORADO WATER LAW at 47 (rev. ed. 1999).

[12]   C.R.S. § 37-92-102(2)(b).

[13]   *Schodde v. Twin Falls Land & Water Co.*, 224 U.S. 107 (1912).

[14]   *City of Colo. Springs v. Bender*, 148 Colo. 458, 366 P.2d 552 (1961).

could not be made to improve the well beyond his economic reach and suggested that the cost of deepening the well might be properly borne by the junior. The Colorado Supreme Court has also stated that it may be reasonable in some circumstances to require senior surface diverters to use wells when it would be a more efficient means of diversion that would maximize use of the entire water resource.[15]

In the context of an original adjudication, the Division Engineer may examine the reasonableness of the diversion, particularly if it is challenged by an objector, and provide the Water Referee with a field inspection report, usually done by the Water Commissioner.

Anti-Speculation

Another doctrine related to the beneficial use requirement is the prohibition in Colorado against appropriating water for speculative uses.[16] The anti-speculation doctrine is also related to the goal of conservation of the water resource because all water in Colorado is deemed to be in public ownership.[17] Individuals may perfect the right to use water, but may not own the public water resource. The anti-speculation doctrine is discussed in more detail in Section 3.3.3.

§ 3.2.5   Diversion

Colorado courts have generally required that water be diverted or removed from the stream to constitute a valid appropriation. For example, in a case involving the Colorado River Water Conservation District, the district sought water rights for flows to be left in the stream for fish propagation and fishing recreation purposes. The Colorado Supreme Court rejected the claim on the basis that actual diversion was required.[18] The court analogized the district's claim to a claim for riparian water rights, which are not recognized in Colorado.

Several early exceptions to the requirement that water must be diverted from the stream were recognized in Colorado, making the law somewhat confusing. For example, in *Empire Water & Power Co., v. Cascade Town Co.*,[19] a federal court interpreting Colorado law suggested that, in order to complete an appropriation of water, a resort

---

15 *Alamosa-La Jara Water Users Protection Ass'n v. Gould*, 674 P.2d 914 (Colo. 1983)

16 C.R.S. § 37-92-103(3)(a), *Colo. River Water Conservation Dist. v. Vidler Tunnel Water Co.*, 197 Colo. 413, 594 P.2d 566 (1979).

17 *Colorado Groundwater Com'n v. N. Kiowa-Bijou Groundwater Mgmt. Dist.*, 77 P.3d 62 (Colo. 2003).

18 *Colo. River Water Conservation Dist. v. Rocky Mountain Power Co.*, 158 Colo. 331, 406 P.2d 798 (1965).

19 *Empire Water*, 205 F. 123 (8th Cir. 1913).

need not construct ditches to irrigate lush vegetation on the walls of a canyon if the natural spray of a waterfall accomplished this goal without an artificial diversion. The court found that there was a clear intent to appropriate water for beneficial uses, as shown by the resort's extensive improvement of its property to allow visitors to experience the scenic beauty of the waterfall. The court ultimately rejected the claim for irrigation by spray from the waterfall, however, finding that the resort had not shown that such use of water in the stream was efficient for the intended purpose, as compared to customary means of irrigation. The Colorado Supreme Court has also held that stock watering in a natural pond may give rise to a valid appropriation without a diversion.[20]

Diversion is statutorily defined as "removing water from its natural course or location, or controlling water in its natural course or location, by means of a ditch, canal, flume, reservoir, bypass, pipeline, conduit, well, pump, or other structure or device...."[21] In 1973, the General Assembly removed the diversion requirement from the definition of appropriation and enacted legislation granting authority to the State of Colorado to appropriate minimum stream flows and lake levels for the preservation of the natural environment. These water rights, generally known as "instream flow" rights because water is left undiverted in the stream, are discussed in Section 3.4.1. Colorado statute still provides that, except for minimum stream flows and lake levels appropriated by the state, no water right may be recognized nor decree therefor granted except to the extent that the waters have been "diverted, stored, or otherwise captured, possessed, and controlled...."[22] Water may be "diverted" by controlling it in its natural course. Thus, the Colorado Supreme Court found that a boat chute and fish ladder constructed in a pre-existing dam controlled water in its natural course by concentrating the flow of the river to allow boats and fish to pass over the dam at low flows.[23] Similarly, water courts have found that man-made kayak course structures functioned to create whitewater features in the creek and therefore controlled water in its natural course for purposes of the statute. In 2001, the Colorado General Assembly adopted legislation that specifically defined and limited so-called "recreational in-channel diversion" water rights. Recreational in-channel diversion water rights are discussed in more detail in Section 3.4.2.

---

20 *Town of Genoa v. Westfall*, 141 Colo. 533, 349 P.2d 370 (1960).
21 C.R.S. § 37-92-103(7).
22 C.R.S. § 37-92-305(9)(a).
23 *City of Thornton v. City of Fort Collins*, 830 P.2d 915 (Colo. 1992).

§ 3.3   CONDITIONAL WATER RIGHTS

§ 3.3.1   Relation Back

Large water development projects often take many years to complete before water can be put to beneficial use. If the developer of such a project could not obtain a water right decree until after water was put to beneficial use, it is possible that in the time that it takes to complete the project other water rights could be perfected, making unappropriated water no longer available in the amount originally estimated when the decision to build the project was made. To provide for some certainty in water development planning, Colorado law recognizes conditional water rights upon a showing that the appropriator has the intent to appropriate water for beneficial use and has taken the "first substantial" step toward initiation of the appropriation.[24] The appropriation date for a conditional water right is the date on which the appropriator performs acts that evidence the appropriator's intent to appropriate and the first step toward initiation of the appropriation. Upon completion of the appropriation with reasonable diligence, the appropriator may obtain an absolute water right with an appropriation date that relates back to the date the first step was completed.

§ 3.3.2   First Step Test

The first step test is a somewhat confusing court-made doctrine. The test is divided into an intent prong and an overt acts prong, although there is some overlap between the two. The first step toward completion of an appropriation is complete when the intent to appropriate water for beneficial use and overt acts sufficient to constitute notice to third parties of the proposed use have both occurred. The requisite intent and overt acts need not occur in any order, but the appropriation date will be the date on which the last of the necessary elements is satisfied.

Intent

The Colorado Supreme Court recently summarized the intent prong as follows:

> Intent to appropriate requires a fixed purpose to pursue diligently a certain course of action to take and beneficially use water from a particular source. The intent must be relatively specific regarding the amount of water to be appropriated, its place of diversion, and its type of beneficial use; but, for the purposes of a conditional water

---

24   *Taussig v. Moffat Tunnel Water & Dev. Co.*, 106 Colo. 384, 106 P.2d 363 (1940).

right decree, the applicant need not know the exact amount of water or point of diversion at the time of the first step. The applicant may demonstrate intent by filing the conditional water right application.[25]

Overt Acts

The overt acts comprising the second prong of the first step test must fulfill three functions. First, the overt acts must manifest the necessary intent to appropriate water and apply it to a beneficial use. The requisite intent may be demonstrated by such acts as filing an application in water court or posting a sign at the proposed diversion point. The councils or boards of cities, counties, and water districts often confirm their intent by passing a resolution stating the intent to appropriate a water right.

Second, the conditional water right applicant must demonstrate the taking of a substantial step toward applying water to a beneficial use. What constitutes a substantial step depends upon the facts of each case. A large project to divert substantial amounts of water will require more activity to satisfy the substantial step function than a small project. Thus, a field survey of the diversion site may constitute a substantial first step for a small project, but may not be sufficient for a large project. The act must also be directly connected to developing water for beneficial use. Substantial activity, if not directly related to initiating the appropriation, will not satisfy the substantial step function. Overt acts that may demonstrate the taking of a substantial step include any useful acts towards effectuating an appropriation, such as planning the appropriation of water, undertaking or financing studies regarding feasibility of the diversion, or applying for required permits. The act of filing a water right application, however, is unlikely by itself to constitute the taking of a substantial step.

Finally, the applicant must demonstrate an overt act constituting notice to other potential or actual appropriators of the nature and extent of the proposed demand upon the water supply. Mere notice of an unrefined intent to appropriate is not enough, but a detailed summary of exact diversion specifications is not required either. Thus, simply staking a diversion point will probably not be sufficient; however, posting a sign that describes the nature and extent of the claimed water rights may be sufficient. Filing a water court application will also satisfy the notice function; however, the water court application must be specific enough to put interested persons on inquiry notice of the nature, scope and impact of the proposed diversion.[26]

---

25   *Vought v. Stucker Mesa Domestic Pipeline Co.*, 76 P.3d 906 (Colo. 2003).
26   *City of Thornton v. Bijou Irr. Co.*, 926 P.2d 1 (Colo. 1996).

> Water rights application forms for a number of different kinds of water rights are available from the water court (more information is included in the Appendix, at § 1.1) at the Colorado Division of Water Resources Web site: http://www.water.state.co.us, or at the Colorado Courts Web site: http://www.courts.state.co.us/chs/court/forms/waterforms/water.htm

Summary

A conditional water right applicant must undertake actions that demonstrate the intent to appropriate water for beneficial use, constitute a first substantial step toward application of water to beneficial use, and provide notice to others of the nature and extent of the proposed appropriation. Any single action is unlikely to satisfy all the requirements of the first step test. For example, in *City of Thornton v. Bijou Irrigation Co.*,[27] adoption of a formal resolution to appropriate water by the City Utilities Board, and posting general notices at and surveying the location of some points of diversion, were held to demonstrate an intent to appropriate and constitute a substantial step toward application of water to beneficial use. However, it was only when the actual water right applications were filed with the water clerk on December 31, 1986, that sufficient notice of the claimed appropriation was given. Thus, the court held that the date of appropriation for Thornton was December 31, 1986.

§ 3.3.3 Anti-Speculation

In *Colorado River Water Conservation District v. Vidler Tunnel Water Co.*, the Colorado Supreme Court held:

> Our constitution guarantees a right to appropriate, not a right to speculate. The right to appropriate is for use, not merely for profit.... To recognize conditional decrees grounded on no interest beyond a desire to obtain water for sale would—as a practical matter—discourage those who have need and use for the water from developing it. Moreover, such a rule would encourage those with vast monetary resources to monopolize, for personal profit rather than for beneficial use, whatever unappropriated water remains.[28]

---

27 *City of Thornton v. Bijou Irr. Co.*, 926 P.2d 1 (Colo. 1996).
28 *Vidler*, 197 Colo. 413, 417, 594 P.2d 566, 568 (1979).

In *Vidler*, the court denied conditional water rights for the water company because the proposed appropriation was being sought by the water company on the assumption that a growing population would produce a general need for more water in the future, but the water company had no contract or agency relationship justifying its claim to represent those with future needs.

In 1979, the General Assembly modified the definition of appropriation to codify the *Vidler* decision regarding speculation.[29] The statute provides that no appropriation shall be held to occur when the proposed appropriation is based upon the speculative sale or transfer of the water rights to persons not parties to the proposed appropriation. A proposed appropriation will be deemed to be speculative if the purported appropriator does not have a legally vested interest or reasonable expectation of procuring an interest in the land or the facilities to be served by the appropriation. An exception is made, however, for governmental agencies to allow some planning and flexibility with respect to future water needs. Thus, a municipal water provider may obtain decreed conditional water rights based on future needs without firm contractual commitments or agency relationships. The amount of water that may be conditionally appropriated, however, is limited to the municipality's "reasonably anticipated requirements based on substantiated projections of future growth."[30] Merely showing that growth can occur if more water is acquired is not sufficient to substantiate a projection of future growth. Future growth considerations can include areas not presently within the municipal boundaries; however, the municipal exception to the anti-speculation doctrine does not apply where the municipality seeks to appropriate water to sell for profit on the open market to users outside its boundaries.[31]

Under the statute, a proposed appropriation will also be deemed speculative if the purported appropriator does not have a specific plan and intent to divert, store, or otherwise capture, possess, and control a specific quantity of water for specific beneficial uses. Again, an exception is made to allow for the reasonable anticipated needs of municipal water providers.

§ 3.3.4 Can and Will Requirement

The so-called "can and will" requirement stems from the following statutory provision:

---

29   C.R.S. § 37-92-103(3).

30   *Bijou Irr.*, 926 P.2d at 38-39.

31   *City of Denver v. Colorado River Water Conservation Dist.*, 696 P.2d 730 (Colo. 1985).

> No claim for a conditional water right may be recognized or a decree therefor granted except to the extent that it is established that the waters can be and will be diverted, stored, or otherwise captured, possessed and controlled and will be beneficially used and that the project can and will be completed with diligence and within a reasonable time.[32]

The can and will requirement is related to the concern that water uses be beneficial, not speculative, and is designed to increase certainty in the administration of water rights. The can and will doctrine is broader than the anti-speculation doctrine because it requires the applicant to prove a substantial probability that the appropriation can and will be completed with diligence based on predictions of future conditions.

As a threshold requirement, the applicant must show that unappropriated water is available for appropriation. The applicant for a conditional water right must prove that sufficient unappropriated water is available for the proposed project, taking into account the actual operation of decrees. The court will consider only the historical use of absolute water rights, and may not consider conditional water rights under which no diversions have been made.[33] Only a showing of reasonable availability is required. The applicant does not have to show that water will always be available to the full extent of the decree. If, however, the applicant cannot prove the reasonable availability of water, the application will be denied. A water engineer or hydrologist is usually required to demonstrate water availability if the issue is raised.

Although not threshold requirements, other factors, such as land ownership, access, and permitting issues, may be considered in determining whether water can and will be put to beneficial use and whether the project will be completed with diligence. Lack of access at the time of the application is not an absolute bar, however, to a conditional water right. The applicant may rely on an unexercised private right of condemnation to show access, unless there are no circumstances under which the applicant can gain access to complete the appropriation. This situation might occur where the water source is located on public land and the private right of condemnation is not available and governmental authorization has been denied in a final action. Similarly, uncertainty about whether the project will obtain all necessary permits in

---

32 C.R.S. § 37-92-305(9)(b).

33 *County Com'rs of County of Arapahoe v. Crystal Creek Homeowners' Ass'n*, 14 P.3d 325 (Colo. 2000).

the future is not likely to be an absolute bar to a conditional water right, unless the circumstances are such that the project clearly cannot obtain the necessary approvals.

§ 3.3.5   Reasonable Diligence

In order for a perfected conditional water right to relate back to the date of completion of the first step, the appropriation must be completed with reasonable diligence. Reasonable diligence is statutorily defined as:

> [T]he steady application of effort to complete the appropriation in a reasonably expedient and efficient manner under all the facts and circumstances. When a project or integrated system is comprised of several features, work on one feature of the project or system shall be considered in finding that reasonable diligence has been shown in the development of water rights for all features of the entire project or system.[34]

Reasonable diligence is a fact-based determination requiring the water court to consider all relevant evidence, including the size, complexity, and economic feasibility of the project; the extent of the construction season; the availability of material, labor, and equipment; the economic ability of the claimant; and the intervention of outside delaying factors.[35] Thus, there is no specific time frame in which a conditional water right must be perfected, and there are many examples of water rights in Colorado that have remained conditional for several decades.

Physical activity, such as initiation of construction, may not be required to show reasonable diligence. The acquisition of rights of way, planning, designing, financing, research, and litigation to protect the subject water rights may be sufficient effort to constitute reasonable diligence under the circumstances. Only effort made during the diligence period will count toward satisfying the reasonable diligence requirement. Where the project consists of several integrated features, work on one portion of the project may be sufficient to show diligence for another portion of the project as long as construction of the first portion of the project is necessary for the operation of the entire project.[36]

Economic conditions beyond the control of the applicant which adversely affect the feasibility of the project are not sufficient to deny a diligence application, as long

---

34   C.R.S. § 37-92-301(4)(b).

35   *Colorado River Water Conservation Dist. v. Twin Lakes Reservoir & Canal Co.*, 171 Colo. 561, 468 P.2d 853 (1970).

36   C.R.S. § 37-92-301(4)(b).

as other facts and circumstances indicate that reasonable diligence has been exercised.[37] In one of a series of recent oil shale conditional water rights diligence cases, the Colorado Supreme Court held that, even though evidence was introduced suggesting that the oil shale project could be delayed until as far in the future as 2085 because of economic considerations, the oil company's diligence application was properly granted when the evidence showed that the company had undertaken activities and expended effort toward developing the project.[38] Lack of one or more necessary governmental approvals was not sufficient by itself to deny a diligence application.[39]

Every six years, the holder of a conditional water right must file an application with the water court seeking a finding that he or she has exercised reasonable diligence toward completion of the appropriation or made the water right absolute by virtue of placing water to beneficial use.[40] The six-year period starts on the date the decree for the conditional water right or any subsequent finding of reasonable diligence is entered. The decree must specify the year and month in which the diligence application must be filed. If the conditional water right holder fails to file an application for finding of reasonable diligence or to make the conditional water right absolute within the six-year period, then the conditional water right may be cancelled.[41]

The water court is required to notify the conditional water right owner at least 60 days in advance of the pending cancellation, by certified or registered mail at the last address appearing on the records of the court.[42] For this reason, it is important (and required by the local water court rules) for the conditional water right owner to notify the court of any change in ownership or address.[43] The diligence filing deadline operates like a statute of limitations to cancel conditional water rights; however, a conditional water right cannot be cancelled until the water court gives notice of the pending cancellation. Where the water court fails to give such notice, the conditional water right owner shall be allowed to file an application for finding of reasonable diligence after the six-year deadline has expired.[44]

---

37 C.R.S. § 37-92-301(4)(c).

38 *Municipal Subdistrict, N. Colorado Water Conservancy Dist. v. Chevron Shale Oil Co.*, 986 P.2d 918 (Colo. 1999).

39 C.R.S. § 37-92-301(4)(c).

40 C.R.S. § 37-92-301(4)(a)(I).

41 C.R.S. § 37-92-301(4)(a)(I).

42 C.R.S. § 37-92-305(7).

43 Uniform Local Rules For All State Water Court Divisions, Rule 9(b) (2003).

44 *Double RL Co. v. Telluray Ranch Props.*, 54 P.3d 908 (Colo. 2002).

§ 3.3.6   Making Water Rights Absolute

Once water is beneficially used pursuant to a conditional water right, the conditional water right owner may file an application in water court to make the conditional water right absolute. The applicant will be required to show when, how, and to what extent the water was first put to beneficial use. The applicant may also be required to show that the water used was legally available in priority. Therefore, the applicant should carefully document all water use to support the application to make the right absolute. Only that portion of the water right that was placed to beneficial use may be made absolute. For example, if the owner of a conditional water right decreed for irrigation, commercial, and domestic uses in the amount of 5.0 cubic feet per second (cfs) diverts and uses 1.0 cfs for irrigation, the water right may be made absolute for 1.0 cfs for irrigation. The remaining amount and other uses will remain conditional as long as the owner makes the required showing of reasonable diligence every six years. Once a water right is made absolute, the owner need not make any further showing of reasonable diligence with respect to that portion or those uses that have been made absolute. Such water right is considered perfected and may be lost only by abandonment or adverse possession, discussed in Sections 16.3 and 16.4. The act of placing a portion of the conditional water right to beneficial use may also count toward satisfying the reasonable diligence requirement for the remaining portion of the conditional water right.

§ 3.4   SPECIAL SITUATIONS

§ 3.4.1   Minimum Stream Flows

In 1973, the General Assembly enacted legislation that gave the Colorado Water Conservation Board (CWCB) authority to appropriate minimum stream flows between specific points or lake levels for preservation of the natural environment to a reasonable degree without removing or otherwise controlling water in its natural course or location.[45] These water rights are commonly known as instream flows. The Colorado Supreme Court upheld the constitutionality of this legislation against a challenge by the Colorado River Water Conservation District, finding that a diversion is not a constitutionally required element of an appropriation.[46] In 1987, the legislature clarified that the CWCB has exclusive authority to appropriate minimum stream flows and lake levels.

---

45   C.R.S. § 37-92-102(3).

46   *Colorado River Water Conservation Dist. v. Colorado Water Conservation Bd.*, 197 Colo. 469, 594 P.2d 570 (1979).

There are several limitations on the amount of water that can be appropriated and how instream flow water rights can be obtained. Appropriations for minimum stream flows and lake levels are limited to the minimum amount needed to preserve the natural environment to a reasonable degree. The CWCB may also acquire other water rights it deems appropriate to preserve or improve the natural environment to a reasonable degree, but such rights may not be acquired for instream flow purposes by the power of eminent domain or condemnation[47]. Private individuals, conservation organizations, or municipalities that desire to protect instream flows may donate existing water rights to the CWCB for instream flow purposes. Because the existing water rights would not be decreed for instream flow uses, a change of water right proceeding must be filed in water court to allow the existing water rights to be used for the new purpose of instream flow purposes. The CWCB cannot, however, acquire and change conditional water rights for instream flow purposes.[48] Changes of water rights are discussed in Section 10.1.

Any new appropriation by the CWCB will be subject to the priority system and will necessarily be a junior priority. In addition, all CWCB appropriations are subject to all existing uses or exchanges of water being made by other water users, regardless of whether such uses or exchanges are decreed. The appropriation of instream flows by the CWCB does not create any public right of access over private lands to gain access to a stream or lake benefited by a CWCB appropriation.[49]

> The CWCB rules and regulations pertaining to instream flow rights are available at http://www.cwcb.state.co.us/isf/Rules/Adopted_Rules.pdf

The CWCB has established rules and regulations for development and protection of instream flow water rights.[50] Pursuant to these rules, any person or entity may make recommendations for the inclusion of stream reaches or natural lakes in the CWCB's instream flow program. Following a recommendation, CWCB staff will review the request and make a recommendation to the CWCB on whether to proceed with an instream flow appropriation. Recommendations for instream flows are considered by the CWCB once a year, in January. Based on a review and recommendation

---

[47] C.R.S. § 37-92-102(3).
[48] C.R.S. § 37-92-102(3)(c.5).
[49] C.R.S. §§ 37-92-102(3)(b), (d).
[50] Rules Concerning the Colorado Instream Flow & Natural Lake Level Program (I.S.F.R.) (codified as amended at 5 C.C.R. § 408-2.

by CWCB staff, the CWCB may declare its intent to appropriate an instream flow water right. Proposed instream flows are then submitted to a public notice and comment procedure, and a hearing if necessary. The CWCB will file an application in water court to obtain judicial confirmation of any instream flow water right the CWCB determines to be appropriate.

§ 3.4.2 Recreational In-Channel Diversion Rights

Recreational in-channel diversion water rights (RICDs) are a recent addition to Colorado water law. Beneficial use now includes the diversion of water by a county, municipality, water district, or water conservancy district for recreational in-channel diversion purposes. Recreational in-channel diversion, in turn, is defined as the "minimum stream flow as it is diverted, captured, controlled, and placed to beneficial use between specific points defined by physical control structures" pursuant to an application filed by a county, municipality, water district, or water conservancy district "for a reasonable recreation experience in and on the water."[51]

RICDs are distinguished from instream flows by the requirement that water be controlled in the channel by "control structures." Water need not be controlled and no structure is required for an instream flow. The RICD statute allows various government entities and quasi-governmental water organizations to appropriate RICDs, while only the CWCB may appropriate instream flows. Another distinction is that RICDs are for the purpose of providing a reasonable recreation experience in and on the water, while instream flows are to preserve the natural environment to a reasonable degree.

Under the statute, only municipalities and public water providers may claim RICDs, and they are limited to the minimum stream flow that is diverted, captured, or controlled by structures and put to beneficial use for a reasonable recreational experience. The CWCB must first review the application and make initial findings of fact and a final recommendation to the water court as to whether the application should be granted, granted with conditions, or denied.[52] The CWCB's findings are presumed valid, subject to rebuttal at trial. The water court must consider several factors in deciding whether to grant an RICD application. The factors that must be considered include whether the RICD would impair the ability of Colorado to fully develop and use the water it is entitled to under interstate compacts, whether exercise of the RICD would cause material injury to instream flow water rights, and whether the RICD would promote maximum utilization of the waters of the state.

---

51   C.R.S. § 37-92-103(10.3).
52   C.R.S. § 37-92-102(b)(5).

> The CWCB has promulgated rules and regulations for review of RICD applications, which are available at the CWCB Web site: http://www.cwcb.state.co.us/isf/Programs/RICD_main.htm. The CWCB's policies concerning RICD water rights are also available at the above Web site.

There are many unanswered questions as to the nature and extent of RICDs. For example, most RICD applications have been for white-water kayaking and rafting uses. It is not clear whether the statute provides for other recreation uses such as tubing, fishing, or aesthetic viewing. Also, it is not known what kind of controlling structure is required or what the standard is for determining if water is diverted, captured, or controlled. You should therefore seek professional assistance early in the process of considering an RICD appropriation.

§ 3.4.3   Meadow Rights

A somewhat anomalous and very old statute in Colorado, known as the "Meadow Act," recognizes that an appropriation may be made without a headgate or a ditch by virtue of using the natural flooding or overflow of a stream to irrigate a meadow.[53] The Meadow Act provides that any person who formerly enjoyed the use of such overflow water for irrigation of meadow land may, if the water supply is diminished, have the right to construct a ditch for the irrigation of such meadow. Any such ditch that is constructed is entitled to a water right with a priority as though the ditch had been constructed at the time the meadow land was first used. While this statute appears to allow the priority for a later decreed meadow right to antedate previously decreed water rights priorities, the Colorado Supreme Court has interpreted the Meadow Act to not allow meadow rights to antedate the priorities fixed by previously awarded decrees.[54] Thus, the Meadow Act is not an exception to the postponement doctrine, and the statute probably has little applicability today.

§ 3.4.4   Seeps and Springs

Another old and confusing statute concerns the rights of landowners to seepage and spring waters arising on their lands. The spring statute provides in part that "the person upon whose land the seepage or spring waters first arise shall have the prior

---

53   C.R.S. § 37-86-113.
54   *Broad Run Inv. Co. v. Deuel & Snyder Imp. Co.*, 47 Colo. 573, 108 P. 755 (1910).

right to such waters if capable of being used upon his lands."[55] The Colorado Supreme Court, however, has made it clear that this provision is applicable only in situations where the water from the seep or spring would not otherwise reach a natural stream and is therefore not tributary in nature. The water in such case might also be recognized as "developed" water, *i.e.*, water that an appropriator makes available for use which would not otherwise be available to a natural stream by any natural means discussed in Section 3.4.5. In Colorado, however, any flowing water, even diffuse runoff and seepage that is not in a defined channel, is presumed to find its way to a stream and be tributary in nature; therefore, a landowner seeking to use the spring or seep must prove that the water is not tributary and thus not subject to the prior appropriation system. This is usually not possible, except in rare situations.

Where a spring or seep is proven to be not tributary to a natural stream, however, and the water is subject to use by others, the statute provides that the owner of the land on which the spring or seep arises has the prior right of use if capable of being used on his lands. Another statute concerning springs provides that waters of natural flowing springs may be appropriated, and the priorities of such appropriations may be determined in accordance with the prior appropriation system; however, if the water from the spring is not tributary, the determination of priorities shall fix the rights of appropriators from the springs among themselves.[56]

In reality, water from most springs and seeps would find its way on the surface or by underground percolation into a natural stream. Thus, the landowner usually does not have a prior right to use the water from most springs and seeps. However, there are many old decrees that determined water sources to be not tributary or independent of other priorities that today would probably be considered tributary. The non-tributary determinations made in these decrees, even if erroneous, are not subject to legal attack because of judicial doctrines of finality, sometimes collectively referred to as *res judicata*. Many of these water rights were initially decreed for irrigation. It is not clear that these sources can be changed to different or more consumptive uses in the future and still maintain their not tributary status.

§ 3.4.5 Developed and Salvaged Water

As noted above, developed water is water that would not be available to a natural stream by any natural means. Developed water belongs to the developer and is not subject to the prior appropriative rights of others. Developed water may be used and reused to extinction like imported or foreign water discussed in Section 3.4.7. The

---

55   C.R.S. § 37-82-102.
56   C.R.S. § 37-82-103.

seminal case involving developed water is *Pikes Peak Golf Club, Inc. v. Kuiper*.[57] In that case, the golf club drained a hayfield that was located above a shallow impervious layer of shale that caused the hay field to have standing water and subirrigation conditions, and used the water to irrigate the golf course. The evidence demonstrated that 240 acre-feet of the water trapped by the shale layer would naturally evaporate or be transpired and never reach the stream. The court found that this amount of water was not historically tributary and not subject to administration by the State Engineer. In reaching this result, the court relied partly on the non-tributary spring statute and earlier cases that held, where a person by his or her own efforts has increased the flow of water in a natural stream, he or she is entitled to the use of the water to the extent of the increase.[58]

Following the *Pikes Peak* decision, a claim was soon made for water independent of the priority system made available by the eradication of phreatophytes (water-loving vegetation, such as cottonwood trees) along the Arkansas River.[59] The Colorado Supreme Court distinguished this case from *Pikes Peak*, however, and ruled that the water made available by elimination of vegetation was "salvaged" water, not developed water. Salvaged water is not new water to the system, but is water that had always belonged to the stream, only now made available for use by the prevention of waste. Since salvaged water is water that always belonged to the river, it is not subject to independent appropriation. From an environmental standpoint, this decision may have been motivated by a desire to avoid wholesale destruction of vegetation for the sake of developing water.

§ 3.4.6   Seepage, Waste Water, and Return Flow

Like the law regarding salvaged water and developed water, the law pertaining to appropriation of seepage, waste water, and return flow water is somewhat confusing. Waste water or return flow is water that is not consumed and returns to the stream after initial application of water to beneficial use. As an example, ordinary household uses typically only consume five to ten percent of the water used. Losses due to the waste water treatment process account for part of the water consumed for these uses

---

[57]   169 Colo. 309, 455 P.2d 882 (1969).

[58]   The Colorado Supreme Court later clarified that the *Pikes Peak* opinion should be read to hold that the transpired water was non-tributary because its source was a non-tributary pool of water trapped by impervious shale, not that water evaporated or transpired from the soil or surface is inherently non-tributary because it does not find its way to the stream. *Giffen v. State*, 690 P.2d 1244 (Colo. 1984).

[59]   *Southeastern Colorado Water Conservancy Dist. v. Shelton Farms, Inc.*, 187 Colo. 181, 529 P.2d 1321 (1974).

before it is returned to the stream as effluent. As another example, typical furrow irrigation of row crops consumes only about one-half of the water diverted. The other half returns to the stream by surface runoff or subsurface percolation. The water that returns to the stream from irrigation is often referred to as irrigation return flow. Seepage may occur as a result of storing or transporting water in unlined reservoirs or ditches.

Seepage, waste water, and return flow from the use of tributary water is water that belongs to the stream and is thus subject to appropriation. Like runoff and diffuse water, seepage, wastewater, and return flow may be appropriated even before reaching a natural stream, but may be subject to prior rights on the stream.[60] Use of underground seepage is subject to the elements of appropriation, however. Thus, where crops are benefited by subirrigation due to seepage from an upland reservoir, the use of such seepage water by subirrigation is not an appropriation because no diversion has been made.[61]

Downstream appropriators are entitled to rely on historical return flows from tributary water. Thus, a water right owner may not, independent of the priority system, enlarge the use of an original appropriation by later reusing or making additional uses of return flow that historically accrued to the stream.[62] Nothing prohibits an appropriator, however, from fully consuming water under an original appropriation for uses that are wholly consumptive, such as industrial and manufacturing. It is also possible to appropriate rights of reuse in connection with an initial use, but the appropriator must make a proper showing of intent to reuse the water combined with overt acts evidencing such intent. A fixed and definite plan for reuse is also required.[63]

Many water rights benefit from or are based on the appropriation of seepage, waste water, or irrigation return flow. Although a junior appropriator may generally object to changes of water rights that cause injury to his water rights, there are special considerations pertaining to seepage, waste water, and return flow. The appropriator of seepage, wastewater, or irrigation return flow cannot compel the continuation of the original use that causes such water to occur, and cannot compel the continuation of waste.[64] Similarly, one cannot force another to exercise his or her water right in order to cause seepage or return flow to occur. In addition, Colorado courts have held that appropriators may not object to a change in the point of *discharge* of wastewater

60   *Comstock v. Ramsay*, 55 Colo. 244, 133 P. 1107 (1913).
61   *Lamont v. Riverside Irr. Dist.*, 179 Colo. 134, 498 P.2d 1150 (1972).
62   *Pulaski Irrigating Ditch Co. v. City of Trinidad*, 70 Colo. 565, 203 P. 681 (1922).
63   *Water Supply and Storage Co. v. Curtis*, 733 P.2d 680 (Colo. 1987).
64   *Burkart v. Meiberg*, 37 Colo. 187, 86 P.98 (1906).

that affects their water rights. Thus, when the City of Denver built a new sewage treatment plant and moved the point of discharge of its effluent downstream to a point on the South Platte River that was below the Burlington Ditch headgate, the Colorado Supreme Court held that the ditch company could not require Denver to maintain the old point of discharge above the ditch headgate.[65]

The *Denver* case must be squared, however, with other cases that firmly hold that the junior appropriator is entitled to maintenance of stream conditions existing at the time of his or her appropriation and a senior appropriator may only change the use of his or her water right if no injury will result to other junior water rights. The *Denver* court made a distinction between a change in the point of return or discharge of waste water and a change in point of diversion or place of use that also causes a change in point of return. Junior appropriators may not assert injury from a change in point of wastewater return when there is no change in point of diversion or place of use. Junior appropriators may challenge, however, a change in point of diversion or place of use that results in relocation of the point of discharge of wastewater that causes injury to other appropriators who have relied on the location and amount of such return flows.

§ 3.4.7   Imported or Foreign Water

Imported or foreign water is water that is introduced to a stream system from an unconnected stream system. The most familiar type of imported water is water that is diverted from the western slope of Colorado to the eastern slope via a transmountain diversion. Water that is imported from one water division to another would in most cases also be considered imported water because, with the exception of the Gunnison River basin (Water Division 4), the streams in one water division do not connect with streams of another water division within the state. Water diverted from one stream to another stream in the same water division may not be considered imported water if the two streams connect within the state.

Imported water is treated differently than native water. Whenever an appropriator has lawfully introduced foreign water into a stream, "such appropriator may make a succession of uses of such water by exchange or otherwise to the extent that its volume can be distinguished from the volume of the streams into which it is introduced."[66] The statute further provides:

---

65   *Metro. Denver Sewage Disposal Dist. No. 1 v. The Farmers Reservoir and Irr. Co.*, 179 Colo. 36, 499 P.2d 1190 (1972).
66   C.R.S. § 37-82-106(1).

To the extent that there exists a right to make a succession of uses of foreign, nontributary, or other developed water, such right is personal to the developer or his successor, lessees, contractees, or assigns. Such water, when released from the dominion of the user, becomes a part of the natural surface stream where released, subject to water rights on such stream in the order of their priority, but nothing in this subsection (2) shall affect the rights of the developer or his successors or assigns with respect to such foreign, nontributary, or developed water, nor shall dominion over such water be lost to the owner or user thereof by reason of use of a natural watercourse in the process of carrying such water to the place of its use or successive use.[67]

Accordingly, the importer of foreign water has a right to use, reuse, use successively, or dispose of the imported water to extinction upon importation of the water. Stated another way, junior appropriators may not rely on return flows from use of imported water because such water would not have been available except for the importer's efforts. A typical example of successive use of foreign water is a city that imports water, uses it in the city's municipal system, and claims credit for effluent discharged to the stream. The city then diverts the effluent credits by exchange at an upstream location, in effect using the water again.

The importer of foreign water may reclaim return flows from the use of such water at any time. The right to make a succession of uses also applies to non-tributary and developed water because such water would not be part of the stream except for the efforts of the developer. Downstream users may use imported water return flows on the basis of their relative priorities, but no right vests as to future use of such return flows. Unlike native water rights, the right to reuse foreign water is not subject to abandonment by non-use and is not dependent on the importer's original intent. In order to make successive uses, the importer must maintain dominion over the imported water, but such dominion need not be physical. Dominion may be established by procedures to quantify and account for the return flows so as to distinguish such water from other native water in the stream.[68] While downstream users in the receiving basin cannot assert injury as a result of a change in use of imported water, water users in the basin of origin may assert injury to their water rights as a result of any change in use that enlarges use beyond the historical diversion.

---

67   C.R.S. § 37-82-106(2).
68   *City of Thornton v. Bijou Irr. Co.*, 926 P.2d 1 (Colo. 1996).

§ 3.4.8 Federal Reserved Water Rights

The federal government generally must appropriate water rights in accordance with state law, except if the water is needed to fulfill a primary purpose of a federal reservation of land from the public domain, in which case the doctrine of federal reserved water rights may apply. The public domain includes land open to settlement, public sale, or other disposition under federal law, and which is not exclusively dedicated to any specific governmental or public purpose. Public domain lands are managed largely by the United States Department of Interior's Bureau of Land Management. Reserved lands are those lands that have been expressly withdrawn from the public domain by treaty, statute, or executive order and are dedicated to a specific federal purpose. Examples of federal reservations include Indian reservations, national forests, national parks, national monuments, public springs and waterholes, and public mineral hot springs.

Federal reserved water rights find their genesis in the Property Clause of the United States Constitution and United States Supreme Court decisions that hold, when the federal government reserves land for a specific purpose, it implicitly reserves unappropriated water sufficient to accomplish the primary purpose of the reservation.[69] Reserved water rights are not lost by non-use. Furthermore, the postponement doctrine did not apply to such rights until the United States was joined in Colorado water court proceedings under the McCarran Amendment as discussed in Section 1.5.2. The United States has now been joined as a party in water court proceedings in all seven water divisions in Colorado. Therefore, any future federal reserved water rights claims will be subject to the postponement doctrine.

The doctrine of federal reserved water rights is superimposed on the state water rights system of prior appropriation. Because many such reservations date back to the early 1900s, federal reserved rights often turn out to be very senior with respect to other decreed priorities. Federal reserved rights are a unique and important overlay on state water law that can affect the relative priority of other water rights long after those rights have been adjudicated. Although the United States has been properly joined in water court adjudications in all of Colorado's water divisions, some reserved water rights claims are still pending. Thus the extent and priority of such pending claims is not yet known. See Section 18.2.2.

The federal reserved water rights doctrine was first enunciated in substantial form by the United States Supreme Court in the 1908 case of *Winters v. United States.*[70]

---

69   *Cappaert v. United States*, 426 U.S. 128 (1976).
70   207 U.S. 564 (1908).

Winters involved a suit by the United States on behalf of several Indian tribes living on the Fort Belknap Indian Reservation in Montana to enjoin several parties from diverting and storing water from the Milk River upstream of the reservation. The upstream diverters developed their water rights after the reservation was created. The court focused on the intent of the treaty whereby the Indians ceded their rights to lands in return for the reservation. The court reasoned that irrigation was necessary for the Indians to make use of the otherwise arid lands of the reservation; therefore, a grant of the necessary water was implied from the grant of the land. The *Winters* opinion did not discuss the priority date of the reserved water rights because the reservation was made prior to development of the upstream uses; therefore, the federal reserved water rights were simply deemed superior to those uses. Later cases, however, made clear that the priority date of the reserved water right relates back to the date of the reservation by the federal government, although some courts have interpreted federal reserved water rights for Indians to predate the reservation date and relate back to "time immemorial."[71]

Federal reserved water rights are recognized only for the primary purpose of the reservation.[72] In *City and County of Denver v. United States*,[73] the Colorado Supreme Court affirmed water rights for several national forests in Water Divisions 4, 5, and 6 for the primary purposes of conserving the watershed and maintaining a continuous timber supply, as such purposes are specifically identified for national forests in the Organic Administration Act of 1897.[74] The court rejected, however, the United States claims for instream flows for recreational, scenic, and wildlife protection purposes within the national forests because these uses are not primary uses set forth in the Organic Act. The court also rejected a claim for instream flows in Dinosaur National Monument for recreational boating, finding that the monument was originally reserved for scientific and historic purposes, not recreational purposes.

In Colorado, federal reserved water rights have been claimed in connection with oil shale reservations, national forests, national parks, public springs and water holes, and other federal reservations. A few federal agencies, however, have not yet asserted claims for reserved water rights in Colorado and may do so in the future.

---

71   *United States v. Adair*, 723 F.2d 1394 (9th Cir. 1983).
72   *United States v. New Mexico*, 438 U.S. 696 (1978).
73   *City and County of Denver v. U. S.*, 656 P.2d 36 (Colo. 1982).
74   16 U.S.C. § 475.

CHAPTER 4 SECURING NEW GROUND WATER RIGHTS

§ 4.1   INTRODUCTION

The process of allocation and determination of ground water rights in Colorado varies by the type of ground water and its location. For example, ground water outside of any designated ground water basin that is tributary to any natural stream is subject to the constitutional right to appropriate under the prior appropriation system. Ground water within any designated ground water basin is subject to a modified system of prior appropriation. Ground water outside of any designated ground water basin that is not tributary to any stream is allocated based on ownership of the overlying land. While the rights to various types of ground water are allocated differently, *all* ground water withdrawals require a well permit issued by the State Engineer's office. Well permits are discussed in the section concerning tributary ground water.

§ 4.2   TRIBUTARY GROUND WATER

§ 4.2.1 Historical Overview

Colorado, like most other western states, recognizes that ground water is usually hydraulically connected to, and therefore influences, surface water. Thus, ground water that is found to be tributary to a natural stream is subject to appropriation in the same way as surface water. Tributary ground water is statutorily defined as water that is in an alluvial aquifer or water that is hydraulically connected to the alluvial aquifer that can influence the rate or direction of movement of water in the alluvial aquifer or the stream.[1] Except for ground water in designated ground water basins and ground water in certain aquifers in the area known as the Denver Basin, all ground water in Colorado is presumed to be tributary in nature unless proven otherwise.[2]

In the early development of Colorado water law, the connection between ground water and surface water was not well understood. Many people believed that ground water was separate from surface water and that the pumping of ground water could not affect surface streams. Consequently, ground water was generally considered to be outside the priority system, and wells were not adjudicated or regulated in Colorado for many years. By the 1960s, however, thousands of irrigation wells had been drilled along the South Platte and Arkansas Rivers, and surface diverters began to assert that ground water pumping affected the surface flow. The legislature responded by passing the Groundwater Management Act of 1965 (1965 Act).[3] The 1965 Act created a special category of ground water within "designated" ground water basins (see Section 4.3.1). It also affirmed the applicability of the prior appropriation system to tributary ground water and directed the State Engineer to administer the distribution of tributary ground water in accordance with the priority system. The 1965 Act also required a well permit from the State Engineer for the construction of a new well.

Even after passage of the 1965 Act, there remained the problem of bringing wells into the priority system. In some cases, unadjudicated wells had been allowed to operate for many years and the well owners believed that their rights to ground water had vested. The General Assembly had given the State Engineer the difficult task of curtailing junior wells for the benefit of senior surface water rights, but the Colorado Supreme Court struck down initial attempts by the State Engineer to shut down some

---

1   C.R.S. § 37-92-103(11).
2   *Sweetwater Dev. Corp. v. Schubert Ranches, Inc.*, 188 Colo. 379, 535 P.2d 215 (1975).
3   C.R.S. §§ 37-90-101 to 37-90-143.

but not all wells in the Arkansas River basin as arbitrary and capricious because the State Engineer had not developed principled rules and regulations for the systematic administration of wells.[4] The problem of administration was aggravated by the fact that there is often a lag time between pumping and the effect on the stream, such that the curtailment of a well would not immediately make more water available for a senior surface diverter.

The Water Right Determination and Administration Act of 1969 (1969 Act)[5] was designed to integrate tributary ground water and surface water use and provide maximum utilization of the water resource by allowing for flexible "plans for augmentation"[6] and by giving the State Engineer discretion to not administer water rights calls in situations where curtailment of junior water rights would not result in more water being made available for a senior appropriator.[7] (Plans for augmentation are discussed further in Section 10.3.) As incentive for the well owners to adjudicate their wells and join the priority system, the 1969 Act provided that water court applications to adjudicate wells filed before July 1, 1972 would not be subject to the postponement doctrine and the wells would be given a priority relating back to the original appropriation date.[8]

§ 4.2.2   Well Permits

> Several useful publications that explain the well permitting process, well permit fees, well permit applications, and instructions are available from the State Engineer's Web site: http://water.state.co.us

Well Permitting Process

The 1965 Act required well permits for the construction of all new wells and for relocating or increasing the supply from all existing wells. The well permit applicant must specify the location of the well and the aquifer from which the water will be withdrawn, as well as the average annual amount of water to be withdrawn, the maximum pumping rate, and the proposed use.[9] If the well penetrates more than one

---

4   *Fellhauer v. People*, 167 Colo. 320, 447 P.2d 986 (1968).
5   C.R.S. §§ 37-92-101 to 37-92-602.
6   C.R.S. § 37-92-103(9).
7   C.R.S. § 37-92-501(1).
8   C.R.S. § 37-92-306.
9   C.R.S. § 37-90-137(1).

aquifer, it must be cased to allow the withdrawal of water from only one aquifer.[10] The State Engineer's office charges a well permit application fee and must act to deny, approve, or return a well permit application for more information within 45 days of receipt, although it often takes much longer in practice.[11] A decision of the State Engineer with respect to a well permit application may be appealed in an administrative hearing process, which is itself subject to judicial review. Because only a licensed well contractor can contract a water well, it is useful to select a driller who can then assist in negotiating the permitting process.

> Rules and regulations for water well construction and pump installation are available at http://www.water.state.co.us/pubs/rule_reg/boe_pump.pdf

A well is defined as "any structure or device used for the purpose or with the effect of obtaining ground water for beneficial use from an aquifer."[12] Thus, a pond constructed below the water table that intercepts ground water is considered a well for purposes of the well permit requirement. Gravel pits that expose ground water to the atmosphere also require a well permit although gravel pits in operation prior to January 1, 1981 are exempt from this requirement.[13] Gravel pit well permits are also subject to additional fees by the State Engineer.

To grant a new tributary well permit, the State Engineer must find that there is unappropriated water available for withdrawal by the proposed well and that the vested rights of others will not be materially injured.[14] As a practical matter, most stream systems are over-appropriated, *i.e.*, there are more decreed water rights than can be satisfied by the physical amount of water available. In such cases, the State Engineer will not issue a well permit for a new well without a judicially decreed augmentation plan or State Engineer approved substitute water supply plan. Augmentation and substitute water supply plans are discussed in more detail in Sections 10.2 and 10.3. The basic function of a plan for augmentation or substitute water supply plan is to replace water used under junior water rights so that such junior rights may divert out of priority without causing injury to senior water rights. Augmentation water is often readily available for domestic wells. The Division Engineer, local water agencies, and water

---

10   Water Well Construction Rules, Rule 10.4, 2 C.C.R. 402-2.
11   C.R.S. § 37-90-142.
12   C.R.S. § 37-90-103(21)(a).
13   C.R.S. § 37-90-137(11)(a).
14   C.R.S. § 37-90-137(2)(b)(I).

attorneys are usually aware of augmentation water for this purpose; the local water commissioner may also know of available water. The augmentation requirement does not apply to ponds and gravel pits if they are lined according to the State Engineer's guidelines to prevent ground water seepage into the pond or pit.

By statute, a well does not include a naturally flowing spring where the natural spring discharge is captured or concentrated by installation of a near-surface structure (less than ten feet in depth) within 50 feet of the spring's natural discharge point, and the owner obtains a water right decree for the structure as a spring.[15] Therefore, a shallow drainage tile system may not require a well permit if it meets the statutory requirements and the owner adjudicates the system as a spring.

Well Spacing

As a general proposition, wells are required to be spaced at least 600 feet apart.[16] Upon submitting a well permit application, the State Engineer's office will help the applicant determine whether any wells are located within 600 feet of the proposed well, and the applicant will be given the opportunity to obtain consent from the owners of any affected wells. If consent cannot be obtained, the applicant may request a hearing and the State Engineer will notify the affected well owners by certified mail. No hearing will be required, however, if (1) the State Engineer notifies the affected well owners and receives no response within 30 days, or (2) the applicant provides such notice as part of a water court application for the well.[17] This affords the affected well owner notice and opportunity to participate and assert potential injury to his or her existing water right in the water court proceeding. If a well spacing hearing is required, the services of a ground water hydrologist will likely be necessary to prove injury or non-injury to an existing well from the proposed well.

Well Completion

> Well completion forms, as well as well spacing and other forms, are available from the State Engineer's office or Web site:
> http://www.water.state.co.us/pubs/wellforms.asp

---

15   C.R.S. § 37-90-103(21)(b).
16   C.R.S. § 37-90-137(2)(b).
17   C.R.S. § 37-90-137(2)(b)(II).

Once issued, a well permit expires after one year unless before the expiration the well owner submits evidence that the well has been constructed and the pump was installed.[18] Water production wells must be constructed by a licensed well contractor. In addition to the statement of beneficial use form, the well owner must also submit a well construction and test report and pump installation report.[19] The well driller may complete these forms; however, the well owner should ensure that they are properly filed with the State Engineer. The well permit may be extended for one additional year upon a showing of good cause why the well was not completed within one year.

If evidence that the well has been constructed and the pump installed has not been received as of the expiration date of the well permit, the State Engineer is required to notify the applicant by certified mail.[20] The notice must give the applicant the opportunity to submit proof that the well was constructed and the pump was installed before the expiration date.

Any structure or device that is a well, including ponds and gravel pits, must be constructed according to the State Engineer's well construction and pump installation regulations.[21] The regulations have very specific requirements for the construction, casing, and pump installation of wells to prevent contamination of the ground water supply. Wells completed in more than one aquifer can only withdraw water from one aquifer. Nontraditional wells such as ponds or subsurface drains will require a variance that may be obtained from the Board of Examiners of Water Well Construction and Pump Installation Contractors.[22]

§ 4.2.3   River Basin Rules and Regulations

In addition to the well permitting statutes, the withdrawal of tributary ground water in the Arkansas and South Platte River basins is subject to additional rules and regulations promulgated by the State Engineer. In these basins, the State Engineer has exercised his general rule-making authority under the 1969 Act to assist in the administration of tributary water. The State Engineer also has authority to make and enforce regulations that will enable the state to meet its interstate compact commitments.[23]

---

18   C.R.S. § 37-90-137(3)(a)(I)(A).
19   Water Well Construction Rules, Rule 16, 2 C.C.R. 402-2.
20   C.R.S. § 37-90-137(3)(c).
21   Water Well Construction Rules, Rule 18, 2 C.C.R. 402-2.
22   Water Well Construction Rules, Rule 17, 2 C.C.R. 402-2.
23   C.R.S. § 37-80-104.

> Well completion forms, as well as well spacing and other forms, and The
> State Engineer's rules for the Arkansas River and the South Platte River
> basins are available from the State Engineer's Office Web site:
> http://www.water.state.co.us/pubs/rule_reg.asp

In response to litigation by the State of Kansas alleging that Colorado had violated the 1949 Arkansas River Compact by allowing depletions from wells with decreed priorities later than the date of the compact, in 1994 the State Engineer adopted amended rules governing well pumping in the Arkansas River basin. The rules generally require wells with decreed priorities later than the compact to curtail pumping unless the depletions from such wells are replaced, and the rules provide that the State Engineer may continually approve annual replacement plans to allow such wells to operate on a long-term basis. The State Engineer does not have authority under the 1969 Act, however, to continually approve replacement plans in the South Platte River basin.[24]

The supreme court rejected proposed rules and regulations governing wells in the San Luis Valley for the benefit of senior surface rights and to satisfy the Rio Grande Compact. The court upheld the water judge's determination that senior surface water rights were not entitled to automatically compel curtailment of junior wells where the surface right owners have the ability to drill and pump their own wells rather than obtain surface supplies through the curtailment of other wells.[25] The legislature has also determined that there is a confined aquifer in the San Luis Valley in Water Division 3 that is hydraulically connected to surface streams tributary to the Rio Grande, and has mandated that the State Engineer promulgate rules for the withdrawal of ground water from the confined aquifer before July 1, 2004.

As of the date of this publication, the State Engineer has not promulgated rules for any other river basins in Colorado.

§ 4.2.4 Exempt Wells and Monitoring Holes

The 1969 Act exempts the following types of small capacity tributary wells from application of the 1969 Act and administration under the priority system:

1) Wells not exceeding 15 gallons per minute of production and used for ordinary household purposes, fire protection, the watering of poultry, domestic

---

24 *Simpson v. Bijou Irr. Co.*, 69 P.3d 50 (Colo. 2003).
25 *Alamosa-LaJara Water Users Prot. Ass'n v. Gould*, 674 P.2d 914 (Colo. 1983).

animals, and livestock on farms and ranches, and for the irrigation of not over one acre of home gardens and lawns but not used for more than three single-family dwellings.

2) Wells not exceeding 15 gallons per minute of production and used for drinking and sanitary facilities in individual commercial businesses.

3) Wells used exclusively for firefighting purposes if said wells are capped, locked, and available for use only in fighting fires.

4) Wells not exceeding 50 gallons per minute that were in production as of May 22, 1971, and were and are used for ordinary household purposes for not more than three single-family dwellings, fire protection, the watering of poultry, domestic animals, and livestock on farms and ranches, and for the irrigation of not over one acre of gardens and lawns.

5) Wells to be used exclusively for monitoring and observation purposes if said wells are capped and locked and used only to monitor water levels or for water quality sampling.[26]

The first four types of wells are commonly known as "exempt" wells. Well permits are required for the first three types of exempt wells. These exempt wells must be constructed within two years of the issuance of the permit, although the State Engineer may extend the period upon a showing of good cause. A well permit is not required for the fourth type of exempt well (in production as of May 22, 1971) unless it is relocated. For monitoring holes (temporary monitoring wells that will be sealed within one year of construction), the owner need only file a notice of intent to construct the hole. Within one year after construction, a monitoring hole must either be plugged and abandoned in accordance with the well construction rules or be converted by permit to a monitoring well or dewatering system. A monitoring hole may not be converted to a water production well.

The legislative policy behind the exempt well provisions is to allow citizens to obtain a water supply in less densely populated areas for in-house and domestic animal uses where other water supplies are not available.[27] The State Engineer's policy is generally not to issue an exempt well permit where water service to the property is available from a municipality or water district.

Before issuing a permit for any tributary well, including an exempt well, the State Engineer must find that the proposed well will not cause material injury to vested

---

26   C.R.S. § 37-92-602(1).
27   C.R.S. § 37-92-602(6).

water rights of others. There is a rebuttable presumption of no injury to other water rights or existing wells if the proposed well meets the first exempt well criteria listed above and (1) will be the only well on a residential site, and will be used solely for ordinary household purposes inside a single-family dwelling and will not be used for irrigation; or (2) will be the only well on a tract of land of 35 acres or more; or (3) will be the only well on a cluster development lot, serving one single-family residence, where the ratio of water usage in the cluster development does not exceed one acre-foot of annual withdrawals for each 35 acres within the cluster development, and the well will be used solely for household purposes, and return flows from such uses will be returned to the same stream system in which the well is located.[28] The practical effect of this provision is that "exempt" well permits may be obtained in over-appropriated areas without regard to the prior appropriation system and without a court-approved augmentation plan, while well permits for other wells in over-appropriated areas will be denied without approved plans for augmentation.

Although exempt wells are not administered under the priority system, they nevertheless have water rights that have vested by virtue of the application of water to beneficial use, just like any other unadjudicated water right. Therefore, in the context of considering whether a non-exempt well will materially injure the vested water rights of others, the State Engineer must consider possible injury to exempt wells. Similarly, in the context of a change of water right, augmentation plan, or exchange, the water court must consider exempt wells in determining whether such change of water right, plan for augmentation, or exchange will cause material injury to vested water rights.[29]

Even though an exempt well is a vested water right, the owner of an exempt well does not have a legally enforceable priority. To have standing to assert injury to an exempt well in water court, the exempt well owner must have filed an application to adjudicate the well priority but need not have obtained a final decree before filing a statement of opposition to a change of water right, plan for augmentation, or exchange application.[30]

The 1969 Act allows an exempt well owner to adjudicate a priority for the exempt well like any other water right, except that the exempt well owner is entitled to a priority date equal to the original priority date of the well, regardless of when the water court application is filed. In other words, the postponement doctrine does not apply to adjudication of exempt wells. Once the exempt well owner obtains a priority, how-

---

28   C.R.S. § 37-92-602(3)(b)(II)(A).
29   *Shirola v. Turkey Cañon Ranch Ltd. Liab. Co.*, 937 P.2d 739 (Colo. 1997).
30   *Shirola*, 937 P.2d 754, n.18.

ever, it is not clear whether the well is then subject to administration on the basis of the adjudicated priority.

§ 4.3   DESIGNATED GROUND WATER

§ 4.3.1   The Ground Water Management Act of 1965

The 1965 Act recognized a type of "designated" ground water that is separate from tributary ground water and is not subject to the pure prior appropriation system laid out in the Colorado Constitution. Designated ground water, as defined by the 1965 Act, is water within the boundaries of a designated ground water basin that is either "not available to and required for the fulfillment of decreed surface rights" or is water in "areas not adjacent to a continuously flowing natural stream" wherein ground water withdrawals have constituted the principal water usage for at least 15 years prior the designation of the basin.[31] Although designated ground water can include ground water in alluvial aquifers connected to surface streams, designated ground water, such as water in the Ogallala aquifer, is often separated from the surface stream and not recharged quickly. In this situation, designated ground water is essentially a non-renewable resource that is "mined," rather than being used and replenished like tributary ground water. The legislature provided for a "modified" prior appropriation system to permit the full economic development of designated ground water resources. The modified prior appropriation system is designed to protect prior appropriations of ground water to a limited degree by maintaining "reasonable" ground water pumping levels, although historical water levels need not be maintained. If pumping is not regulated, mining of designated ground water will ultimately result in the water table being lowered below the level from which water may be economically withdrawn.

The 1965 Act established the Colorado Ground Water Commission (Commission) to designate ground water basins and regulate the use of ground water within the basins. The 1965 Act also provided for the formation of ground water management districts within designated basins. The Commission may delegate to the State Engineer any of the Commission's functions, except the determination of a designated ground water basin and creation of ground water management districts. The Commission has designated eight different designated ground water basins in eastern Colorado to date. The State Engineer's Office has maps of the various designated ground water basins and will help a prospective ground water user determine if he or she is within a designated ground water basin.

---

31   C.R.S. § 37-90-103(6)(a).

Example 1: Map of Designated Ground Water Basins in Colorado

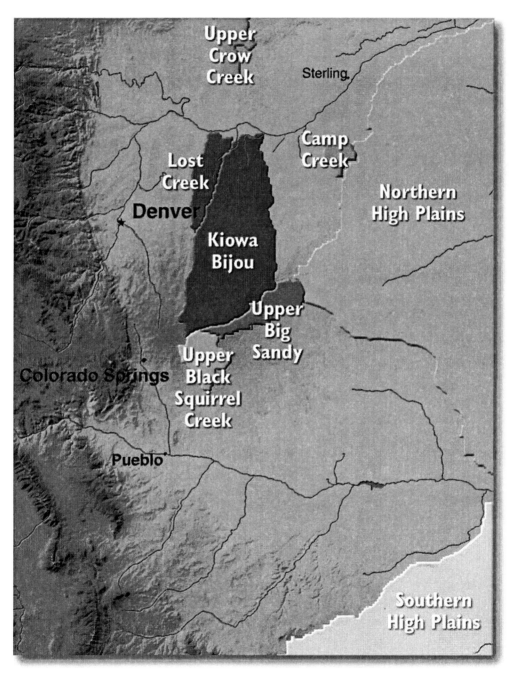

Courtesy of Colorado Foundation for Water Education

§ 4.3.2   Determination of Rights to Designated Ground Water

Under the 1965 Act, the Commission, rather than the water court, has jurisdiction to determine the right to withdraw designated ground water, although there may be decrees for surface and ground water rights in designated basins that pre-date formation of the designated basin. Ground water within designated basins is presumed to be not tributary, unless proven otherwise before the Commission.[32] The Commission issues final well permits, rather than decrees. To initiate a designated ground water use, the prospective user must first apply to the Commission for a conditional well permit. The applicant must specify the location of the proposed well, the name of the owner of the land on which the well will be located, the estimated average annual amount of water to be withdrawn in acre-feet, the estimated maximum pumping rate, and the proposed use.[33] The water may only be used on the land designated in the application, and the place of use cannot be changed without authorization of the Commission.

> Applications for conditional well permits and instructions are available from the State Engineer's Web site:
> http://www.water.state.co.us/pubs/wellforms.asp

Upon receipt of an application, the Commission is required to make a preliminary evaluation of the application to determine if it may be granted. In practice, this determination is made by the State Engineer's staff, not the Commission. If the staff believes that the application can be approved under existing policies, it will publish the application in a newspaper of general circulation in each county concerned, once each week for two successive weeks. Written objections to the application may be filed with the Commission within 30 days following the date of the last publication. Like all water in Colorado, designated ground water is a public resource that is to be conserved; therefore, the well permit applicant must demonstrate to the Commission the intent to appropriate for beneficial use rather than for speculation. As a practical matter, many designated groundwater basins are considered to be over-appropriated and it is not possible to obtain a large capacity well permit in these basins without a plan to replace the well's depletions. If no objections are filed, the Commission will grant the application if it finds that the proposed appropriation will not unreasonably impair existing water rights from the same source and will not create unreasonable

---

[32]   *Danielson v. Vickroy*, 627 P.2d 752 (Colo. 1981).
[33]   C.R.S. § 37-90-107(1).

waste. The State Engineer will then issue a conditional permit. If objections have been filed within the specified time, the Commission must set a date for a hearing on the application and the objections. If after such hearing it appears that there are no unappropriated waters in the designated source or that the proposed appropriation would unreasonably impair existing water rights from the source or would create unreasonable waste, the application will be denied; otherwise it shall be granted. The Commission has exclusive jurisdiction to consider the approval or denial of permits for large capacity wells in designated basins, but the Commission must consider any recommendation by the affected ground water management district.[34]

After receiving a conditional well permit, the permit holder must construct the well within one year and submit well completion information or the permit will expire. If the well completion information is not submitted within the required time, the Commission is required to notify the applicant and give the applicant the opportunity to submit proof that the well was completed within the required time, and that the applicant failed to submit the evidence of completion on time due to mistake, inadvertence, or neglect. After completion of the well, the well owner must submit a sworn statement that water from the well has been put to beneficial use within three years after the date of issuance of the permit. The statement of beneficial use will be considered *prima facie* evidence of the beneficial use of water as claimed; however, the claim is subject to objection by others, including an affected ground water management district and any inquiry or verification the Commission deems appropriate. If the statement of beneficial use is not submitted within three years, the Commission is required to notify the applicant and give the applicant the opportunity to submit proof that water from the well was put to beneficial use and that the applicant failed to submit the statement of beneficial use on time due to mistake, inadvertence, or neglect.[35]

Upon submission of the required information and affidavit, the Commission will consider the issuance of a final permit after publication. To the extent that the Commission finds that water has been put to a beneficial use and that any other terms of the conditional permit have been complied with, it will order the State Engineer to issue a final well permit containing such limitations and conditions as the Commission deems necessary to prevent waste and protect the rights of others.[36] As a practical matter, the State Engineer's office is in some cases many years behind in the issuance of final well permits in some designated ground water basins.

---

34   C.R.S. § 37-90-107(8).
35   C.R.S. § 37-90-108.
36   C.R.S. § 37-90-108(3).

The 1965 Act requires the Commission to maintain a priority list for all wells within a designated ground water basin. For wells that were put to beneficial use before May 17, 1965, the priority date is the date on which the water was first beneficially used. For all other wells that are completed and beneficially used, the priority date relates back to the filing of the original permit application.[37]

Commission decisions are appealable by filing an appeal within 30 days in the district court in the county in which the water rights involved are situated, not the water court. For each designated ground water basin, one district court judge is assigned each year by the Colorado Supreme Court to be the designated ground water judge to hear such cases.[38]

§ 4.3.3   Ground Water Commission Rules and Regulations

The Commission has promulgated rules and regulations for the management and control of designated ground water.[39] The rules set forth criteria by which applications for new appropriations or changes of existing uses in the various designated basins will be evaluated. No application for a permit to withdraw water from any aquifer within a designated ground water basin, except the Denver Basin aquifers and certain other aquifers, will be granted for a well within one-half mile of an existing large capacity well unless a waiver is obtained from the owner of such existing well or unless the commission, after a hearing, finds that issuance of the permit is justified under the particular circumstances.[40]

> The Ground Water Commission's rules and regulations are available at
> http://www.water.state.co.us/cgwc/rules-regs/DBRulesApril2004withFigs.pdf

Applications for new wells are subject to different rules depending on the designated basin and the aquifer. For the Ogallala and White River aquifers within the Northern High Plains Designated Ground Water Basin, the availability of unappropriated water is determined by projecting a three-mile circle around the proposed well and calculating the total amount of water available and the amount already claimed in the circle. The total combined amount of withdrawal in the circle cannot exceed 40 percent depletion in a period of 100 years. The Colorado Supreme Court has recognized the unique situation presented by ground water mining and upheld

---

37   C.R.S. § 37-90-109(1).
38   C.R.S. § 37-90-115.
39   Rules & Regs. For the Mgmt. & Control of Designated Ground Water, 2 C.C.R. 410-1.
40   Designated Ground Water Rules, Rule 5.2.1.

the reasonableness of the three-mile circle rule.[41] As a practical matter, most areas of the Ogallala and White River aquifers are fully appropriated, and it is not possible to obtain large capacity well permits in these areas.

The alluvial aquifers in several other designated ground water basins have been deemed to be over-appropriated; therefore, no new applications for large capacity wells in these alluvial aquifers will be granted without a "replacement plan" approved by the commission. By definition, a replacement plan is a detailed program to allow the use of a new well while preventing injury to other water rights by developing new sources of water or water exchange projects, pooling water resources, or providing substitute supplies of water.[42] A replacement plan is similar to a court-approved plan for augmentation. The rules and regulations of the commission specify standards that the replacement plan must meet. The main requirements are that the applicant show the plan has adequate substitute supplies to replace depletions that would be injurious to other water users and provide adequate monitoring and reporting of water use and replacement.[43] Applications for replacement plans are subject to publication and a hearing before the Commission like conditional well permit applications.

In the absence of a ground water management district, the commission has authority to supervise and control the exercise and administration of designated ground water priorities. The Commission may by summary order "prohibit or limit withdrawal of water from any well during any period that it determines that such withdrawal of water from said well would cause unreasonable injury to prior appropriators."[44] However, a prior designated ground water appropriator is not entitled to the maintenance of the historic water level or any other water level below which water still can be economically withdrawn "when the total economic pattern of the particular designated ground water basin is considered."[45] No curtailment order by the commission shall take effect, however, until six months after its entry. To date, there has been little attempt by the commission to curtail existing wells on the basis of priority once they are permitted.

§ 4.3.4   Ground Water Management Districts

The 1965 Act also provides that citizens may establish ground water management districts within designated basins through a petition and election procedure when the

---

[41]   *Fundingsland v. Colorado Ground Water Com'n*, 171 Colo. 487, 468 P.2d 835 (1970).
[42]   C.R.S. § 37-90-103(12.7).
[43]   Designated Ground Water Rules, Rule 5.6, 2 C.C.R. 410-1.
[44]   C.R.S. § 37-90-111(1)(a).
[45]   C.R.S. § 37-90-111(1)(a).

Commission has approved the proposed creation of the management district and its boundaries.[46] The purpose of management districts is to give local ground water users some measure of control over the distribution and administration of designated ground water in the area. Within the boundaries of a ground water management district, the district, not the Commission, has the authority to administer designated ground water priorities, issue curtailment orders, and resolve disputes between well owners. The State Engineer has authority to enforce orders of a ground water management district or the Commission. Perhaps the most important power possessed by ground water management districts is the authority to promulgate rules that control the use of ground water outside the boundaries of the district.[47]

§ 4.3.5 Small Capacity Wells

Similar to the exemption in the 1969 Act for household use and livestock wells, the 1965 Act exempts certain "small capacity" wells in designated basins from regulation by the Commission. The State Engineer may approve permits for the following types of wells in designated basins without regard to the provisions of the 1965 Act: (1) wells not exceeding 50 gallons per minute and used for no more than three single-family dwellings and the irrigation of no more than one acre of land; (2) wells not exceeding 50 gallons per minute and used for watering of livestock on range and pasture; (3) wells not exceeding 50 gallons per minute if limited to one well used in one commercial business; (4) wells to be used exclusively for monitoring and observation purposes; and (5) wells to be used exclusively for firefighting purposes.[48]

§ 4.3.6 Designated Ground Water in Denver Basin Aquifers

Designated basins may contain another kind of statutorily recognized ground water in four deep aquifers, called the Dawson, Denver, Arapahoe, and Laramie-Fox Hills aquifers, and located within the area known as the Denver Basin. The Denver Basin and these aquifers underlie much of the Front Range between Greeley and Colorado Springs and extending east to Limon. About one-half of the land overlying the Denver Basin and the so-called "Denver Basin" aquifers is within designated ground water basins. Ground water in the Denver Basin aquifers within designated ground water basins is considered non-tributary, but is not subject to the modified

---

46   C.R.S. § 37-90-118.
47   C.R.S. § 37-90-130(2)(f).
48   C.R.S. § 37-90-105.

prior appropriation system that governs other ground water in designated basins. Rather, non-tributary ground water in the Denver Basin aquifers is allocated in all cases on the basis of ownership of the overlying land. The rate of withdrawal for the Denver Basin aquifers is limited to allow an aquifer life of at least 100 years, as described below.

The Commission has jurisdiction to determine rights to use non-tributary ground water in Denver Basin aquifers within a designated ground water basin, while the water court has jurisdiction to determine the right to use water in the Denver Basin aquifers located outside of a designated ground water basin upon applications filed under the procedures of the 1969 Act. The method of allocation of Denver Basin ground water, based on ownership of the overlying land, is the same whether the right is determined by the water court or the Commission. If the right to use Denver Basin ground water within a designated basin is determined by the Commission, no conditional well permit is required; the water right vests upon determination by the Commission. Non-tributary ground water in the Denver Basin is discussed in Section 4.4.2.

§ 4.3.7   Anti-Speculation

All water within Colorado, including designated, non-tributary and not non-tributary ground water, is a publicly owned resource. A person may obtain a right to use such water, but no person may own the public's water. Even though designated ground water is allocated and managed differently than tributary surface and ground water, the Colorado Supreme Court recently held that the anti-speculation doctrine applies to designated ground water within the Denver Basin aquifers.[49] As discussed in Section 3.3.3, the anti-speculation doctrine precludes the appropriator who does not intend to put water to use for his own benefit, and has no contractual or agency relationship with one who does, from obtaining a water right. Thus, a person who intends to hold the right only to sell it or dispose of it for profit in the future, rather than acquire it for the purpose of applying water to an identified beneficial use, is not entitled to a determination of a water use right. If the use will occur on land not owned by the applicant in determination of a water right, the applicant must demonstrate that he or she has a contract or agency relationship with another entity for the water's beneficial use.

---

[49]   *Colorado Ground Water Com'n v. N. Kiowa-Bijou Groundwater Mgmt. Dist.*, 77 P.3d 62 (Colo. 2003).

§ 4.4   NON-TRIBUTARY GROUND WATER

The history of allocation of non-tributary ground water in Colorado is long and complicated. Since at least 1963, Colorado courts have recognized that non-tributary ground water is not subject to the constitutional doctrine of prior appropriation.[50] However, in the absence of clear allocation rules, and because of lack of specific knowledge of the non-tributary nature of many aquifers, water users and courts often treated non-tributary ground water as being subject to appropriation and adjudication. As a result, appropriation decrees for such water were entered in many parts of the state, even though the courts did not have jurisdiction under the water adjudication statutes to enter such decrees.[51]

In 1973, with the adoption of Senate Bill 213, the Colorado legislature for the first time provided a specific method for allocation of non-tributary ground water based on the ownership of the overlying land.[52] Recognizing past history, the legislature, in 1983, provided that the method adopted in 1973 does not apply to rights to use ground water that were initiated prior to July 6, 1973.[53] Finally, in 1985, rights to non-tributary ground water were made subject to adjudication in the water courts, and prior water court decrees adjudicating such rights were validated.[54]

§ 4.4.1 Basis for Allocation

Colorado statutes now define non-tributary ground water as water located outside the boundaries of any designated ground water basin in existence on January 1, 1985, "the withdrawal of which will not, within one hundred years, deplete the flow of a natural stream…at an annual rate greater than one-tenth of one percent of the annual rate of withdrawal."[55] Rights to non-tributary ground water are now allocated based on ownership of the overlying land.[56] The annual withdrawal rate for non-tributary ground water is set at one percent per year of the total volume of water under the land in question, to provide for an aquifer life of 100 years. To encourage economic development of the non-tributary ground water resource, the legislature

---

50   *Whitten v. Coit*, 153 Colo. 157, 385 P.2d 131 (1963).

51   *State of Colo. v. Southwestern Colo. Water Conservation District*, 671 P.2d 1294, 1318-19 (Colo. 1983).

52   C.R.S. § 37-90-137(4).

53   C.R.S. § 37-90-137(5).

54   C.R.S. § 37-92-203(1).

55   C.R.S. § 37-90-103(10.5).

56   C.R.S. §§ 37-90-102(2), 37-90-137(4)(b).

further provided that well pumping which reduces the hydrostatic (*i.e.*, "artesian") pressure or water level in the aquifer does not constitute injury to other vested non-tributary rights.[57]

The owner of land does not own the non-tributary ground water under that land. However, the landowner or a person with consent of the landowner has an inchoate right to seek a decree from the water court determining a non-tributary ground water right or to obtain a well permit from the State Engineer to allow withdrawal of the non-tributary ground water.[58] The same basis—an aquifer life expectancy of 100 years—is used for determining the amount of water that may be withdrawn whether the use right is determined by the water court or a well permit is obtained from the State Engineer. If a well permit is obtained from the State Engineer, the applicant must file notice of completion of the well within one year after the permit is issued or the permit will be cancelled. If a person seeks to obtain a vested non-tributary ground water right without drilling a well, he or she may apply for a water court determination of the right to use non-tributary ground water. Until the water right vests by water court decree or well permit, the inchoate right to obtain a vested water right may be modified or limited by the legislature in the future. Therefore, many people believe one should adjudicate rights to non-tributary ground water, even if the owner has no immediate plans to use the water.

Except in certain aquifers within the area known as the Denver Basin and designated ground water basins, ground water is presumed to be tributary unless proven otherwise.[59] The determination of whether ground water is non-tributary is based on aquifer conditions existing at the time of the application, except, as explained below, in the Denver Basin.

§ 4.4.2 Non-Tributary Ground Water in the Denver Basin Aquifers

> Maps showing the location and extent of the Denver Basin aquifers are available for a small fee from the State Engineer's office. See Appendix § 1.1.

Colorado statutes recognize a special class of non-tributary ground water in four aquifers within the area known as the Denver Basin. The Denver Basin is generally

---

[57] C.R.S. § 37-90-137(4)(c).

[58] *Bayou Land Co. v. Talley*, 924 P.2d 136 (Colo. 1996).

[59] *American Water Dev. Inc. v. City of Alamosa*, 874 P.2d 352 (Colo. 1994).

kidney-shaped, lying along the front range of Colorado and stretching from Greeley on the north to Colorado Springs on the south and Limon on the east. The Denver Basin is composed of four sedimentary and mostly confined aquifers, which lie underneath each other, separated by layers of impermeable materials. The four aquifers in descending order are known as the Dawson, Denver, Arapahoe, and Laramie-Fox Hills aquifers. The Dawson and Arapahoe aquifers are sometimes divided into upper and lower aquifers.

As noted above, the determination of whether ground water is non-tributary is usually based on aquifer conditions existing at the time of the application. For ground water within the four Denver Basin aquifers, however, a relaxed formulation is applied for determining whether such water is tributary or non-tributary. Whether located inside or outside the boundaries of a designated ground water basin, it is assumed that the hydrostatic pressure in each Denver Basin aquifer has been lowered at least to the top of that aquifer throughout the aquifer, such that the ground water is not considered to overflow into surface waters.[60] Without this assumption, the Denver Basin aquifers would be considered to be under artesian conditions. Thus, Colorado statutes assume that the water contained in each Denver Basin aquifer is less hydraulically connected to surface water than it may be in fact.

The legislature established this exception because the discharge from the Denver Basin aquifers into surface streams is thought to be so small as to be unimportant and the reliance of municipalities on this water is great. The non-tributary assumption is somewhat offset by the statutory requirement that the user of such water may consume only 98 percent of the water withdrawn and must relinquish two percent of the water to the surface stream system.[61] The legislature also recognized and protected pre-1973 uses in the four Denver Basin aquifers that were established based on appropriation rather than land ownership.[62] The special rules afforded ground water in the Dawson, Denver, Arapahoe, and Laramie-Fox Hills aquifers located within the Denver Basin do not apply, however, to ground water in these aquifers located outside the Denver Basin.[63]

§ 4.4.3 Not Non-Tributary Ground Water

Not non-tributary ground water is ground water located within those portions of the Denver Basin aquifers that are outside the boundaries of any designated basin that

---

60   C.R.S. § 37-90-103(10.5).
61   C.R.S. § 37-90-137(9)(b).
62   C.R.S. § 37-90-137(5).
63   *Park County Sportsmen's Ranch, LLP v. Bargas*, 986 P.2d 262 (Colo. 1999).

Example 2: Denver Basin Aquifer System

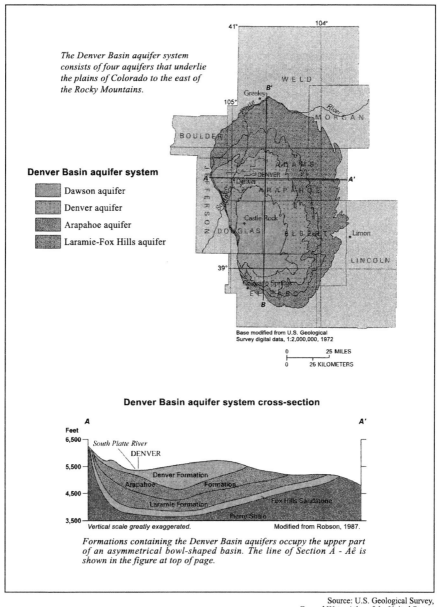

The Denver Basin aquifer system consists of four aquifers that underlie the plains of Colorado to the east of the Rocky Mountains.

Denver Basin aquifer system

- Dawson aquifer
- Denver aquifer
- Arapahoe aquifer
- Laramie-Fox Hills aquifer

Base modified from U.S. Geological Survey digital data, 1:2,000,000, 1972

0   25 MILES
0   25 KILOMETERS

Denver Basin aquifer system cross-section

Vertical scale greatly exaggerated.   Modified from Robson, 1987.

Formations containing the Denver Basin aquifers occupy the upper part of an asymmetrical bowl-shaped basin. The line of Section A - Aê is shown in the figure at top of page.

Source: U.S. Geological Survey,
Ground Water Atlas of the United States.

will, within 100 years, deplete the flow of a natural stream at an annual rate greater than one-tenth of one percent of the annual rate of withdrawal. Thus, not non-tributary ground water is water in the Denver Basin aquifers that does not meet the statutory definition of non-tributary ground water (withdrawal will not deplete the stream within 100 years at a rate greater than one-tenth of one percent of the rate of withdrawal), even when applying the hydrostatic pressure assumption. Absent the legislative classification, this water would be considered tributary and therefore be subject to prior appropriation. Nevertheless, the legislature provided that this water will be allocated on the basis of land ownership and an aquifer life of 100 years.

To avoid injury to surface water rights, however, the law requires a judicially approved augmentation plan before not non-tributary ground water can be pumped and used. The augmentation requirements are different based on the aquifer in question and the location of the well with respect to the stream/aquifer connection. For wells completed into the Dawson aquifer, the user is required to replace actual stream depletions to the extent necessary to prevent any injurious effect on surface water rights, based on actual aquifer conditions in existence at the time of the augmentation decree. For wells in the Denver, Arapahoe, and Laramie-Fox Hills aquifers, the water user must replace four percent of the annual withdrawal to the affected stream if the well is more than one mile from the connection between the aquifer and the stream. If the well is closer than one mile from the stream/aquifer contact point, the water user must augment actual injurious depletions using the assumption that the hydrostatic pressure level in each aquifer has been lowered at least to the top of the aquifer throughout the aquifer. Well pumping will eventually lower the water level in a not non-tributary artesian aquifer, causing it to lose its hydrostatic head and perhaps to become non-tributary over time; however, by statute not non-tributary ground water in the Denver Basin shall not become non-tributary as a result of the aquifer's hydrostatic pressure level dropping below the alluvium of an adjacent stream due to pumping. Thus, to protect surface water rights, the augmentation requirement for not non-tributary ground water will continue even after pumping has rendered the aquifer non-tributary in fact. Because pumping of not non-tributary ground water may have lagged effects on the stream, post-pumping depletive effects on the stream must also be augmented. This makes planning for not non-tributary augmentation plans extremely difficult, because post-pumping depletions can go on for hundreds of years after pumping ceases in some cases. It is possible to avoid the augmentation requirement in limited circumstances by obtaining an "exempt" well permit for ground water in not non-tributary aquifers. For more information on exempt well permits and their limitations, see Section 4.2.4.

§ 4.4.4 Rules and Regulations

Non-tributary ground water can occur anywhere in the state; therefore, the State Engineer has adopted statewide non-tributary ground water rules (statewide rules) that apply to all non-tributary ground water (except within a designated basin), including non-tributary ground water within the Denver Basin.[64] The statewide rules set forth the methodology for determining the amount of non-tributary and not non-tributary ground water underlying a parcel of land that may be withdrawn on an average annual basis. The average annual withdrawal amount in acre-feet per year is based upon the number of acres of the overlying land, the saturated thickness and specific yield of the aquifer, and an aquifer life of 100 years. All wells to withdraw non-tributary ground water must be located on the overlying land; however, the overlying land may be made up of separate parcels if they are adjacent or partially contiguous.[65] The State Engineer may consider parcels to be contiguous if they are separated by a public road. The owner of non-contiguous parcels may withdraw the combined annual amount attributable to all parcels as long as the well is located so that the cylinder of appropriation of the well, as determined by the State Engineer, overlaps, at least in part, each of the non-contiguous parcels. The cylinder of appropriation is determined by drawing a circle on a map around the well that is equal in area to the combined acreage of all the non-contiguous parcels. If well capacity is limited, additional wells may be permitted to withdraw some or all of the average annual amount allocated to the original well.

> The Denver Basin Rules are available at
> http://www.water.state.co.us/pubs /rule_reg/denverbasin.pdf

In addition, the State Engineer has promulgated rules and regulations applying exclusively to the withdrawal of ground water from the Dawson, Denver, Arapahoe, and Laramie-Fox Hills aquifers within the Denver Basin, commonly referred to as the "Denver Basin Rules." The Denver Basin Rules provide presumptive specific yields for the different aquifers and maps that show the location and presumptive thickness of the different aquifers throughout the Denver Basin. The presumptive specific yield and saturated thickness values given in the Denver Basin Rules may be used to determine the amount of ground water available for withdrawal where no site-specific data is available, but the presumptive values may be overcome with site-specific well log data that indicates that actual aquifer characteristics are different at the location in question.

---

64   Statewide Nontributary Ground Water Rules (codified as amended at 2 C.C.R. 402-7).
65   The Denver Basin Rules (codified as amended at 2 C.C.R. 402-6).

> The Statewide Nontributary Ground Water rules are available at
> http://www.water.state.co.us/pubs/rule_reg/nontributary.pdf

The statewide rules provide that the amount of water withdrawn in any year may exceed the average annual amount allowed, provided the total volume of water withdrawn from the well does not exceed the product of the number of years since the date of the well permit or the decree (whichever comes first) times the allowed average annual amount of withdrawal.[66] Thus, if a non-tributary or not non-tributary well does not withdraw the total amount allowed within a year, the difference between the amount pumped and the amount allowed to be pumped is "banked" and can be withdrawn in later years.

When estimating the average annual amount of withdrawal that will be available, it is important to check the local county's land use regulations. In an effort to conserve this finite resource, some counties, such as El Paso County, require proof of a 300-year water supply as a condition of land use approval, rather than the 100-year withdrawal schedule permitted under the statewide rules. In other words, the average annual amount of withdrawal is calculated by dividing the total amount of non-tributary ground water available by 300 years, rather than 100 years.

§ 4.4.5 Implied Consent

As explained above, a landowner has an inchoate right to apply for a well permit or determination of a non-tributary ground water right by the water court. The landowner may also consent to the withdrawal of the non-tributary ground water under his or her land by another. (Such consent is commonly expressed in the form of a deed to the non-tributary ground water rights.) If the landowner has consented in writing, the holder of such consent may also apply for a well permit or determination of a non-tributary ground water use right from the water court. Consent may also be deemed to exist or be implied, pursuant to statute.[67]

Under the applicable statute, consent may be deemed to exist by virtue of a municipal ordinance or quasi-municipal district resolution in effect prior to January 1, 1985, if such consent was the subject of a water court application for determination of non-tributary ground water rights filed by the municipality or quasi-municipal district before January 1, 1985. This provision is commonly known as the

---

[66] Nontributary Ground Water Rules, Rule 8.A., 2 C.C.R. 402-7.
[67] C.R.S. §§ 37-90-137(4)(b)(II), (8).

"Lakewood" provision because it validates a 1980 ordinance passed by the City of Lakewood concerning the consent of overlying landowners to that city's water court application for determination of non-tributary ground water rights under land within the city limits. The ordinance provided that the overlying landowner would be deemed to have consented to Lakewood's appropriation of the non-tributary ground water under his or her land unless he filed a notice of non-consent with the city clerk and recorder.

Municipalities or quasi-municipal water suppliers may adopt ordinances or resolutions that incorporate ground water from the Dawson, Denver, Arapahoe, or Laramie-Fox Hills aquifers underlying areas included within the entity's service area as of January 1, 1985, if the entity was obligated to serve the area by law or contract in effect prior to that date. Upon lawful adoption of the ordinance or resolution, the affected landowners will be deemed to have consented to the withdrawal of all such water by the water supplier. The implied consent does not apply where water service from the public supplier is not reasonably available to the land, and where consent to withdraw was conveyed, reserved, decreed, or permitted to anyone other than the public supplier prior to adoption of the ordinance or resolution. See Section 16.5 regarding steps that a landowner should take to protect against implied consent resolutions.

CHAPTER 5 PURCHASING EXISTING WATER SUPPLIES

Because of their relative seniority in the priority system, existing water rights often provide a more reliable water supply than new appropriations. The acquisition of senior rights typically involves a substantial up-front purchase cost. Depending upon the purchaser's intended use, acquisition of these rights may also involve a more costly and time-consuming trip to the water court to obtain required approvals for that use. See Section 10.1, discussing change of water rights. Often, however, at least some of the facilities that the purchaser needs to use the existing water rights are in place.

To justify and protect their investment, water right buyers need to do two things: (1) conduct an adequate pre-purchase "due diligence" investigation into the legal status and suitability of the water right for its intended use; and (2) make sure that the purchase will include all interests necessary for full use of the water right.

§ 5.1   DUE DILIGENCE INVESTIGATIONS

§ 5.1.1   In General

While a water right evaluation can provide benefits to an owner at any time, it is most useful before a buyer pays too much money for too little water. Title or other problems are best addressed by a seller still eager to close the transaction, who may be induced to pay for any necessary curative work. This is also the best time to obtain affidavits and other information concerning the historic use of the water rights from knowledgeable people, which will help water engineers to calculate transferable water yield in a later water court change of water right proceeding if necessary. Finally, these types of evaluations can uncover additional or different water rights than the seller thinks he or she owns. Frequently the buyer can then specifically include such rights in the deed to eliminate title questions and add value to the transaction.

How much diligence is due diligence? It will depend on the absolute and relative value of the water rights involved. In one commentator's words, "One would naturally recommend a more detailed or expert investigation on a million dollar purchase than on a thousand dollar one."[1]

Where the buyer only intends to continue the existing decreed or permitted uses of the water (*e.g.*, for irrigation or livestock watering), some but certainly not all risks to the buyer dwindle. For starters, buyers in such cases still should obtain and review the relevant decrees and/or permits. Almost always, buyers should look behind these documents to ensure they will receive "wet water" instead of simply "paper water."

§ 5.1.2   Purchase Contract Language

Water right buyers should consider requesting inclusion of the following water right due diligence provision in contracts to purchase water rights of significant value:

> Buyer's obligations under this Contract are expressly conditioned upon Buyer, at Buyer's expense, having obtained, on or before 90 days after the effective date of this Contract, a water opinion prepared by an attorney or other qualified person of Buyer's choosing, which water opinion shows the Water Rights to be in a status of title, quantity, and condition satisfactory to Buyer, at Buyer's sole discretion. The legal description of the Water Rights shall be determined

---

1   Ward Fischer, Water Title Examination, 9 COLO. LAW, No. 10, p. 2043, 2050 (1980).

from such water opinion. If this condition is not met on or before such date, and Buyer has given written notice of such fact to Seller within the time for such condition to have been met, Buyer, at Buyer's sole option, shall have the right to terminate this Contract and, upon such termination, to receive all amounts previously paid to Seller hereunder, and both parties shall be relieved of all further obligations hereunder.

§ 5.1.3 Types of Existing Water Supplies

Water right buyers should take care to evaluate the nature of the interest in water in question, as it may be an interest in real property (ownership of a water right itself), an interest in personal property (ownership of a contractual right to use water owned by another), have attributes of both real and personal property (such as shares of stock in a mutual ditch or reservoir company), or be an allotment contract with a water conservancy district.

In Colorado, water rights are conveyed like real estate, either with or without the land where they were used historically.[2] As other parts of this book describe, these rights can vary by source (tributary, non-tributary, or "not non-tributary"), manner of use (storage, direct flow, or augmentation/exchange), and degree of vesting (conditional or absolute). Each of these potential distinctions can create unique risks to the legal status of the water right in question and, as outlined below, can generate different tasks in a due diligence investigation.

Mutual ditch and reservoir companies typically own tributary surface water rights, which are allocated to the owners of shares of stock in the non-profit company. The ownership of a share of stock in the company usually entitles the holder to a pro rata share of the water supply physically and legally available to the company. Conversely, the company usually assesses the shareholders pro rata for the anticipated costs of operating and maintaining the company water facilities for the coming year. Non-payment of assessments can result in curtailment of water deliveries to the delinquent shareholder or, worse, forfeiture or sale of the shares.[3] See Section 15.3.

Statutes provide that company shares "shall be deemed personal property and transferable as such in the manner provided by the [company] bylaws," often by signing an assignment form on the back of the stock certificate and delivering it to the company secretary for transfer in the company stock book. However, mutual

---

2   C.R.S. § 38-30-102; *Navajo Dev. Co. v. Sanderson*, 655 P.2d 1374 (Colo. 1982).
3   C.R.S. § 7-42-104(3)-(4).

companies hold only the bare legal title to the water rights decreed to company structures, and the shareholders' equitable interest in those rights make them the owner in all material respects.[4] Thus, it is common to transfer full ownership of water rights represented by mutual company shares by both a deed and an assignment of the stock certificate.

The mutual ditch or reservoir company's corporate documents and water right decrees may affect the use of company water by a shareholder. A potential share buyer may intend to use the water in a manner not currently authorized by the company's water right decrees (*e.g.*, most such decrees are for irrigation only). In addition to the typical terms and conditions associated with court approval of a change application, such a buyer may need to leave a portion of his or her pro rata entitlement in the company's ditch to help maintain ditch flows, and to obtain the company's consent to the change.[5] While a company shareholder has the right to inspect a list of all shareholders, the scope of shareholder rights to inspect other corporate documents is not well defined.[6]

Water conservancy districts cover many areas of the state. Some districts have existing water supplies that are available for use within district boundaries. Conservancy districts typically allocate their water supply through the use of "allotment contracts" for specified types of uses. Some districts provide treated water supplies, while others only provide raw water that their allottees use for irrigation or treat for drinking.

The use (and possible transfer) of conservancy district water supplies is governed by the Water Conservancy Act, by regulations, rules, and policies adopted by the district's board of directors; and by the terms of the allotment contract. As in the case with water from other water providers, a potential buyer of conservancy district supplies should evaluate carefully the reliability and suitability of those supplies for the particular uses at issue. The transfer of allotment contracts usually must be approved by the district's board of directors. While these transfers are usually approved, there is no legal right to obtain the board's approval of a transfer.

For more information on mutual ditch and reservoir companies and water conservancy districts, see Sections 15.3 and 15.7.

Contract rights to water abound, both historically and today. Unfortunately, it is difficult to generalize concerning their nature and reliability because they vary

---

4   C.R.S. § 7-42-104(4); *Jacobucci v. Dist. Court*, 189 Colo. 380, 541 P.2d 667 (1974).
5   *Farmers Water Dev. Co. v. Barrett*, 151 Colo. 140, 376 P.2d 693 (1962); *Fort Lyon Canal Co. v. Catlin Canal Co.*, 642 P.2d 501 (Colo. 1982).
6   *Left-Hand Ditch Co. v. Hill*, 933 P.2d 1 (1997).

widely according to their specific terms. For this reason, potential buyers of contract rights should almost always hire an attorney to help with the interpretation of these documents. The conduct of the parties prior to any dispute over the meaning of contract terms may be a particularly fruitful interpretive aid.[7]

§ 5.1.4 Title to Water Rights

Historically, the express transfer of water rights by recorded deeds in a "chain of title" has been notoriously sloppy. Descriptions of water rights, whether tributary, non-tributary, or not non-tributary, frequently do not appear in deeds at all, or include only some of the water rights historically associated with land also described in the deed. Deeds also can describe water rights that long ago passed from a former owner's hands. Moreover, *standard land title insurance policies issued in real estate transactions do not insure against defects in title to associated water rights.* What obscures this fact from many buyers of land with water rights is the common (but erroneous) practice of basing the amount of title insurance coverage upon the combined purchase price of both assets and the fact that water related documents (including decrees) may be listed in the "Exceptions" portion of the title insurance policy.

To reduce the risk of buying water rights from someone who does not own them, a buyer can either (1) attempt to purchase specific water rights title insurance, which has only recently become available;[8] or (2) obtain a formal water right title opinion from an attorney. Both of these approaches will require time and money from a buyer to obtain, and typically remain subject to a list of exceptions and limitations as to the scope of the policy or opinion. As an alternative to a full-blown title opinion, a buyer may wish to obtain a less extensive evaluation of the chain of title from an attorney who only looks at a portion of the time the water right has existed. For purchases where water rights are a meaningful part of the purchase price, a buyer who considers foregoing any title evaluation should ask: Does this deal still make sense if I don't receive any of the water rights?

A water right title opinion or report will typically address documents of record, including water rights decrees, well permits, and documents recorded in the chain of title that expressly refer to the water right at issue. A water right decree, which may or may not be recorded, does not determine or establish title to the water right. It only determines who claims to own the water right and the existence of the water right. Water right title opinions or reports may be prepared based on an abstract of title. However, this review may be incomplete because water right transactions may not

---

7   *Greeley & Loveland Irr. Co. v. McCloughan*, 140 Colo. 173, 342 P.2d 1045 (1959).
8   Stewart Water Information LLC, *available from* info@stewartwater.com.

have been included in the abstract, or because the water rights transaction was recorded in something other than the standard grantee-grantor indices (*i.e.*, a "Ditch Book" kept by the county clerk and recorder), or not recorded at all.

In addition, because tributary water rights can be conveyed under the standard appurtenancy clause of a deed, even a complete review of the documents of record may not, by itself, clearly establish the status of record title.[9] In cases involving the conveyance of the inchoate (*i.e.*, unpermitted and unadjudicated) right to develop non-tributary and not non-tributary ground water, the Colorado Supreme Court has held that, because the right to withdraw such ground water "is so tied to land owner-ship, courts should presume that such right passes with the land in a deed and is encumbered by a deed of trust encumbering the land unless these water rights are explicitly excepted from the deed or deed of trust."[10]

§ 5.1.5 Other Investigations

Even if a water right's chain of record title is without kinks (very rare), a host of other, more elusive risks to the legal status of the right remain. As noted previously, the diversion and use of a water right for beneficial purposes is what creates the right. Similarly, the originally decreed rate of flow for a water right is only a maximum allowance under that priority. Historical use of a water right in quantities or at rates below the decreed amounts (very common) can decrease the value of a water right in several ways.

First, non-use of a water right for an "unreasonable" period of time can result in the complete or partial loss of the right under principles of abandonment. Section 16.3 covers this topic in greater detail. Most noteworthy in a due diligence investiga-tion is the rule holding that a continuous chain of title conveying a water right is "not enough" proof to rebut a presumption of abandonment created by non-use.[11]

Second, non-use or marginal use of a water right can significantly limit the transferable yield of the water right for a new, non-decreed use and/or place of use. Section 10.1 discusses the requirements to change the use of a water right (*e.g.*, from irrigation to a municipal use). Because the value of a water right often depends on its historical consumptive use (based in part on its relative seniority), a buyer should evaluate and preserve proof of historical use for any later change proceeding.

---

9   *Kinoshita v. N. Denver Bank*, 181 Colo. 183, 508 P.2d 1264 (1973).
10   *Bayou Land Co. v. Talley*, 924 P.2d 136, 150 (Colo. 1996); *see also Chatfield E. Well Co. v. Chatfield E. Prop. Owners Ass'n*, 956 P.2d 1260 (Colo. 1998).
11   *Haystack Ranch, LLC v. Fazzio*, 997 P.2d 548, 554 (Colo. 2000).

Historical use evaluations require the work of a trained hydrologist or water engineer. Prior to closing on the purchase of a water right that will require a change of use, such an evaluation would typically assess historic patterns of use of the water right through the review of diversion records maintained by the Colorado State Engineer's Office, aerial photographs, crop records, interviews with knowledgeable people, and an actual inspection of the property. The water right buyer should consider having this evaluation done in coordination with the water attorney because confidentiality of the report's findings may become an issue.

Additional investigations may also disclose other potential problems with the water right's legal status, such as adverse possession claims by neighbors, cancellation of conditional water rights for failure to obtain required reasonable diligence findings (see Section 3.3), discrepancies between decreed and actual uses and diversion points, unacceptability of the water right for dedication to a treated water provider to satisfy raw water requirements (see Section 15.9.4), or future limitations on use of the water right due to the presence of water supply facilities on federal land or federally listed threatened or endangered species downstream, (see Sections 11.2 and 11.3).

Finally, if the water supply at issue is a contract right or associated with a mutual ditch company, water conservancy district, or other entity, the water right title opinion or report should also address the legal requirements and obligations created by these entities (including articles of incorporation, bylaws, rules and regulations, or other expressions of policy).

§ 5.1.6 Discovering Unidentified Water Rights

In addition to the water rights that the seller specifically mentions as "appurtenant" to the land up for sale, there may be associated rights or interests in water not mentioned by (or known to) the seller. This is particularly likely if the longtime owner or tenant of the property is deceased. While it may be possible to acquire such unenumerated rights and interests in a catch-all "together with all other water rights" clause, research and identification of such rights prior to purchase will head off later questions. Accordingly, a buyer should search available records in the State Engineer's Office by location, to learn if any listed points of diversion or wells were shown to be located on the property. This search would not necessarily locate all possible appurtenant water rights, (*e.g.*, undecreed rights, unpermitted wells, or rights that divert upstream from but are used on the property).

§ 5.2   CLOSING ON THE PURCHASE

§ 5.2.1   The Deed

Standard real estate forms are often acceptable for water right transfers. Due to the many risks to the legal status of water rights just discussed, however, sellers typically resist requests to give title warranties for water rights, or to warrant the fitness of a water right for a new purpose. For conveyances of land and water, this may require the use of two deeds (or at least careful drafting) to clarify what title warranties, if any, apply to the conveyance of water rights.

§ 5.2.2   Description of Water Rights

Describe water rights as specifically as possible in the deed (generally, the more detail the better). For example:

> The water right and priority to 8.3 cfs decreed to the Dry Creek Ditch out of Dry Creek by decree of the Dry County District Court in the general adjudication of October 11, 1906, with an appropriation date of June 18, 1896; including without limitation all rights and uses of said water right, and under such terms and conditions, adjudged and decreed in the Findings and Ruling of the Referee and Decree of the Water Court in Case No. 89CW071, entered June 29, 1990, Concerning the Application for Change of Water Rights filed therein (hereinafter the "Water Right"), together with all easements, rights of way, ditches, headgates, and other structures and interests necessary to divert and deliver the water from its point of diversion to the property described on Exhibit A attached hereto.

"Catch-all" language for unenumerated water rights (for example, "all water rights and rights-of-way and structures associated therewith appurtenant to, used on, or in any way associated with the Property") may be added if that is the intent of the parties.

§ 5.2.3   Financing Documents

Generally, the same considerations applicable to deeds apply to deeds of trust and other security instruments. Lenders should be careful concerning the perfection and protection of security interests in "hybrid" interests in water such as mutual ditch company shares. Many such companies assert the right to sell the shares of delinquent shareholders for nonpayment of annual assessments, so a bank's possession of original share certificates may not be sufficient protection. Security interests in some conservancy district allotment contracts must comply with the requirements of both Article 9 of the Uniform Commercial Code and the applicable rules of the district.

§ 5.2.4 Miscellaneous Closing Items

Sellers should limit any affidavits concerning the historical use of the water right to their own knowledge and recollection. Signing such affidavits will not preclude the possible subpoena of the seller to testify in the buyer's water rights change case. Additionally, buyers who anticipate seeking court approval of a change of the water right generally should obtain non-irrigation or "dry-up" covenants on the historically irrigated land, in order to prohibit the use of other portions of the same water right from expanding onto that land and potentially causing injury to other water rights. "Floating shares" of mutual ditch company stock (*i.e.*, those lacking a dry-up covenant on historically irrigated land), in particular, may not be suitable for a water court change case.

Assignments of mutual ditch company share certificates sometimes are included within the deed to the water rights represented by such shares, but check with the company beforehand concerning the acceptable form of share assignment. The State Engineer currently does not require proof of assignment of a well permit; a change of ownership form signed by the new owner/permit holder, plus a fee, will suffice.

§ 5.3 TEMPORARY USE AGREEMENTS

Temporary use agreements, including rentals and leases, interruptible supply contracts, and water banks offer highly flexible means for water users to adjust to annual fluctuations in supply and demand. For example, low snowfall reduces supply, and hot and dry summers conversely increase demand. Temporary use agreements almost always involve irrigation water and municipal, commercial, or industrial interests simply because agriculture uses 90 percent of the water in Colorado, and municipal, commercial, and industrial organizations have greater financial incentives and resources to secure necessary water supplies. However, farm-to-farm transactions are also common.

§ 5.3.1 Renting and Leasing

A water rental or lease is an agreement between a water owner and a new user providing for a temporary water right transfer of a pre-determined quantity and duration. Seasonal rentals and decades-long leases are both common. Short-term rentals are often driven by economics. For example, due to a severe drought in 2002 and 2003, many South Platte River irrigators found they could make more money renting their water for municipal, commercial, and industrial uses than farming.

Farm-to-farm rentals are similarly driven by inadequate supplies—that is, where drought constrains irrigation, some farmers fallow their land for the year and rent their water to another farmer on the same ditch who has a crop that year. Water rights leases should state clearly the parties' understanding of the duration, renewability, and terminability of the lease (*e.g.*, some municipalities have charter provisions that prohibit the vesting of rights to lease water extraterritorially).

Longer term leases of water often involve owners with excess supplies in need of a place to "park" them until needed. Lessees may be parties needing interim supplies while seeking a permanent source of water, or may be responding to a drought crisis. For example, Aurora leases 5,000 acre-feet per year from Pueblo for a term of 15 years, with a ten-year option. Other communities, such as Commerce City, have declined lease offers from Pueblo, due to a strong bias for permanent supplies. This reluctance is evidence of a general municipal fear of anything less than total control over their water supplies. The enormous potential for future problems of supplying permanent development with temporary water supplies is the basis for this fear.

The rental market for Colorado-Big Thompson (C-BT Project) water is the most developed in Colorado. Before the 2002 drought, annual rentals were in the range of 25,000 to 30,000 acre-feet per year, 10 to 15 percent of C-BT annual supply. Historical rental rates were in the range of $25 to $30 per acre-foot to agricultural producers. Municipal and urban users took over the market during the drought, raising the rental price to $400 to $500 per acre-foot, although the volume rented did not dramatically increase. The fact that the approximate economic value of C-BT water for producing hay is $400 per acre-foot may explain the rental price.

> Owners of C-BT units can rent their water to another user within the district. Information is available on the district's Web site: http://www.ncwcd.org

There are a growing number of water brokers who function in the rental and leasing market. Some of these can be found by searching the Internet, whereas others rely on word of mouth. Other water professionals are often aware of brokers active in the geographic area of their practice.

§ 5.3.2 Water Banks

Water banks are analogous to water markets, except that water banks seek to coordinate temporary, rather than permanent, water transfers. A water bank is a formal mechanism for pooling surplus water rights for rental to other water users. The Northern Colorado Water Conservancy District's rental program functions as a water bank by facilitating temporary transfers. The Colorado legislature enacted a pilot water-banking program for the Arkansas River Basin in 2001,[12] and expanded it statewide in 2003.[13] The purpose of the legislation is to test the concept of a water bank to "simplify and improve the approval of water leases, loans, and exchanges, including interruptible supply agreements…[and to] reduce the costs [of] such transactions."[14] The Arkansas River water bank is the only one up and running, but there is not much activity. This may be due to unrealistic expectations of profits by Arkansas Valley irrigators.

> The Arkansas River water bank may be accessed through its Web site: http://www.coloradowaterbank.org

§ 5.3.3 Interruptible Supply Contracts, a.k.a. Dry-Year Options

One strategy for increasing water supply reliability is an interruptible supply contract, also known as a dry-year option agreement, or land following agreement. A dry-year option allows temporary water transfers during specified hydrologic conditions. As the name implies, dry-year options normally allow the senior rights holders to continue to use the water (in most cases for irrigation) in normal years and give the option holder (typically a municipal user) a way to make its supply more reliable during dry years. In exchange for the option arrangement, the municipality pays a fee to the irrigator for entering into the agreement, plus additional amounts for exercising the option and actually transferring the water. This can be an important source of supplemental agricultural income.

Dry-year options theoretically provide a win-win situation for both the agricultural and municipal or business sectors. They allow farmers to retain ownership of water rights, to augment their income through fees collected when entering into the agreement, and to receive compensation for production losses experienced when a municipality exercises its option in dry years. For the municipality or business, a dry-year option provides a means of drought protection that could be much more cost-effective or at least less controversial than the purchase of senior agricultural water rights, and perhaps more importantly, the construction or expansion of storage facilities, although storage may still be required to implement a successful dry-year leasing program.

---

12   Arkansas River Pilot Water Banking Act of 2001, C.R.S. §§ 37-80.5-101 to 37-80.5-107.
13   C.R.S. §§ 37-80.5-102 to 37-80.5-106.
14   C.R.S. § 37-80.5-102.

Dry-year options are not common in Colorado. The need to adjudicate a change of water right to permit use for additional purposes, to divert at a different point, and to use water at a different place or time than originally decreed is partly responsible, as discussed in Section 10.1. This process can be expensive and time-consuming, particularly for transactions that involve relatively small quantities of water or multiple owners of a single water right. However, it is now possible for the State Engineer to approve "substitute water supply plans" for 90 days on an emergency basis, or for a limited duration up to five years. Additional statutory authority exists to implement interruptible water supply agreements. These mechanisms are discussed in Section 10.2.

To succeed, an interruptible supply contract must adequately address the interests of both parties. The municipality needs assurance that the water will be available when needed. The owner needs compensation for losses caused by the exercise of the option, plus some incentive to enter into the agreement. It may be necessary to create a schedule of compensation based on the date the municipality exercises its option. For example, if exercised before planting, the farmer will have avoided some costs and compensation should correspond accordingly. However, if exercised later, the farmer will have unrecoverable costs that require greater compensation. There may also be concerns about calculating the value of lost productivity, and possible third-party effects such as greater difficulty among other ditch users in delivering their water.

Colorado agricultural interests have historically found dry-year options unattractive, for fear that they will impede the outright sale of their water rights to another provider who needs a permanent annual supply. There is also substantial anecdotal information that irrigators hold unrealistic expectations of the lease value of their rights, and are unwilling to give up control of their water in a dry year. This has discouraged municipalities who find it economically infeasible to lease a water right for approximately the purchase value without obtaining an ownership interest. In contrast, municipal lessors in California have overcome irrigator concerns by offering compensation that *exceeds* the current sales value of the water they lease. Colorado municipalities have yet to adopt this strategy, although the 2002 drought has loosened their purse strings to some extent. Aurora is moving in that direction with its above-market lease of water from the Highline Canal for $300 per acre-foot, an interruptible supply contract allowing the diversion of up to 10,000 acre-feet per year from Arkansas River Basin for three years out of ten. Irrigator enthusiasm for this deal—it was substantially over-subscribed—may signal the start of an era of interruptible supply contracts as an alternative to outright municipal purchase and dry-up agricultural water rights.

§ 5.3.4 Leaseback Arrangements

Leaseback arrangements are the mirror image of dry-year option agreements. In a leaseback, a municipality (for example) purchases the water right outright, adjudicates the necessary changes in water court, and then leases the water back to the seller. There are two principal variations of this scenario.

The first is most analogous to a dry-year option agreement and occurs when the purchaser only needs the water rights in case of drought. In average or wet years, the buyer meets its needs with other water rights, and leases the water back to the original seller. This leaseback approach allows for the possibility of retaining long-term agricultural use. Examples abound in the Northern Colorado Water Conservancy District, where municipalities have purchased some C-BT units solely for use during drought. In average or wet years, they rent the water back to farmers through annual agreements.

The second situation may be more typical in Colorado. Here, a municipality acquires the agricultural water rights it needs to meet future growth. It then leases the water back to the seller for continued agricultural use until the growth materializes. Pueblo, for example, annually leases excess water to irrigators. These leasebacks defer the impacts of agricultural transfers until municipal growth creates the need for water.

The potential and promise for leaseback arrangements is high given the efforts of municipal water providers to drought-proof their water systems. Many municipalities plan to meet a 30- to 50-year drought without cutbacks, while trying to stay 20 to 50 years ahead of projected population demands. This means that in average or wet years, most municipalities have substantial excess water supplies they can make available for agricultural or other uses. Unfortunately, some agricultural lands do not respond well to periodic cycles of being dried up and then irrigated. For example, it is impossible to return the lands irrigated by the Rocky Ford Ditch that were purchased by Aurora to productivity within a single irrigation season following several years of being dry.

§ 5.4 CONSERVATION EASEMENTS

A conservation easement is a legally enforceable agreement between a property owner and an easement holder (a land trust or public agency) that permanently protects conservation values by restricting future development and other deleterious activities. A conservation easement is usually established for a specific purpose, such as retaining or protecting agricultural, natural, scenic, or open-space values of the property, and may include requirements for the continuation of agricultural and irrigation activities. Conservation easements are a useful tool for property owners to voluntarily preserve property in its current state while also receiving substantial federal and state tax benefits.

In the last quarter-century, conservation easements on land evolved into an established and widely used mechanism to protect the natural values of real property and historic buildings in perpetuity. Water rights often support conservation easements on open space and agricultural lands in Colorado, and may be material to maintain associated conservation values such as irrigated agriculture, wildlife habitat, and wetlands.

Conservation easements offer an economically attractive way to maintain irrigated agriculture, wildlife habitat, and wetlands for less than fair market value because their value is based on the incremental value of the development rights, rather than the entire fee estate. Donors of conservation easements receive substantial federal and state tax advantages from irrevocable dedications of real property for conservation purposes. Federal law provides for an income tax deduction as a charitable contribution for the donation of a qualified conservation contribution.[15] State law provides for a state income tax credit up to $260,000 for the donation of a conservation easement.[16] Additionally, conservation organizations benefit by obtaining property below market value. The public benefits from the protection of important social values by private landowners and non-profit land trusts.

Colorado law now allows the creation of conservation easements that include water rights beneficially used on the land or water area that is the subject of the easement.[17] The law requires 60 days' notice to the company when encumbering shares in a mutual ditch and reservoir.[18]

The following model language on water and water rights was originally developed by the Colorado Water Trust, and could be used in any conservation easement in the state.

a) **Water Rights Included.** The "Property" includes any and all water and water rights beneficially used on the land described in Exhibit _____ that are owned by the Grantor, and all canals, ditches, laterals, headgates, springs, ponds, reservoirs, water allotments, water shares and stock certificates, contracts, units, wells, easements and rights of way, and irrigation equipment associated therewith (the "Water Rights"). The Water Rights include surface water rights

---

15   C.R.S. § 39-22-522.
16   26 U.S.C. § 170(f)(3)(B)(iii).
17   C.R.S. § 38-30.5-102.
18   C.R.S. § 38-30.5-104(5).

and ground water rights, whether tributary, non-tributary or not non-tributary, decreed or undecreed *[where specific water rights are known add the following:* ", including, but not limited to, those water rights or interests specifically described on Exhibit _____ attached hereto."] The parties agree that it is
appropriate to include the Water Rights in this Conservation Deed pursuant
to C.R.S. § 38-30.5-102.

b) **Permitted Water Right Uses.** The Water Rights are included in this Deed of
Conservation Easement in order to retain or maintain the Water Rights pre-
dominantly for agricultural productivity, wildlife habitat, open space character, scenic qualities, horticultural, wetlands, recreational, forest, or other uses
consistent with the protection of open land, environmental quality or life-
sustaining ecological diversity (the "Permitted Uses"). The Water Rights are
hereby dedicated and restricted to support, enhance, and further the
Permitted Uses. The Permitted Uses include, but are not limited to, the continuation of the historic use of the Water Rights on the Property. Grantor
shall have the right to use and enjoy the Water Rights on the Property consistent with historic practices and this Deed of Conservation Easement.
Grantor shall have the right to maintain, repair, and if destroyed, reconstruct
any existing facilities related to the Water Rights (such as ditches, wells, and
reservoirs) unless the Conservation Values of the Property would be adversely impacted thereby, as determined by the Grantee in its sole judgment.

c) **Restrictions on Water Rights.** The Water Rights may never (i) be changed to
or used for municipal, industrial, commercial, or any other new uses, (ii) be
changed for use other than on the Property, (iii) be sold, leased, encumbered
separately from the Property, or otherwise legally separated from the
Property, or (iv) have their points of diversion, or their type or place of use
within the Property changed, except after a written determination by Grantee
that such changes are consistent with the Permitted Uses and do not impair
the Conservation Values of the Property. Grantor shall not construct, or
permit others to construct, any new water diversion or storage facilities upon
the Property, shall not develop any conditional water rights for use on the
Property, and shall not otherwise undertake any new development of
water resources for use on the Property, without the prior written approval
of the Grantee. The Grantee shall record the Deed of Conservation Easement
as an encumbrance on all shares of ditch and reservoir companies listed on
Exhibit _____.

d) **Protection of Water Rights.** The intent of the parties is that the Grantor will
continue the historic use of the Water Rights on the Property. Grantor shall

provide Grantee annually a report on the nature and extent of use of the Water Rights on the Property during the prior year, including any reports submitted to the State or Division Engineer or local water commissioner. If Grantor fails to maintain the historic use of the Water Rights, or the Water Rights are otherwise subject to threat of abandonment, Grantee shall have the right, but not the obligation, to (i) enter upon the Property and undertake any and all actions reasonably necessary to continue the use of the historic Water Rights, or (after 90 days written notice to Grantor) to (ii) seek to change the Water Rights to another Permitted Use.

e) **Effect of Loss.** No loss of any or all of the Water Rights through injury or abandonment, or conservation of the Water Rights as set forth above, shall be considered a severance or other transfer of the title to the Water Rights from the Property for federal or state tax or other purposes.

The Colorado Water Trust Web site has additional information on the water rights aspects of conservation easements. The Water Trust will also assist land trusts and governmental entities with acquiring water rights in conservation easements. See http://www.coloradowatertrust.org.

CHAPTER 6 CONDEMNATION OF
WATER RIGHTS AND RELATED INTERESTS

Condemnation, or eminent domain, is a process whereby authorized persons and entities may acquire, involuntarily from another person, a property interest for specific purposes upon payment of "just compensation" determined in a court proceeding. The topic deserves separate treatment in this book for two reasons. First, condemnation frequently has generated controversy—not only with the owner of the condemned property, but also in the Colorado General Assembly. Second (and more importantly), the power to condemn real property interests necessary to divert water from a stream for use elsewhere has been an essential feature of Colorado's prior appropriation system.

§ 6.1   CONDEMNATION OF WATER RIGHTS

The Colorado Constitution's Water Use "Preference" Provision

Section 6 of Article XVI of the Colorado Constitution provides in part:

> Priority of appropriation shall give the better right as between those using the water for the same purpose; but when the waters of any natural stream are not sufficient for the service of all those desiring the use of the same, those using the water for domestic purposes shall have the preference over those claiming for any other purpose, and those using the water for agricultural purposes shall have preference over those using the same for manufacturing purposes.

Case law indicates that, rather than constituting an exception to the "first in time" system of water allocation (as seems explicit in the text), this provision instead simply provides a grant of condemnation authority to the "preferred" user.[1]

---

[1]   *Town of Sterling v. Pawnee Ditch Extension Co.*, 42 Colo. 421, 94 P. 339, 340 (1908); *Black v. Taylor*, 128 Colo. 449, 264 P.2d 502, 506 (1953).

The Water Rights Condemnation Act

In 1973, the City of Thornton commenced a condemnation action against the Farmers Reservoir and Irrigation Company (FRICO) to acquire water rights represented by shares in FRICO's Standley Lake Division. The Colorado Supreme Court held that the shareholders of FRICO, whose interests in the company's water rights were the subject of the condemnation, were "indispensable parties" whom Thornton had to name individually in the litigation.[2]

While the case was pending, opponents of Thornton's proposed acquisition secured passage of the Water Rights Condemnation Act.[3] Among other requirements, the Act purported to require any "town, city, city and county, or municipal corporation having the powers of condemnation" which seeks to condemn water rights to follow certain special procedures, including (1) the appointment of a commission of three landowners who, after a review of a detailed municipal growth plan and a study of alternatives to and effects of the taking, would determine whether the condemnation was necessary; and (2) a prohibition on condemning water rights for any anticipated or future needs in excess of 15 years. The district court then dismissed Thornton's condemnation action for failure to comply with these procedures.

On appeal, the supreme court held that the General Assembly could not enact legislation that limits the determination of necessity under the power of eminent domain granted to "home-rule" municipalities such as Thornton in the Colorado Constitution.[4] Specifically, the court invalidated the commission/necessity procedure and the 15-year "future needs" provision as applied to Thornton. The court limited the applicability of its holding to home-rule municipalities, however, and did not rule whether other procedural requirements of the act could constitutionally apply to such municipalities. A significant number of the state's larger cities have organized themselves as home-rule cities, and thus would be exempt from at least two significant requirements of the act.

Other Limits on Condemnation of Water Rights

Various other statutory enactments prohibit the condemnation of water rights, depending upon the legal identity of the acquiring entity. For example, water and sanitation districts may not acquire water rights by eminent domain,[5] and water

---

2   *Jacobucci v. Dist. Court*, 541 P.2d 667 (Colo. 1975).
3   C.R.S. §§ 38-6-201 to 38-6-216.
4   *City of Thornton v. Farmers Reservoir and Irr. Co.*, 194 Colo. 526, 575 P.2d 382 (Colo. 1978).
5   C.R.S. § 32-1-1006(f).

conservancy districts may condemn "any property necessary" to exercise their enumerated powers, except "title to or beneficial use of vested water rights for transmountain diversion."[6]

Appraisal of Water Rights

Any action to condemn water rights will require at least one formal appraisal of their value. It is difficult to find anyone who is proficient in appraising the value of water rights, particularly under the glare of a condemnation courtroom. The appraiser's chief difficulty is in finding sales of truly "comparable" water rights from which to generate a reliable market value. Water rights engineering and real estate appraisal are careers in themselves, and a mixture of equal parts of these careers (with some water law thrown in) is probably the best recipe for accuracy. The definition of "real estate appraiser," to whom the statutory licensing requirement applies, does not include "any person who conducts appraisals strictly of water rights."[7] Readers of water right appraisals thus should review them carefully, and question the appraiser's assumptions and qualifications.

§ 6.2   CONDEMNATION OF WATER-RELATED RIGHTS OF WAY

As explained in Section 1.1, Colorado's prior appropriation doctrine represented a rejection of the riparian water system prevalent in the rainier eastern United States. Water needed to be transported away from streams to allow development in the vast areas of the West devoid of water. Thus, the doctrine could not tolerate a system where control of the land beside the streams would effectively lock up the development potential of the uplands. The ability to condemn rights-of-way across the lands of another for water facilities—even privately owned facilities—has been an integral part of prior appropriation.

Condemnation by Specific Water Providers

Statutory and constitutional provisions empower a number of entities that provide water to condemn property for water-related purposes, including water conservancy districts, municipalities, water and sanitation districts, and "any corporation formed for the purpose of constructing a road, ditch, reservoir [or] pipeline."[8]

---

6   C.R.S. § 37-45-118(1)(c).
7   C.R.S. § 12-61-702(5).
8   C.R.S. § 37-45-118(1)(b)-(c), COLO. CONST. art. XX, § 1; C.R.S. § 31-15-707; C.R.S. § 32-1-1006(f); C.R.S. § 38-2-101.

Condemnation for Private Use

Section 14 of Article II of the Colorado Constitution provides: "[p]rivate property shall not be taken for private use unless by consent of the owner, except for private
ways of necessity, and except for reservoirs, drains, flumes or ditches on or across the
lands of others, for agricultural, mining, milling, domestic or sanitary purposes."[9]
Section 15 of the same article provides in part that "[p]rivate property shall not be
taken or damaged, for public or private use, without just compensation."[10]

Both the United States Supreme Court and the Colorado Supreme Court have
upheld such private-use condemnations against claims that they deny constitutional
due process guarantees. The latter court stated that, because they promote the full utilization of water in western states, private water development uses "are so closely connected with the public interest as to be at least quasi public."[11]

The general condemnation statute provides counterpart language to the constitutional grant that authorizes condemnation for private use, for the identical purposes.[12] Case law establishes that the statutory grant has provided an adequate basis of
authority to condemn private property for private use.[13] An additional statutory
grant of condemnation authority (available to public or private persons) relates to the
property needed to construct a water storage reservoir.[14]

Condemnation for Water Transportation

Section 7 of Article XVI of the Colorado Constitution provides broad authority
to condemn rights-of-way for water transportation purposes:

> All persons and corporations shall have the right-of-way across pub-
> lic, private and corporate lands for the construction of ditches,
> canals and flumes for the purpose of conveying water for domestic
> purposes, for the irrigation of agricultural lands, and for mining and
> manufacturing purposes, and for drainage, upon payment of just
> compensation.[15]

---

9   COLO. CONST. art. II, § 14.
10   COLO. CONST. art. § 15.
11   *Pine Martin Mining Co. v. Empire Zinc Co.*, 90 Colo. 529, 537, 11 P.2d 221, 225 (1932);
     Clark v. Nash, 198 U.S. 361 (1905).
12   C.R.S. § 38-1-102(3).
13   *State Dep't of Highways v. Denver & Rio Grande W. R.R. Co.*, 789 P.2d 1088 (1990); *Kaschke
     v. Camfield*, 46 Colo. 60, 102 P. 1061 (1909).
14   C.R.S. § 37-87-101(1).
15   COLO. CONST. art. XVI, § 7.

While this constitutional provision does not appear to require implementing legislation,[16] special statutes relating to the use of ditches at least partially provide any needed authority.[17] More importantly, this provision grants private interests the authority to condemn most publicly owned property for the transport of water. The provision is limited, however, and does not address condemnation of land for storage of water.[18]

§ 6.3   CONDEMNATION AND THE "CAN AND WILL" TEST

While private-use condemnations for water facilities are relatively rare these days, the presence or absence of condemnation authority has more frequently affected the ability of an applicant to obtain confirmation of new water rights or otherwise develop a water project.

Trespass and Initiation of Water Rights

It is unclear in Colorado whether a water right may be initiated by trespassing on the property of others. The closest Colorado courts have come to the issue is the case of *Bubb v. Christensen*,[19] where two water right claimants obtained a conditional water right decree for a spring located on property which they did not own. The Colorado Supreme Court reviewed a consolidated action to (1) make the conditional water right absolute (the claimants had trespassed again to install water delivery facilities); (2) restrain the owners of the land where the water right was located from interfering with those facilities; and (3) permit the water rights claimants to proceed to condemn an easement for their water diversion and delivery facilities. The court held that, because the condemnation action would compensate the landowners for the value of the easement (and a trespass action, if necessary, would allow for recovery of any other damages), "[n]o useful purpose would be served" if the court denied entry of an absolute decree until conclusion of the condemnation action. The court declined to address whether trespass was a defense to the initial adjudication of the *conditional* right, however, because the landowners had failed to object to entry of the initial decree and had thus waived any such defense.

---

16   *Town of Lyons v. City of Longmont*, 54 Colo. 112, 129 P. 198 (1913).
17   C.R.S. § 37-86-104.
18   *In re Gibbs*, 856 P.2d 798 (Colo. 1993).
19   610 P.2d 1343 (Colo. 1980).

Proving the Ability to Acquire Property Necessary to Appropriate Water

The existence of, or lack of, condemnation authority is becoming more important for the initiation of new water rights. A water right claimant may be required to show that it can obtain rights of way and other lands necessary to instruct a proposed project, even from unwilling landowners, in order to obtain a decree for a new conditional water right. See Section 3.3.4 on "can and will."

In *FWS Land & Cattle Co. v. State Division of Wildlife*, a 1990 case, the Colorado Supreme Court affirmed the denial of a conditional water right application because the applicant lacked, and apparently could not acquire, the real property interests necessary to complete the appropriation from two state agencies, which owned most of the affected land.[20] The trial court had held that the applicants thus could not show "that the waters can be and will be diverted, stored or otherwise captured, possessed, and controlled," which is part of the proof required to adjudicate a conditional water right.[21] The court did not directly address the applicants' alternative argument that it had the authority to condemn the needed state lands to complete its water appropriation until three years later. In that case, the Court allowed use of the prospective right of condemnation to satisfy the can and will test unless there are "no circumstances" under which condemnation could secure needed access rights.[22]

That same year, the Colorado Court of Appeals held that neither a home-rule municipality nor a water and sanitation district has the authority to condemn state-owned park property.[23] These entities wished to use the land (part of Castlewood Canyon State Park) for a reservoir project. The court reached this conclusion despite a statute which provides:

> Condemning public land – petition. Whenever any corporation authorized to appropriate for a public use by the exercise of the right of eminent domain lands, rights-of-way, or other rights or easements in lands requires, needs, or desires to appropriate lands...which belong to the United States, the state of Colorado, or any other state or sovereignty, such corporation [may take the further steps outlined to file and prosecute its condemnation action].[24]

---

20   *FWS Land & Cattle Co. v. State Div. of Wildlife*, 795 P.2d 837 (Colo. 1990).
21   *FWS*, 795 P.2d 839 *quoting* C.R.S. § 37-92-305(9).
22   *In re Gibbs*, 856 P.2d 798, 803 (1993).
23   *Town of Parker v. Colo. Division of Parks*, 860 P.2d 584 (Colo. Ct. App. 1993).
24   C.R.S. § 38-3-101.

A condemnor's present lack of needed governmental approvals will not bar the condemnation of other, private property needed for a reservoir site. However, a government land use permitting agency's active opposition to (and previous denial of a special use permit for) water development on government land may preclude confirmation of a conditional water right.[25]

---

25   *Gibbs*, 856 P.2d at 803; *Denver Power & Irr. Co. v. Denver & Rio Grande R.R.*, 30 Colo. 204, 69 P. 568 (1902); *West Elk Ranch, LLC v. United States*, 65 P.3d 479 (Colo. 2002).

CHAPTER 7 WATER FACILITY AND WATER RIGHT ACQUISITION FUNDING

---

§ 7.1   STATE FUNDING

A variety of state, federal, and private financing programs are available to support water projects. In Colorado, two entities, the Colorado Water Conservation Board (CWCB) and the Colorado Water Resources and Power Development Authority, have financing programs. The CWCB is authorized to loan to public and private entities while the Colorado Water Resources and Power Development Authority may only loan to government agencies and irrigation districts.

The Colorado Water Conservation Board administers construction fund loans, which are annually authorized by Colorado's General Assembly. However, the CWCB can loan up to $5 million without legislative project approval. See Appendix § 1.1. Loans can be obtained for new construction, repair, or rehabilitation of existing water storage and delivery systems, municipal and agricultural water treatment, and distribution systems. Loans have also been made to acquire existing rights. The loans are financed at below-market interest rates and funding is available for project planning and feasibility. Not surprisingly, requests for funding from the construction fund far outstrip availability and requests for funding are often seen on a multi-year basis.

The CWCB also administers funding from the Colorado Mineral Severance tax. The tax is assessed on mineral extraction to alleviate the impacts of extraction. The CWCB receives 25 percent of these taxes for its water projects. The Colorado Department of Local Affairs receives 50 percent of the Colorado Mineral Severance tax and can use these funds for development of water projects in counties impacted by mineral extraction. Current total funding provides for $20 to $30 million in CWCB loans annually. Outstanding loans total $360 million.

The Colorado Water Resources and Power Development Authority issues its own bonds and lends the proceeds to third parties. Its Web site address is found in Appendix § 1.1. This authority was created by the Colorado legislature in 1981 and provides funding for water and wastewater projects throughout the state of Colorado. The authority can now fund loans up to $500 million per borrower per project.

The authority has funded basin-wide studies and reservoir projects, including the controversial Animas-La Plata Project. It has a fund for small water resources projects and a drinking water revolving fund. The Small Water Resources Projects Program finances water supply projects up to $10 million without legislative review. The authority administers a water revenue bond support program for local water providing government entities, which pays the costs of issuance of debt, including the costs of surety bonds, trustees, and other necessary front-end expenses.

§ 7.2   FEDERAL FUNDING

At the federal level, a variety of resources are also available. The United States, through the U.S. Department of the Interior, Bureau of Reclamation, which is best known for its dams, power plants, and canals constructed throughout the West over the last century (including in Colorado), funded numerous projects in the past. Each reclamation project is specifically authorized by Congress for specific uses and in partnership with a local sponsoring entity. Funding for Bureau of Reclamation projects is a long-term and political process. The two largest projects in Colorado are the Colorado-Big Thompson project, sponsored by the Northern Colorado Water Conservancy District, and the Frying Pan-Arkansas project, sponsored by the Southeastern Colorado Water Conservancy District. Reclamation now has few large construction projects and primarily administers existing projects. The Bureau of Reclamation has recently developed new programs and initiatives covering topics such as desalinization, reuse, and dam rehabilitation. In 2003, the U.S. Department of the Interior launched its Water 2025 program aimed at helping western communities develop conservation, efficiency, and water marketing initiatives in order to stretch existing supplies over increasing demands. See Appendix § 1.2.

The United States Department of Agricultural Rural Development Program provides loans and other funds for development of rural drinking water infrastructure. The USDA maintains field offices in Golden, Sterling, Loveland, Frisco, Grand Junction, Durango, Monte Vista, Pueblo, and Lakewood. See Appendix § 1.2.

§ 7.3   PRIVATE FUNDING

Lastly, private funding through the municipal bond market is also available to governmental entities based on traditional bonding criteria. While this is normally available only to established cities, towns, and districts, it has become widely used in Colorado as a funding source, and financial entities are becoming increasingly familiar with western water issues. Banks and other financial institutions often secure an interest in water rights, together with land, to collateralize a loan. This practice is discussed in Section 5.2.3 on financing documents.

SECTION THREE: USING WATER

CHAPTER 8 ADMINISTRATION OF THE PRIORITY SYSTEM

§ 8.1   RECORDING AND REPORTING

Administration of water rights is overseen by the State Engineer's Office, a division of the Colorado Department of Natural Resources. Actual administration is performed by the Division Engineers through water commissioners.

§ 8.1.1   The State Engineer

The State Engineer and the Division Engineers have exclusive authority to "administer, distribute, and regulate the waters of the state."[1] The State Engineer may adopt rules and regulations to assist in the administration of the waters of the state. The regulation of water use is limited by the constitution, naturally including the priority system. Rules issued by the State Engineer also must recognize that each basin and aquifer has unique characteristics.[2] As a result, rules for the administration of waters of the state are generally applied on a basin-wide basis. The State Engineer's Office has issued, or is in the process of revising, rules in the Arkansas and South Platte River basins.

---

1   C.R.S. § 37-92-501.
2   C.R.S. § 37-92-501(2).

§ 8.1.2 The Division Engineer and Water Commissioners

The State Engineer appoints a Division Engineer for each of the seven water divisions of the state. The divisions are: (1) South Platte; (2) Arkansas; (3) Rio Grande; (4) Gunnison, including Dolores and San Miguel; (5) Colorado (except for Gunnison and White), (6) Yampa; and (7) San Juan/Animas. The Division Engineer, in turn, may appoint water commissioners for districts created within the division.[3] While the State Engineer is responsible for administration and distribution of the waters of the state, the Division Engineers accomplish the administration and distribution within each division.[4]

Water commissioners are the individuals most directly responsible for the day-to-day administration of the waters of the state in every division. Through modeling developed by the Division Engineers and through experience and observation of the conditions in each division, the water commissioners are initially responsible for determining how water should be allocated so that senior water rights are fully satisfied under varying stream conditions. The water commissioners observe diversions in their district, communicate directly with individual appropriators and ditch riders, and receive and keep records of diversions, which become the official record of water use. Most importantly, the Division Engineer and water commissioners have the authority to prevent and stop water users from diverting water when they are not in priority.

§ 8.1.3 Recording and Reporting Diversions

> Diversion records are compiled by the Division Engineers and are available online at http://cdss.state.co.us/db/viewdata_structures.asp

Water rights owners are responsible for recording their amount of water diversions and reporting those diversions, and can be made to provide such records. The water commissioners collect and keep the records for their districts, and through observation of the diversions within the district may confirm the records. In many cases, reporting diversions may simply be a matter of measuring the amount of water taken at the headgate, requiring relatively simple forms. However, in the case of structures that divert under multiple priorities, recordkeeping may be more complex. In the case of water rights with changed uses, or that are used in augmentation plans, the

---

3   C.R.S. § 37-92-202(3).
4   C.R.S. § 37-92-301.

reporting requirements are likely to be dictated by the change or augmentation decree and will often include requirements to project available supplies, particularly in the case of augmentation plans for wells where the depletions to the river are delayed and the water user must make sure that future supplies sufficient to offset those depletions will be present.

Failure to report diversions may be a violation of the terms and conditions of a decree. Even if no reporting is specified in a decree, failure to report any diversions for a long period of time may result in the Division Engineer placing the water right on the abandonment list. The preparation of the abandonment list is a formal process that occurs every ten years and can result in the complete or partial loss of water right. See Section 16.3. Furthermore, the Division Engineer has the authority to, and most often does, require water users to install measuring devices such as well meters or Parshall Flumes at their own expense.[5]

§ 8.2   CALLS

§ 8.2.1   In General

A "call" is the common term for an order issued by the Division Engineer to stop diversions when the water is needed by senior water rights holders.[6] "A call is placed on a river when a senior appropriator forces upstream juniors to let sufficient water flow to meet the requirements of the senior priority."[7] Because of water scarcity on the Front Range, calls frequently occur in the summer on the South Platte, Arkansas, and Colorado Rivers. Calling rights are often senior rights from the early 1900s or late 1800s.

> Information on calls currently in place for each water district is available online at http://cdss.state.co.us/db/viewdata_calls.asp

§ 8.2.2   Futile Call

One of the most critical considerations of the Division Engineers and water commissioners in determining how to administer a call is the statutory requirement that no "discontinuance shall be ordered unless the diversion is causing or will cause

---

5   C.R.S. § 37-92-502.

6   C.R.S. § 37-92-502.

7   *Empire Lodge Homeowners' Ass'n v. Moyer*, 39 P.3d 1139, 1144 n.5 (Colo. 2001), *modified by denial of rehearing* (Feb. 11, 2002).

material injury to such water rights having senior priorities."8 This is known as the "futile call doctrine." A call is "futile" and cannot be enforced as to a particular junior water user if the order stopping diversions does not provide additional water to the senior appropriator.9 For example, if two diverters are on the same stream with the senior downstream, the call the senior makes may be "futile" if additional water will not be made available to the senior when the water is needed. This often occurs when stream flows are low in mid-summer and the water sinks into the streambed and ceases to flow downstream.10

Depending upon conditions on the river, therefore, a water user may be able to continue diverting, even though his or her priority is junior to the diversion making a call. In administering a call, the Division Engineer must consider "factors [that] include the current and prospective volumes of water in and tributary to the stream from which the diversion is being made; distance and type of stream bed between the diversion points; the various velocities of this water, both surface and underground; the probable duration of the available flow; and the predictable return flow to the affected stream."11

§ 8.2.3 Interstate Obligations

Although Colorado is a headwaters state, we do not retain full ownership or control of the waters that originate here. As a result of interstate compacts and litigation between Colorado and other states, Colorado has many obligations to deliver water to the state line for the benefit of downstream states. These obligations limit the amount and timing of water that can be diverted and consumed within the state. The State Engineer is responsible for administering water to meet Colorado's obligations to other states.12

An interstate compact is an agreement negotiated between states that is ratified by the affected state legislatures and Congress. Once ratified, it has the force and effect of law. The State Engineer makes and enforces regulations for the delivery of water to enable Colorado to meet its compact commitments to other states, including regulations to curtail diversions.13 An order from the State Engineer to curtail diversions to meet a compact obligation is sometimes referred to as a "compact call."

---

8   C.R.S. § 37-92-502(2)(a).
9   *Empire Lodge*, 39 P.3d at 1145 n.7.
10   *Empire Lodge*, 39 P.3d at 1145.
11   C.R.S. § 37-92-502(2)(a).
12   C.R.S. § 37-80-102(1)(a).
13   C.R.S. § 37-80-104.

Colorado is party to nine interstate water allocation compacts:

- The 1922 La Plata River Compact allocates La Plata River water between Colorado and New Mexico.[14]

- The 1922 Colorado River Compact divides Colorado River water between the states of the Upper Basin (Colorado, Utah, New Mexico, Wyoming) and Lower Basin (Arizona, Nevada, California) with Lee Ferry, Arizona as the dividing point.[15]

- The 1923 South Platte River Compact distributes South Platte River water between Colorado and Nebraska.[16]

- The 1938 Rio Grande Compact allocates Rio Grande waters among Colorado, New Mexico, and Texas.[17]

- The 1942 Republican River Compact allocates Republican River water among Colorado, Kansas, and Nebraska.[18]

- The 1946 Costilla Creek Compact (as amended in 1963) provides an equitable division and apportionment of Costilla Creek water between Colorado and New Mexico.[19]

- The 1948 Arkansas River Compact allocates Arkansas River water between Colorado and Kansas.[20]

- The 1948 Upper Colorado River Compact between Arizona, Colorado, New Mexico, Utah, and Wyoming apportions Colorado River water among the Upper Basin states.[21]

- The 1968 Animas-La Plata Project Compact between Colorado and New Mexico describes potential operation of an Animas La-Plata Federal Reclamation Project.[22]

Colorado has been a party to a number of interstate water conflicts that culminated in litigation before the United States Supreme Court. In these cases, the

---

14   C.R.S. §§ 37-63-101 to 37-63-102.
15   C.R.S. §§ 37-61-101 to 37-61-104.
16   C.R.S. § 37-65-101.
17   C.R.S. §§ 37-66-101 to 37-66-102.
18   C.R.S. §§ 37-67-101 to 37-67–102.
19   C.R.S. §§ 37-68-101 to 37-68–102.
20   C.R.S. §§ 37-69-101 to 37-69–106.
21   C.R.S. §§ 37-62-101 to 37-62–106.
22   C.R.S. § 37-64-101.

Supreme Court has applied the legal doctrine of "equitable apportionment" to allocate water between the states. The doctrine allows a state to bring an original action before the Court to protect its right to an equitable share of the water of an interstate stream flowing along or across its borders.[23] Important equitable apportionment cases that affect Colorado include:

- *Wyoming v. Colorado*, 259 U.S. 419 (1922) – Wyoming sued Colorado and two Colorado corporations to stop a proposed diversion in Colorado from the Laramie River. A decree was entered that enjoined the diversion of more water than the excess available over existing prior appropriations in the two states.

- *Nebraska v. Wyoming*, 325 U.S. 599 (1945) – Nebraska sued Wyoming to determine the equitable shares between Nebraska, Wyoming, and Colorado of the North Platte River. The Court entered a stipulated modified decree to settle subsequent litigation, apportioning the river's flow during the irrigation season and including limitations on the amount of irrigated acres, storage for irrigation, and diversions out of the basin in specific reaches of the river in Colorado and Wyoming.

- *Colorado v. New Mexico (I)*, 459 U.S. 176 (1982) – Colorado sued New Mexico in an attempt to claim partial use of the Vermejo River, a river that arises in Colorado before flowing into New Mexico where most of the water is consumed. In this and subsequent litigation (*Colorado v. New Mexico (II)*, 467 U.S. 310 (1984)), Colorado failed to prove that potential benefits to new Colorado appropriators would offset impacts to existing New Mexico water users. The case was ultimately dismissed.

---

23   *Kansas v. Colo*, 206 U.S. 46 (1907).

CHAPTER 9 WATER FACILITIES

§ 9.1   FACILITY MAINTENANCE: RIGHTS AND RESPONSIBILITIES OF DITCH AND RESERVOIR OWNERS

Ditches are the arteries that sustain irrigated agriculture. Many farmers and ranchers, and even some municipalities, have historically relied upon ditches to deliver irrigation water. Ditch owners typically hold easements to operate and maintain the ditch across the lands of others. Very old ditches may be entitled to easements by prescription because they have existed for decades, but these easements have never been formalized or recorded in real property records.

§ 9.1.1   Rights of Ditch and Reservoir Owners

The rights of a ditch or reservoir owner, like the rights of any owner of an interest in real property, are determined by the interest the owner has acquired. Where the ownership is by easement, the extent of the easement right is a significant issue. While an easement document may spell out the rights of the ditch or reservoir owner, there may be additional rights implied by law. For easements created by prescription or implication, where there is no document stating the rights of the easement holder, those rights are determined entirely by law.

The legal right to operate an existing water facility on private land usually arises in one of five ways: as a deeded "fee simple" (*i.e.*, full ownership) interest in a specifically defined strip of land; as a deeded easement (*i.e.*, a use right) over such a strip; as a deeded easement over a broad area that lacks a specific location (or even a width); as an easement by prescription; or as what courts have sometimes referred to as an easement by acquiescence.

In the case of ditch rights-of-way, prescriptive rights (essentially obtained by "adverse possession" of the underlying land from another) are the most common. Because prescriptive easement rights have almost never appeared in recorded deeds conveying the underlying property, their existence and scope often cause the most controversy. But their absence from the chain of title does not mean that they are not enforceable rights.

§ 9.1.2   Easement vs. Fee

Even where the facility right-of-way is granted in a deed, it may be unclear whether the right-of-way is a fee interest or an easement. Much depends on the precise wording of the deed, and there is a statutory presumption in ambiguous cases that a fee simple interest was intended.[1]

The easement versus fee question most often requires an answer when the owner of land adjacent to the facility seeks to make some sort of use of the facility, or to cross it with a road, pipeline, or other structure. If the ditch or reservoir right-of-way is a fee, its owner has an absolute right to prevent such uses (absent condemnation). If the right-of-way is an easement, however, the general rule is that the underlying owner of land "burdened" with an easement (called the servient estate) may use the easement (called the dominant estate) so long as such use does not "unreasonably interfere" with the easement owner's use.[2]

An actual case may help illustrate this principle. The owner of a ditch sued the owner of land on both sides of the ditch. The landowner, a farmer, had placed railroad ties across the ditch in several places to permit the wheels of an irrigation sprinkler to pass over the ditch and irrigate the land on each side. The ties cut into the ditch bank and the irrigation increased weed growth along the ditch, both of which hampered the ditch owner's ability to operate and maintain the ditch. The Colorado Court of

---

1   *See Farmers Reservoir & Irr. Co. v. Sun Production Co.*, 721 P.2d 1198 (Colo. Ct. App. 1986).
2   *Osborn & Caywood Ditch Co. v. Green*, 673 P.2d 380 (Colo. Ct. App. 1983).

Appeals agreed that the landowner's actions constituted unreasonable interference with the ditch easement, and forbade them. The court also concluded, however, that the trial court's absolute ban on any crossings of the ditch whatsoever was too broad, because alternate crossings that did not unreasonably interfere with the ditch easement were theoretically possible.[3]

§ 9.1.3 Prescriptive Easements

> Because of Colorado's long history of irrigated agriculture, it is quite common for properties to be crossed by ditches where there has been no written grant of right-of-way.

In order to create a ditch or reservoir easement by prescription, the user of the easement must meet the usual criteria for creating any easement by prescription. This means the use of the easement must be (1) adverse to the landowner; (2) for the period of prescription; and (3) continuous and uninterrupted. The period of prescription in Colorado is 18 years.[4] Continuous possession for the prescriptive period creates a presumption of adverse use.[5]

Use of a ditch or reservoir easement is continuous even though water is not run in the ditch or stored in the reservoir during every season. "[T]he requirement of continuous possession in order to establish a right-of-way by prescription does not mean that the claimant must physically possess it every moment of the day."[6] The right that is claimed must be continuously asserted. Where the claimed right is only to run the ditch during the irrigation season, or where it includes the ability to completely empty a reservoir, continuity is not broken by these seasonal or annual variations in use.

§ 9.1.4 Easements by Acquiescence

In addition to prescription, Colorado courts have held that a ditch or reservoir easement may be created by the acquiescence of the landowner. Like a prescriptive easement, an easement created by acquiescence is not written and relies on the use of a property for a significant period of time for the easement's creation. Unlike a prescriptive easement, creation of this type of easement assumes the underlying

---

3   *Osborn & Caywood Ditch Co. v. Green*, 673 P.2d 380 (Colo. Ct. App. 1983).
4   C.R.S. § 38-41-101.
5   *Gleason v. Phillips*, 172 Colo. 66, 470 P.2d 46 (1970).
6   *Gleason*, 470 P.2d at 48.

landowner's consent to the easement creation; therefore, it is not necessary to show that use of the easement was adverse to the underlying landowner.

The Statute of Frauds requirement of a written conveyance of interests in land is not strictly applicable to ditch easements. This relaxation of the Statute of Frauds is justified on the basis of the statutory and constitutional grants of a right to transport water across the lands of others, and the need for irrigation in order to make the land in the state agriculturally productive.[7]

> There is no law which forbids one to grant permission to his neighbor to dig an irrigation ditch across his land without first purchasing a right-of-way and getting a deed to it. When, under such circumstances, the ditch actually is excavated and put into use without objection, or by approval, the owner of land traversed thereby may not thereafter withdraw his consent, deny the right of maintenance or destroy the ditch. Such consent need not even be in writing. Where the ditch has been in existence for any appreciable time, consent to its original construction is presumed.[8]

Under this reasoning, courts have held that if a ditch is dug and the landowner does not object in time, consent is considered to have been granted.[9] Constructive consent to the construction of the ditch is given if the owner knew about the construction of the ditch and did not object.[10] The amount of time the ditch must be in existence to infer consent is determined on a case-by-case basis. It is not necessary for the general 18-year period of adverse possession to run.

§ 9.1.5 Extent of the Easement Rights

If an easement was created by a written document, the scope of the rights granted is determined by the intent of the parties to the easement as evidenced in the language of the grant of easement. "The rights of an easement holder are defined by the nature and purpose of the easement."[11] "[T]he owner of the easement, or dominant estate, may do whatever is reasonably necessary to permit full use and enjoyment of the easement."[12]

---

7   *Yunker v. Nichols*, 1 Colo. 551 (1872).
8   *Leonard v. Buerger*, 130 Colo. 497, 502-03, 276 P.2d 986, 989 (1952).
9   *Shrull v. Rapasardi*, 33 Colo. App. 148, 517 P.2d 860 (1973).
10   *Leonard v. Buerger*, 130 Colo. 497 at 503, 276 P.2d at 986 (1952).
11   *Bijou Irr. Dist. v. Empire Club*, 804 P.2d 175, 183 (Colo. 1991).
12   *Osborn & Caywood Ditch Co. v. Green*, 673 P.2d 380, 383 (Colo. Ct. App. 1983).

The extent of an easement created by prescription will be the same as the prescriptive use that created the easement. "The extent of an easement created by prescription is fixed by the use through which it was created."[13] Similarly, the extent of an easement created by acquiescence will be the same as the use of the easement when the consent for the ditch construction was implied to have been given.

§ 9.1.6   The Right to Maintain the Ditch

A ditch or reservoir easement specifically carries with it by implication the right to maintain the facilities, including the right to cross other property for reasonable access, and reasonable use of property adjacent to the structure.

The owner of the easement may do whatever is reasonably necessary to gain the benefit of an easement, including repairs, ingress and egress, and additional space as necessary for those activities, as long as the easement is not expanded and the owner of the servient estate is not unnecessarily inconvenienced.[14] "However, a ditch owner is not permitted to place a greater servitude or burden on the land than that which existed at the time the ditch was constructed or was reasonably necessary to operate it properly."[15] When the owner proposes an additional use of an easement that was acquired by prescription, the additional use is compared with the original use with respect to physical character, purpose, and relative burden on the servient estate, as well as the "needs arising from normal evolution in the use of the dominant tenement and the effect of this increase upon the servient tenement...."[16]

Under this standard, a ditch owner has the right to enter property that is crossed by the ditch in order to perform routine maintenance, as well as more significant repairs and replacements. However, an expansion of a ditch to increase capacity significantly beyond the historic capacity would probably be beyond the scope of the easement, and therefore access for enlargement purposes would probably not be implied to be part of the original easement.

---

13   *Wright v. Horse Creek Ranches*, 697 P.2d 384, 388 (Colo. 1985) (*quoting* RESTATEMENT (FIRST) OF PROPERTY § 477 (1944)).

14   *Hayes v. City of Loveland*, 651 P.2d 466 (Colo. Ct. App. 1982).

15   *Hitti v. Montezuma Valley Irr. Co.*, 42 Colo. App. 194 197, 599 P.2d 918, 921 (1979).

16   *Hayes*, 651 P.2d at 468 (*citing* RESTATEMENT (FIRST) OF PROPERTY § 478-79 (1944)).

§ 9.2   RESPONSIBILITY FOR FACILITIES

§ 9.2.1   Injuries Caused by Facility Failure or Overflow

A reservoir owner's liability for injury caused by an overflow or the failure of the reservoir structures is limited to injury proximately caused by the owner's negligence.[17] The Colorado legislature long ago repealed the common-law rule of strict liability for the failure of a dam or reservoir. Similarly, a ditch owner has a duty to "carefully maintain the embankments...so that the waters of such ditch may not flood or damage the premises of others."[18]

§ 9.2.2   Trespass

A ditch or reservoir owner may also be liable for damages for a trespass caused by seepage or leakage against the lands of others. A trespass claim requires proof that the actor physically intruded upon the land of another without the landowner's proper permission. "A landowner who sets in motion a force which, in the usual course of events, will damage property of another is guilty of a trespass on such property."[19] Causing water to flow across another person's property will therefore give rise to a trespass action.[20] However, the Colorado Supreme Court has suggested that a cause of action in trespass for underground seepage either does not exist, or requires proof that the seepage caused interference with the use and enjoyment of the surface.[21]

§ 9.2.3   Dam Safety Rules

In addition to the common law duties of facility owners outlined above, dam owners also must follow the Dam Safety and Dam Construction Rules issued by the State Engineer.[22] These rules govern construction and safe operation of all but the smallest dams in the state.

A "dam" for purposes of the Dam Safety Rules may not appear to be a dam at all on first glance because of the rules' broad definition. The rules define a "dam" as "a

---

17   C.R.S. § 37-87-104.
18   C.R.S. § 37-84-101.
19   *Hoery v. United States*, 64 P.3d 214 (Colo. 2003).
20   *Burt v. Beautiful Savior Lutheran Church*, 809 P.2d 1064 (Colo. Ct. App. 1990).
21   *Board of County Com'rs v. Park County Sportsmen's Ranch, LLP*, 45 P.3d 693 (Colo. 2002).
22   Rules & Regs. For Dam Safety & Dam Constr. 2 C.C.R. 402-1. The Dam Safety Rules are available on the Web site of the State Engineer's Office. See Appendix.

man-made barrier, together with appurtenant structures, constructed above the natural surface of the ground for the purpose of impounding water."[23] The rules govern dams over ten feet in height, or that create a reservoir more than 20 acres in area or with a capacity of 100 acre-feet or more.[24] However, the rules do not apply to structures that were not built for the purpose of impounding water, such as highways and railroad embankments and many diversion dams.[25] The rule also lists several exempt dams. The regulations provide varying levels of requirements on construction or modification of dams, depending on the size of the reservoir formed by the dam and the amount of loss of life and property projected to be caused by a failure of the dam. One of the most significant design aspects is spillway size, since the spillway of a dam must be designed to safely pass greater amounts of water the larger a dam is or the greater the damage from its failure would be.

The State Engineer has significant authority to regulate existing dams by determining the safe storage level of a dam.[26] The State Engineer also has the authority to review the classification of dams based on the consequences of failure of the dam. The combination of these authorities means that the State Engineer may issue an order limiting the amount of water that may be stored in a reservoir where encroaching development causes an increase in the potential damage from dam failure, rendering the existing spillway inadequate. As a result, increasing development close to a dam could force a reservoir owner to choose between expensive repairs to increase spillway capacity or abandonment of a reservoir that can no longer be operated at an efficient capacity.

The rules are enforced by requiring a permit prior to construction, through periodic safety inspections of all permitted structures, and by complaint or other specific concern that is provided to a dam safety inspector. Such concerns may include vegetation growing on the face of a dam, extraordinary seepage, or overtopping of a dam after a large precipitation event. If you have questions about permitting or concerns about the safety of a structure, safety inspectors can be easily reached by telephone through the office of the State Engineer, which is referenced in Appendix § 1.1.

---

23   Rule 4.A.(6), Dam Safety Rules.
24   Rule 4A(b)(a), Dam Safety Rules.
25   Rule 18.A, Dam Safety Rules.
26   Rule 13, Dam Safety Rules.

§ 9.3   PROTECTING FACILITIES FROM INTERFERENCE BY THIRD PARTIES

§ 9.3.1 In General

Landowners, either because they do not receive water from the ditch or because they are recent purchasers of the land burdened by the ditch (or both), often do not appreciate the ditch owner's complex needs (and superior right) to use the easement area for ditch operation and maintenance. Related conflicts can arise over the exercise of water storage rights and maintenance activities in reservoirs, where adjacent landowners float upon false hopes that they own "lakefront" property.

Many new landowners view ditches at best as a nuisance, which cause invasions of their perceived privacy and undesirable impacts to the adjacent land when inspection, operation, or maintenance activities take place. Others, who are intensively redeveloping the surrounding land, view historic ditches as a constraint on their development plan unless the ditch can be bridged, piped, or relocated. The boldest (and least informed) among them may assume that they may take water running in the ditch, or add storm drainage water into the ditch, to benefit their development. In the case of reservoir rights, recreational access to the water surface, or water level fluctuations themselves, may generate friction.

As noted above, a landowner cannot unreasonably interfere with a ditch easement or its use. But, who makes the decision whether a particular activity constitutes unreasonable interference with an easement? When do they make that decision? Colorado law strongly discourages the "unilateral alteration" of ditches by underlying landowners, and encourages landowners either to reach an agreement with the ditch owner or go to court to prove that the proposed action is reasonable.

The recent case of *Roaring Fork Club v. St. Jude's Company* provides guidance. In this case, a ditch owner filed a civil trespass action after the landowner excavated within the right-of-way, graded and destroyed ditch banks and parts of ditches, realigned ditch channels, diverted ditch water flows, piped portions of ditches, constructed cabins and golf course greens within the easements, and temporarily piped wastewater into the ditch.

In upholding an injunction prohibiting such activities (and ordering restoration), the court held:

> Clearly, the best course is for the burdened owner and the benefited owner to agree to alterations that would accommodate both parties' use of their respective properties to the fullest extent possible.

> Barring such an agreement, we do not support the self-help remedy that [the developer/landowner] exercised here.[27]

In effect, the court's ruling precludes the owner of property burdened by a ditch easement from moving or altering that easement unless (1) that owner has the *consent of the owner* of the easement; or (2) that owner *first obtains a declaratory judgment* from the court that the proposed changes will *not* (a) *significantly lessen the utility* of the easement; (b) *increase the burdens on the easement owner*, or (c) *frustrate the purpose* for which the easement was created.

Not addressed directly in the opinion is whether it also covers crossing a ditch with a buried utility line. It has been common for many pipeline owners to negotiate with ditch owners to seek formal approval of such crossings. In the absence of such an agreement, it might be possible to bore completely underneath a ditch and thus arguably not interfere (much less unreasonably interfere) with ditch operations. Such "self-help," a far cry from the developer's conduct in *Roaring Fork Club*, nonetheless might now require advance court approval.

§ 9.3.2 Ditch Owner Impacts and Agreements

Despite the *Roaring Fork Club* opinion, ditch owners should obviously try to learn of any new landowner's plans to modify their ditch in advance. If the owner is not forthcoming, a call to the county planning department may not only provide needed details, but also give the ditch owner a chance to put potential impacts to the ditch on the county's list of concerns when county officials consider any permit needed by the landowner. At that point, the belatedly enlightened landowner may be willing to enter into an agreement with the ditch owner.

Agreements should specify what activities will affect the ditch, require at least sketches (and possibly engineered plans) for any modifications or crossings, and should include an indemnity from the landowner for any third-party damages caused by the planned modifications. (Some government entities may not agree to grant indemnification under such circumstances.) It is not uncommon for such agreements to require payment of a small crossing fee, and reimbursement of reasonable attorney, engineering, or inspection fees actually incurred by the ditch owner. A ditch owner whose easement is merely prescriptive or otherwise not specifically located in a deed may wish to specifically define a legal description in any agreement reached with a developing landowner, to eliminate potential confusion later.

---

27   *Roaring Fork Club, L.P. v. St. Jude's Co.*, 36 P.3d 1229, 1237 (Colo. 2001).

§ 9.3.3 Recreational Use

Recreational access to reservoirs has arisen occasionally as a disputed issue between underlying landowners and reservoir owners. Court rulings have left these waters murky.

When it ruled as a matter of law that a reservoir easement obtained under federal law was exclusive—and therefore denied recreational use rights to the underlying landowner—the Colorado Supreme Court made several critical observations about water storage reservoirs in general:

> The scope of the [reservoir easement owner's] rights as defined by the easement's nature and purpose necessarily includes construction and maintenance of the reservoir and storage of water appropriated for irrigation…. The practical considerations incident to administration of a reservoir and application of these waters to irrigation use support recognition of the right of the appropriator to control the stored water. In administering water stored in a reservoir to maximize beneficial use, it is sometimes necessary to lower or raise the water level significantly in a short period of time…. It is essential for purposes of public protection and liability control, therefore, that the reservoir owner carefully monitor the condition of the dams, maintain only that amount of water in storage consistent with safety, and assure that the processes of filling and discharging from the reservoir do not create hazards for reservoir users.[28]

Despite these pronouncements, the Supreme Court declined to overrule a prior court of appeals case that determined that a non-exclusive reservoir easement allowed surface recreational use by the underlying landowner.[29] The primary reason given was that the prior case gave the court no evidentiary record to review. The court also noted that the prior case involved "construction of an instrument granting a private easement,"[30] so the universal application of the later opinion restricting recreational use rights remains uncertain.

Merely because the underlying landowner does not have the right to recreational use of the surface of a reservoir does not mean that the reservoir water right and easement owner has that right either. In *Bijou*, the irrigation district held its easement

---

28 *Bijou Irr. Dist. v. Empire Club*, 804 P.2d 175, 183-184 (Colo. 1991).

29 *Bergen Ditch & Reservoir Co. v. Barnes*, 683 P.2d 365 (Colo. Ct. App. 1984).

30 *Bijou*, 804 P.2d at 185; *Bergen Ditch*, 683 P.2d at 366.

through a federal grant that allowed use of the right-of-way for "water transportation, domestic purposes, and development of power, each 'subsidiary to the main purpose of irrigation,' [and] 'for purposes of a public nature.'"[31] The court concluded that using the easement for recreation would "overburden the easement and would intrude on the rights of the Landowners as owners of the servient estate."[32]

Determining whether an easement holder or underlying landowner has a right to use a reservoir surface for recreation depends upon a close scrutiny of the grant of easement. Where the subject is addressed explicitly, of course, the easement grant ends the matter. Where the easement grant is silent on the matter, however, the question can often be a close one. Generally, it is unlikely that the underlying landowner will have the right to use the surface for recreation. If the types of water use are enumerated in the easement, it is also quite possible that the reservoir owner will not have a recreational right. In any case, landowners adjacent to the reservoir are unlikely to own any rights to use the reservoir surface absent grants or agreements with those parties that own such rights.

---

31   *Bijou*, 804 P.2d at 187 (citations omitted).
32   *Bijou*, 804 P.2d at 187.

CHAPTER 10 CHANGES OF WATER RIGHTS, PLANS FOR AUGMENTATION, AND EXCHANGES

One of the most basic and valuable aspects of a water right in Colorado is the right to change its use, while maintaining its priority. In other words, the point of diversion, type of use, place of use, time of use, and other aspects of a water right can all be changed, and after the change, the water right can still be exercised under its original priority and adjudication date, so long as other water rights are not injured.

> Changes of water rights normally require the assistance of a water attorney and water engineer or hydrologist.

§ 10.1   PERMANENT CHANGES OF WATER RIGHTS

§ 10.1.1 Tributary Water Rights

Both absolute and conditional water rights can be changed. A change of water right is now statutorily defined as:

[A] change in the type, place, or time of use, a change in the point of diversion, a change from a fixed point of diversion to alternate or supplemental points of diversion, a change from alternate or supplemental points of diversion to a fixed point of diversion, a change in the means of diversion, a change in the place of storage, a change from direct application to storage and subsequent application, a change from storage and subsequent application to direct application, a change from a fixed place of storage to alternate places of storage, a change from alternate places of storage to a fixed place of storage, or any combination of such changes. The term "change of water right" includes changes of conditional water rights as well as changes of water rights.[1]

Permanently changing the use of a water right requires approval of the water court. The use of a water right cannot be changed unilaterally by its owner.[2] The water court is required by statute to approve a proposed change of water right *if the change will not injure other water rights.*

A change of water right or plan for augmentation, including water exchange project, shall be approved if such change or plan will not injuriously affect the owner of or person entitled to use water under a vested water right or a decreed conditional water right.[3]

The applicant for approval of the change of use of a water right has the burden of proving in water court that the change will not cause injury. The requirement that the change not injure other water rights means that the change cannot cause other water rights to receive less water than they historically received before the change occurred. The requirement applies to water rights that are both senior and junior to the water right being changed. In practice, the Colorado Supreme Court now applies a two-part test to determine whether a proposed change of water right meets the non-injury requirement:

[C]hange of use involves two primary questions: (1) What historic beneficial use has occurred pursuant to the appropriation that is

---

1   C.R.S. § 37-92-103(5).
2   *Santa Fe Trail Ranches Prop. Owners Ass'n v. Simpson*, 990 P.2d 46 (Colo. 1999).
3   C.R.S. § 37-92-305(3).

proposed for change? and (2) What conditions must be imposed on the change to prevent injury to other water rights?[4]

The "historic beneficial use of a water right" means the amount and timing of water that was historically diverted and beneficially used under the water right. The extent of historical beneficial use limits the amount of water that can be changed to another use. It includes consideration of the amount of water diverted, the rate of diversion, the time of diversion, the place of use, the use to which the water was put, and the return flows back to the stream system that occurred as a result of the use.

The determination of the historic beneficial use of a water right is a complicated matter that generally requires the services of a water engineer. However, in simple terms, it seeks to determine two things: (1) the timing, location, and amount of water diverted from the stream, and (2) the timing, location, and amount of water that returned to the stream.

For example, consider a water right that was diverted from the Cache la Poudre River in Larimer County only for irrigation during the period of April 1 to September 30 each year. It was decreed for a rate of diversion of eight cfs, but was historically diverted at no more than five cfs, for an average of 50 days per year. Historic records indicate that, on average, 400 acre-feet of water per year were diverted under the water right that was used to irrigate 150 acres of crops. Water used for irrigation is not completely consumed or removed from the hydrologic system. Part of the water seeps into the ground (either from the irrigation ditch or from the field) and recharges the tributary aquifer that is associated with the surface stream; part of the water flows on the surface and back to the stream system; part of the water is incorporated into the plants that are grown; and part of the water evaporates. Engineering studies can generally determine, with limits of accuracy that vary from case to case, the amount of water that is consumed through plant growth and evaporation (historic consumptive use) and the amount of water that returns to the tributary stream system either through subsurface seepage or surface flows (return flow). In this hypothetical case, engineering studies could indicate that 44 percent (176 acre-feet) of the water diverted from the stream eventually returned to the stream system as return flow, and 56 percent (224 acre-feet) was consumed by the plants and evaporation.

Under the non-injury standard, the water right owner would only be allowed to consume a maximum of 224 acre-feet in a new use of the water right after a change proceeding. The other 176 acre-feet would have to be left undiverted in the stream

---

4   *Santa Fe*, 990 P.2d at 53.

system or, if diverted, returned to the stream system consistent with historical patterns of return flows.

However, the analysis does not stop at determining the relative quantities of water that can be diverted. The court would also place limits on the place, time, and rate of diversion of the water right so that the historic pattern is not exceeded in the future. In particular, the time of diversion of a water right usually cannot be changed without injuring other water rights. However, time of use can be shifted by storing the water for later use. In this case, it is likely that after the change the water right could only be diverted between April 1 and September 30 at or near its historical point of diversion, its rate of diversion would be limited to five cfs or less, its average days of diversion would be limited to 50, and the overall amount of water consumed in the new use would be limited to 224 acre-feet. In addition, the court may limit the amount of water that could be diverted in any one month to more accurately mimic the historic pattern of diversion for irrigation. These limitations would be necessary to assure that other water rights senior or junior to the water right being changed do not receive less water after the change than they historically enjoyed.

Water rights that are junior to the water right being changed have a right to the continuation of stream conditions as they existed at the time of their appropriation, meaning that any return flows from the use of the changed water right, which occurred at the time that the junior water rights were created must be maintained after the change.[5] Thus, if there are junior water rights that divert water below the place of irrigation with our hypothetical changed water right, and which historically received some part of their supply from the 176 acre-feet of return flows from the changed water right, the court is likely to require that the historic pattern of return flows be maintained after the change is implemented. Depending on the location of these junior water rights, this may entail not diverting a small portion of the water right, diverting a portion of the water right and allowing the water to seep into the ground through recharge ponds at or near the original place of irrigation, conducting the water through ditches to a point above the point of diversion of the junior water rights, or even storing a portion of the return flow water and releasing it back to the stream system after the end of the irrigation season to replace return flows that occurred in the non-irrigation season.

The amount of historic consumptive use of an irrigation water right is dependent not only on the amount of water historically diverted, but is also dependent upon the amount of water that was actually necessary to irrigate the crops. Part of a historic use

---

5   *Orr v. Arapahoe Water & Sanitation Dist.*, 753 P.2d 1217 (Colo. 1988).

analysis involves determining the amount of water that the historically irrigated crops actually needed to grow, considering natural precipitation, temperature, altitude, and other relevant factors. In some cases, the amount of water applied to a crop through irrigation may be less than the amount that the crop actually needed (this is called a water short system). In other cases, the amount of water applied to a crop through irrigation may exceed the amount that the crop actually needed (this is called a water long system). In cases where more water is applied than the crop actually needed, the amount of historic consumptive use that may be transferred to new uses is limited to the amount of water that the crop actually needed. For instance, going back to the hypothetical irrigation water right, if the historical average diversions had been 500 acre-feet, but the crop water need was still only 224 acre-feet, the historic consumptive beneficial use would still be limited to 224 acre-feet per year, and the return flows would have been 276 acre-feet. In this way, wasteful water use practices are not rewarded in change of use proceedings.

Changes in point of diversion involve additional analysis. The point of diversion of a water right may be changed, but within limits necessary to prevent injury. A point of diversion may be moved upstream or downstream on the same stream, if the change does not cause other water rights to receive less water. After the change, the water right is usually limited to diverting water only in the amounts and at the times that water was legally and physically available at the original point of diversion.[6] In other words, a water right owner cannot obtain an improved water supply by moving the point of diversion to a better point on the stream.

It is also sometimes possible to move the point of diversion of a water right to a new point on a different stream that is located in the same stream system as the original point of diversion. The same non-injury standard applies to such a change.

While the same non-injury standard applies to changes of conditional water rights, the fact that, by definition, conditional water rights have not yet been put to beneficial use, requires a different analysis. The courts have approached this issue by analyzing the draft on the stream that was planned at the time of the original appropriation, called the "contemplated draft." The contemplated draft includes consideration of the amount of water that would have been diverted as well as the amount of water that would have been consumed. If the draft on the stream after the change of the conditional water right is equal to or less than the draft contemplated at the time of the original appropriation, the change is determined to be non-injurious.[7] The contemplated draft must be determined based on the original intentions of the

---

6   *City of Thornton v. Clear Creek Water Users Alliance*, 859 P.2d 1348 (Colo. 1993).
7   *Twin Lakes Reservoir & Canal Co. v. City of Aspen*, 193 Colo. 478, 568 P.2d 45 (1977).

appropriator of the conditional water right, which may be shown by number of acres intended to be irrigated, number of homes intended to be served, engineering reports, and other competent evidence.

In practice, a change of water right proceeding in court is an iterative process. The applicant will propose the change of water right and some terms and conditions on the use of the water right after the change to prevent injury to other water rights. Objectors, usually owners of other water rights, may then raise claims of potential injury involving additional factors that the applicant may not have addressed initially, which may cause the applicant to propose additional terms and conditions to alleviate the problems identified by the objectors. If the water court finds that the change of water right as proposed with terms and conditions would cause injurious effects to other water rights, the court is required to afford the applicant or an objector an opportunity to propose additional or different terms and conditions to prevent the injurious effects.[8] The change of water right will then be approved in a water court decree after the parties have reached agreement on the extent and nature of the terms and conditions necessary to prevent injury, or after a full trial on the merits and the water court has determined the necessary terms and conditions.

While a change of water right is relatively simple in concept, it is complicated in practice. In particular, it is usually impossible to determine how much water might be available for use from a water right after a change, or what conditions might be imposed on the change, based solely on the original decree and diversion records. As shown in the example, if the water right has not been diverted to the maximum allowed by its original decree, or if the amount diverted exceeded the beneficial use needs, the use after the change will be more limited than the decree or diversion records would suggest. Further investigations of historic use by a competent water rights engineer or other professional are usually required. However, if the historic use of a water right has been determined in a prior water court case, that determination is likely to control a subsequent change of use proceeding, absent changes in the use of the water right or other events that occurred subsequent to the prior change proceeding.[9] This is particularly true under a mutual ditch system where the determination of the historic use of one share of stock is likely to set a precedent for the historic use of other shares in subsequent proceedings. See Section 15.3 for discussion of mutual ditch companies.

The water court is required to retain jurisdiction of changes of water rights for some period of time after the decree is entered to reconsider the question of injury to

---

8   C.R.S. § 37-92-305(3).

9   *Williams v. Midway Ranches Prop. Owners Ass'n Inc.*, 938 P.2d 515 (Colo. 1997).

the vested rights of others.[10] See Section 10.3 on plans for augmentation for a further description of retained jurisdiction procedures.

§ 10.1.2 Mitigation Requirements for Large Changes of Tributary Irrigation Water Rights

Changes of large tributary irrigation water rights from rural areas to urban municipal uses have become increasingly controversial in recent years because of the adverse effects such transfers can have on the areas from which the water is transferred. For example, large old irrigation water rights in the lower Arkansas River basin have been purchased by cities and towns in the Denver and Colorado Springs metro areas and transferred to municipal uses elsewhere. The result has been substantially reduced irrigated agriculture in the area from which the water rights were transferred, causing reduced real estate property tax revenues and reduced economic activity.

As a result of these concerns, large water right changes from one county to another that are not subject to local county land use regulations authorized by Article 65.1 of Title 24 of C.R.S. (commonly known as 1041 regulations, see Section 11.5.2) are now subject to non-water mitigation for the benefit of the area of origin of the water. This is an entirely new concept in Colorado water law, which historically has only focused on the water aspects of water transfers.

Any removal of water that results in the transfer of more than one thousand acre-feet of consumptive use of water per year by a single applicant from irrigated agricultural use in one county to a use not primarily related to agriculture in another county requires special procedures and consideration of economic mitigation.[11] In such cases, the applicant is required to provide actual notice of the application to:

(1) The board of county commissioners of the county from which the water is being removed;

(2) The board of the school district that includes the land from which the water is being removed;

(3) The offices of every water conservancy and water conservation district from which the water is to be removed;

(4) The secretary of every ditch company whose water is involved in the change; and

---

10   C.R.S. § 37-92-304(6).
11   C.R.S. §§ 37-92-103(10.4), (10.6), 37-92-302(3.5), 37-92-305(4.5)(b).

(5) The governing body of every town, city, and city and county, that includes land from which the water is being removed.

This requirement is met by mailing a copy of the application to the various persons and entities within ten days after filing the application in the water court.

In these cases, the water court is authorized to impose mitigation payment requirements on the applicant as a condition of approving the change of water right. These mitigation payments can be of two types: transition mitigation payments and bonded indebtedness payments. Presumptively, the payments must be made for 30 years from the date on which local tax revenues are reduced by the physical removal of the water, but this time period can be lengthened or shortened by the water court. In addition, the water court has flexibility to determine the actual start date of payments. The payments are made to the county from which the water is removed, and the county commissioners are then required to distribute the funds to the affected entities based on their entitlement under the statute.

Transition mitigation payments are made to the governmental entities listed above to compensate them for lost real estate property tax revenue caused by the lands being changed from irrigated to dry-land farming or no farming. Generally speaking, irrigated farmlands are worth more, and generate more real estate property tax revenues, than non-irrigated farmlands or vacant lands. These payments are similar to more traditional payments in lieu of taxes sometimes paid by the federal government to local governments to compensate for the fact that federal lands are not subject to real estate property taxes, but require the expenditure of local government funds for law enforcement, etc.

Bonded indebtedness payments are based on the bonded indebtedness on the property that is to be removed from irrigation. The statute does not state that the mitigation is limited to the bonded indebtedness of the entities listed above. The payment is to be equal to the reduction in bond payment revenues that is attributable to the removal of water in the transfer. In other words, the amount of real estate property taxes that would have been paid on the irrigated lands to support previously issued bonds must continue to be paid after the transfer, even though the assessed valuation of the now dry land would be lower. This provision is primarily aimed at helping school districts in rural areas.

The water court may reduce these payments if the assessed valuation of the land in question increases because of a change of land use that increases tax revenues. This could occur if the formerly irrigated land were developed for a more valuable use, such as a shopping center or residential subdivision. The water court is also required to take into account any beneficial impact to the county from which the water is to be transferred in setting the level of the payments.

There are three exemptions to the mitigation payment requirement. First, the mitigation payment requirement does not apply to water rights that the applicant owns, has changed, or for which a change application was pending as of August 3, 2003. Also, mitigation payments are not required for water rights that are subject to a water right change decree entered as of August 3, 2003, but which continue to be subject to the water court's retained jurisdiction.

Second, mitigation payments are not required if the change of water right is within the service area of the applicant as defined by the following conditions:

(1) The change is undertaken by a water conservancy district, water conservation district, special district, ditch company, other ditch organization, or municipality;

(2) The water was beneficially used within the boundaries or service area of such entity before the removal; and

(3) The water will continue to be beneficially used within such entity's boundaries or service area.

For instance, this exemption would apply if a water conservation district sought to change an irrigation water right that was historically used within the boundaries of the water conservation district, even though the change would have the effect of removing lands from irrigation and moving the use of the water right to an urban area hundreds of miles away from the original area of irrigation, so long as the location of the new municipal water use is within the water conservation district's boundaries.

Third, mitigation payments are not required where the new place of use is within a 20-mile radius of the historic place of use, even though the new place of use is in a different county. The distance between the historic place of use and the proposed new place of use are to be measured between the most proximate points in the respective areas.

The water court may impose these mitigation payments, but they are not absolutely required. To the authors' knowledge, no water court decree has yet been entered in a case subject to these provisions.

§ 10.1.3 Non-Tributary, Developed, and Imported Water

While the same non-injury standard applies to changes of use of non-tributary water, developed water, and water diverted from one river basin to another (imported or transmountain water), the injury analysis is much simpler because other water users do not have a right to rely upon or use the return flows from the use of such water.[12] Those who import water from one river basin to another, or who discharge water from non-tributary water sources to surface stream systems, have a right to successively use and reuse that water, including its return flows, to extinction. Thus, in this type of change of water right, there is no consideration of loss of return flows, or change in return flow patterns, as they may affect other water users. The owner of the non-tributary water or water right for imported water owns all rights of reuse and successive use, and can claim and use all return flows to the extent that they can be quantified in time and amount in the stream system.

The only injury legally possible from changes of imported or transmountain water is from changes in the historical amount, rate, or time of diversion that may adversely affect junior priorities in the basin of origin.[13] Hence, in changes of this type, the court is likely to require only terms and conditions that ensure that the amount of water diverted from the basin of origin, and the rate and time of diversion, do not change compared to historical practices.

Since transmountain water rights have impacts in two different divisions of the water courts, two water courts potentially have jurisdiction over applications to change these water rights. In cases where the applicant seeks to change the point of diversion of a transmountain water right, the water court of the basin of origin of the water has jurisdiction over the application. In cases where the applicant seeks to change the type or place of use of the water, the water court in the basin of use of the water has jurisdiction.[14]

In a number of instances in the past, particularly in the Cache la Poudre River basin in the early 1950s, Colorado courts adjudicated water rights as being not tributary to surface streams in factual circumstances where it is now generally believed that they are in reality tributary.[15] These are often referred to as Coffin wells or Coffin water rights, after the judge who decreed them. While the doctrines of *collateral estoppel* and *res judicata* prevent these decrees from being reopened, and the water rights are now treated as being not tributary to the surface streams, the water courts might not treat these water rights as not tributary if an owner seeks to change their type or place of use. No reported appellate cases have yet addressed this issue.

Change of use of non-tributary ground water that is diverted pursuant to rights based on land ownership pursuant to statute is not subject to the requirement of

---

12   C.R.S. § 37-82-106(1); *City of Thornton v. Bijou Irr. Co.*, 926 P.2d 1 (Colo. 1996).

13   *Twin Lakes Reservoir & Canal Co. v. City of Aspen*, 193 Colo. 478, 568 P.2d 45 (Colo. 1977).

14   *Colo. Dep't of Natural Res., Div. of Wildlife v. Ogburn*, 194 Colo. 60, 570 P.2d 4 (1977).

15   *City of Thornton v. Bijou Irr. Co.*, 926 P.2d 1 (Colo. 1996).

examining historic diversions.[16] So long as the rates and amounts of withdrawal do not exceed the amounts allowed by applicable permits or decrees, no injury can legally result to other water rights from a change in use and changes can be approved without further injury analysis.

As explained in Section 4.4.1, prior to the adoption of the statute allocating non-tributary ground water based on overlying land ownership in 1973, wells withdrawing non-tributary ground water were permitted and adjudicated based on appropriation. Although the matter has not yet been decided by the Colorado courts, changes of use of these appropriated water rights for non-tributary water may be limited so that the amount of water withdrawn from the well after the change does not exceed the historic amounts withdrawn. This limitation could be imposed because, being water rights based on the doctrine of prior appropriation, the wells may be subject to the rules applicable when appropriated water rights are changed, including the limitation to the amount of water historically diverted (discussed above in Section 10.1).

§ 10.1.4 Designated Ground Water

Designated ground water is subject to a modified doctrine of prior appropriation, as explained in Section 4.3. Water rights to designated ground water can be changed, subject to the same legal standards of non-injury to other water rights as those used for tributary water rights.[17] Authority to approve such changes is vested in both the Ground Water Commission and in ground water management districts formed under the Colorado Ground Water Management Act.[18] The Ground Water Commission is empowered to authorize such changes of use except to the extent that similar authority is vested in a ground water management district that has jurisdiction over the water right.[19] Ground water management districts have authority, among other things, to adopt control regulations to conserve, preserve, and protect the ground water and to "prohibit, after affording an opportunity for a hearing before the board of the local district and presentation of evidence, the use of ground water outside the boundaries of the district where such use materially affects the rights acquired by permit by any owner or operator of land within the district...."[20] Pursuant to this authority, ground water management districts have adopted rules governing changes in use of designated ground water rights and the export of water from the district.

---

16   C.R.S. § 37-90-137(4).
17   *Danielson v. Kerbs Ag., Inc.*, 646 P.2d 363 (Colo. 1982).
18   C.R.S. § 37-90-118.
19   C.R.S. § 37-90-111(1)(g).
20   C.R.S. § 37-90-130(2)(e), (f).

§ 10.1.5 Mutual Ditch Company Stock Shares and Contract Rights to Water

The owner of shares of stock in a mutual ditch company has the same right to seek a change of water right for the water rights represented by his or her shares as any other appropriator. However, the board of directors of a mutual ditch company has the authority to adopt and enforce company bylaws imposing reasonable limitations upon the right of a shareholder to change the water rights represented by his or her shares for the purpose of preventing injury to the ditch, the company, and other shareholders from the proposed change.[21] Such bylaws can generally only be enforced against shareholders who acquired their shares after the bylaw was adopted. The water court has jurisdiction to review (under an arbitrary, capricious, or abuse of discretion standard) the decision of the mutual ditch company board of directors in any change of water right proceeding brought to obtain judicial approval of the change of water rights.

In some cases, particularly under old irrigation ditches, rights to obtain and use water may be represented by contracts or deeds, and not water right decrees or shares of stock. For instance, ditch companies sometimes compensated owners of lands crossed by the ditch by providing rights to use certain amounts of water from the ditch under contracts. These documents often contain limitations on the use of the water provided that are not present in normal water right decrees. The rights represented by these contracts or other documents are not water rights with a statutory right to change the use.[22] The courts generally enforce any limitations contained in the relevant documents. Thus, the use of the water provided by these contracts and other documents generally can only be changed if the proposed new use is allowed by the terms of the document.

§ 10.1.6 Minimum Stream Flow Water Rights of the Colorado Water Conservation Board

As explained in Section 3.4.1, the Colorado Water Conservation Board (CWCB) has the exclusive authority under Colorado law to appropriate and hold water rights for minimum stream flows and lake levels.[23] Unlike other water right owners, and due to the unique statutory basis of these water rights, the CWCB cannot unilaterally seek and obtain court decrees to decrease the amounts of these water rights. Instead, the

---

[21]   *Fort Lyon Canal Co. v. Catlin Canal Co.*, 642 P.2d 501 (Colo. 1982).
[22]   *Merrick v. Fort Lyon Canal Co.*, 621 P.2d 952 (Colo. 1981).
[23]   C.R.S. § 37-92-102(3).

CWCB is required to hold public meetings and take evidence regarding any proposal to decrease its minimum stream flow and minimum lake level water rights.[24] The CWCB must then make a written determination regarding the proposal to decrease these water rights, which is then filed with the water court.

Any party who appears in the proceedings before the CWCB can seek judicial review of the CWCB decision based on the administrative record. The reviewing court can only overturn the CWCB decision if it finds that the decision is arbitrary or capricious; a denial of statutory right; contrary to constitutional right, power, privilege, or immunity; in excess of statutory jurisdiction, authority, purposes, or limitations; not in accord with applicable procedures; an abuse or clearly unwarranted exercise of discretion; based upon findings of fact that are clearly erroneous on the whole record; unsupported by substantial evidence when the record is considered as a whole; or otherwise contrary to law.[25] If no party seeks review of the CWCB decision, the water court is required to enter a decree decreasing the water right as determined by the CWCB.

§ 10.2   ADMINISTRATIVELY APPROVED CHANGES OF WATER RIGHTS

In certain circumstances the State Engineer or Division Engineer has the authority to administratively approve temporary and limited changes in the use of water rights. This authority is fairly narrow and specific. The procedural requirements for each circumstance are slightly different, although all of the applicable statutes require a finding of non-injury to other water rights for approval of the temporary change.

§ 10.2.1 Temporary Changes of Water Rights and Substitute Water Supply Plans

The State Engineer may approve temporary changes of use of water rights under certain circumstances. The authority to approve the temporary changes is contained in several statutes, all of which have similar procedural and substantive requirements (discussed below). In all situations, the proposed temporary change can only be approved if it will not cause injury to other water rights.

If a change of water right application has been filed with the water court, the State Engineer may approve the change of water right as a substitute water supply plan for one year if certain statutory criteria are met.[26] The criteria include filing an

---

24   C.R.S. § 37-92-102(4).
25   C.R.S. § 24-4-106(6), (7).
26   C.R.S. § 37-92-308(4).

application with the State Engineer, notice to objectors in the pending water court case, opportunity for the objectors to comment on the proposal, and a finding by the State Engineer that the proposed temporary change of use will not cause injury to other water rights and decreed conditional water rights, including water quality and continuity to meet the requirements of use to which the senior appropriation has normally been put, and will not impair compliance with any interstate compacts. The State Engineer can impose terms and conditions on the proposed change to ensure that these standards are met, and a State Engineer's decision approving or denying a substitute water supply plan can be appealed to the water court. No hearings are required to be held on the application. The State Engineer's decision does not create any presumption, shift the burden of proof, or serve as a defense in any water court case or legal action regarding the substitute water supply plan.[27] The approval of the substitute water supply plan can be renewed by the State Engineer for up to four more years after the initial one-year approval. After the State Engineer has approved the plan for five years, the applicant must demonstrate to the water court that the delay in obtaining a decree is justifiable and that not being able to operate under the substitute water supply plan will cause undue hardship to the applicant.[28]

If a change of water right application is not pending in the water court, the State Engineer can approve a change of water right as a substitute water supply plan if the depletions associated with the change of use will be for a limited duration not to exceed five years.[29] This means that the depletions caused by the changed water right cannot affect the flows in the surface stream system for longer than five years after the change is authorized, and has the practical effect of preventing this authority from being used to allow temporary changes of use of water rights associated with most tributary wells whose diversions do not immediately deplete the stream. The procedures and applicable standards for approval are otherwise the same as when a water court change of water right application is pending. Years of approval of substitute water supply plans before a change of water right application is filed with the water court are counted toward the five-year limit on the State Engineer's authority to approve temporary changes after an application has been filed with the water court.[30]

During 2003, 2004, and 2005, the State Engineer has the authority to approve annual substitute supply plans for wells operating in the South Platte River basin that

---

27   C.R.S. § 37-92-308(4)(c).
28   C.R.S. § 37-92-308(4)(b).
29   C.R.S. § 37-92-308(5).
30   C.R.S. § 37-92-308(4)(b).

had been operating pursuant to substitute water supply plans approved before 2003.[31] This is a temporary authority intended to allow the owners of such wells to continue to operate while they prepare to file an application for approval of a plan for augmentation with the water court, and seek temporary approval of that plan under the procedures described above. The approval can only be given after an appropriate application has been filed, there has been notice and comment, a public hearing has been held, and the State Engineer has found that the proposal will not injure other water rights or decreed conditional water rights, including water quality and continuity to meet the requirements of use to which the senior appropriation has normally been put, and will not impair compliance with the South Platte River Compact.

Finally, in cases of emergency affecting public health or safety, the State Engineer has the authority to approve substitute water supply plans, which can include temporary changes of water rights, for up to 90 days, if the State Engineer determines that the plan will not cause injury to the vested water rights or decreed conditional water rights of others or impair compliance with interstate compacts.[32] No notice to or opportunity for comment by potentially affected parties is provided. As with approval of the other substitute water supply plans, approval of such an emergency plan creates no presumptions, does not shift the burden of proof, and does not provide a legal defense in any legal action involving the plan. Initially, the State Engineer has limited approval of these emergency plans to situations involving municipal water supply shortages, although the State Engineer has indicated that this authority may be used to approve emergency plans for feedlots.

§ 10.2.2 Loans of Water Rights

The Division Engineer has the authority to approve loans of water rights from one water user to another in limited circumstances. The owner of an agricultural irrigation water right may loan all or a portion of the water right to another owner of an agricultural irrigation water right on the same stream system for up to 180 days per calendar year. An application for approval of the loan must be made in advance to the Division Engineer. The Division Engineer can only approve the loan if it will not injure other existing water rights.[33] As with substitute water supply plans, notice of the proposed loan must be provided to persons on the substitute water supply plan notification list, who have 15 days to comment on the proposal. Any party may appeal

---

31   C.R.S. § 37-92-308(3).
32   C.R.S. § 37-92-308(7).
33   C.R.S. § 37-83-105(1).

an adverse decision of the Division Engineer to the water court within 15 days after the date on which the decision of the Division Engineer is served on the parties.

The Division Engineer also has the authority to approve loans of water rights to the Colorado Water Conservation Board (CWCB) for use as instream flows in any basin or county in which the Governor declares a drought emergency or in which any other emergency is declared. The CWCB must make an application to the Division Engineer. The Division Engineer can only approve the loan if it will not injure other existing water rights. Procedures for approval of loans to the CWCB are the same as for loans of an agricultural irrigation water right.

§ 10.2.3 Interruptible Water Supply Agreements

The State Engineer has the authority to approve and administer interruptible water supply agreements that permit a temporary change in the point of diversion, location of use, and type of use of an absolute water right. An interruptible water supply agreement is an agreement between two or more water right owners under which one owner agrees to stop using his water right upon the request of the other party, and the other party then temporarily uses the water right for another purpose.[34]

For example, a municipality or other water provider could enter into such an agreement with the owner of an irrigation water right as a drought protection strategy, and as a way of avoiding permanent cessation of agricultural irrigation. The municipality or other water provider would only use the irrigation water right in drought years, and the water right could continue to be used for irrigation in other years. The owner of the irrigation water right would be appropriately compensated with money or replaced crop production for the times when he cannot use the water right for irrigation purposes. Interruptible water supply agreements cannot be exercised for more than three years in a ten-year period for which only a single approval is required. Notice must be given to the persons who filed comments with the State Engineer on the proposal by March 1 or earlier of any year in which the option to use the water for the changed purpose will be exercised.

Similar to the other temporary authorities, an application must be filed with the State Engineer, notice of the proposal must be given to persons on the substitute water supply plan notification list, there is a 30-day comment period, and the State Engineer can only approve the proposal if its operation will not cause injury to other water rights or decreed conditional water rights and will not impair compliance with

---

34   C.R.S. § 37-92-309(2).

any interstate compact. Parties may appeal an adverse decision of the State Engineer to the water court within 30 days.

§ 10.3   PLANS FOR AUGMENTATION

With the enactment of the Water Right Determination and Administration Act of 1969, the Colorado General Assembly created a new and innovative method for managing water and water rights, called a plan for augmentation. A plan for augmentation is:

> [A] detailed program, which may be either temporary or perpetual in duration, to increase the supply of water available for beneficial use in a division or portion thereof by the development of new or alternate means or points of diversion, by a pooling of water resources, by water exchange projects, by providing substitute supplies of water, by the development of new sources of water, or by any other appropriate means.[35]

A plan for augmentation does not include water salvaged by the eradication of phreatophytes (water-loving plants such as cottonwood trees), or tributary water collected from impermeable surfaces such as parking lots or roofs.

As they have developed over the years, plans for augmentation have become an important tool for providing water for new water uses where water is not available for appropriation in the traditional manner. In its simplest form, a plan for augmentation is a plan to replace the out-of-priority depletions caused by the use of a junior water right, in time, place, rate of diversion, and amount, with a substitute water supply. For instance, one might use the historic consumptive use credit of an existing senior water right to replace the depletions to the stream that will occur under the junior water right.

As an example, consider a senior irrigation water right that is determined to have diverted an average of 140 acre-feet of water per year, which resulted in the consumption of 60 acre-feet of water during the April 1 to September 30 irrigation season, with an average of 10 acre-feet of consumptive use per month. The owner of this water right wishes to supply water to a new water use that will also consume 60 acre-feet of water per year, but the consumption will occur all year long, and the new use will require diversion of 600 acre-feet per year. Such a new use could be an industrial facility, a housing development or any other beneficial use. Under a plan for

---

35   C.R.S. § 37-92-103(9).

augmentation, the owner would obtain a change of water right decree for the senior water right quantifying the historic consumptive use. In addition, the owner would obtain a decree allowing that 60 acre-feet of historic consumption to be used for the new uses, and to store it during the irrigation season for later use during the remainder of the year. The owner would also obtain a new water right decree that would allow diversions of water up to the 600 acre-feet per year that the new use will require. This 600 acre-feet of water diversions will result in return flows of 540 acre-feet, and consumptive use of 60 acre-feet. The owner would then adjudicate a plan for augmentation under which he or she would commit to use the 60 acre-feet per year of historic consumptive use from the senior water right to replace to the stream system the 60 acre-feet of consumptive use caused by the new junior water right. The consumptive use water from the senior water right would be stored in a reservoir and then released to the stream at the same time that the junior water right is causing depletions to the stream system and in the same amount. In this way, the full 600 acre-feet of diversions of the junior water right would be returned to the stream system through the return flows from the new use (540 acre-feet), and through the release of the historic consumptive use credit of the senior water right (60 acre-feet). A plan for augmentation decree contains a description of the manner in which the plan is intended to operate, and provides that the junior water right can be diverted without regard to the priority system so long as the plan is followed. It also must contain a finding by the court that the plan, if operated in accordance with its terms, will not cause injury to other water rights.

Besides being required to provide the quantity of water to prevent injury, a plan for augmentation must also provide the water at the correct time and of a quality so as to meet the requirements for which the water of the senior appropriator has normally been used.

Augmentation plans are often used to allow junior well water rights to continue to divert water when they would otherwise be out of priority. However, the pumping of tributary wells can often cause depletions to the surface stream months or even years after the pumping occurs because water in alluvial aquifers moves relatively slowly. A plan for augmentation for such a well must take this delay in the timing of depletions to the surface stream into account and be designed to provide water to replace the depletions at the time that they actually occur to the surface stream, which could be months or years after the well pumping actually occurred.

Plans for augmentation are now routinely required for the operation of sand and gravel open-mining operations. These operations are almost always conducted in alluvial deposits near streams and rivers. In the process of removing the sand and gravel, ground water is exposed to the atmosphere, which results in evaporation that did not occur before the ground water was exposed. The evaporation directly depletes the alluvial aquifer and connected stream system. The amount of water lost can be substantial.

These operations are now required to obtain a well permit and adjudicate a plan for augmentation to replace the depletions to the stream system caused by the evaporation of the exposed ground water.[36] However, as to ground water exposed to the atmosphere in connection with the extraction of sand or gravel prior to January 1, 1981, no well permit, plan for augmentation, or replacement of depletions is required. In effect, sand and gravel operations as they existed on January 1, 1981, are grandfathered. However, if a sand and gravel operation that ceased activity before January 1, 1981 is reactivated, the operator is required to obtain a well permit and approval of a plan for augmentation to replace evaporation.

In summary, the factors to be considered by the water court in approving a plan for augmentation are:

> [T]he depletions from an applicant's use or proposed use of water, in quantity and in time, the amount and timing of augmentation water that would be provided by the applicant, and the existence, if any, of injury to any owner of or persons entitled to use water under a vested water right or a decreed conditional water right. A plan for augmentation shall be sufficient to permit the continuation of diversions when curtailment would otherwise be required to meet a valid senior call for water, to the extent that the applicant shall provide replacement water necessary to meet the lawful requirements of a senior diverter at the time and location and to the extent the senior would be deprived of his or her lawful entitlement by the applicant's diversion.[37]

Plans for augmentation can rely upon a supply of water that is of a limited duration, for instance a lease or contract, so long as the terms and conditions of the plan prevent injury to other vested water rights. This can often be accomplished by a term that prohibits diversions of water under the plan until the plan operator has sufficient augmentation water available to replace future depletions to the stream system that will occur as a result of operating the plan.

The quality of the water used to replace depletions under a plan for augmentation must be suitable for the use of the senior appropriators that receive the water. This is

---

36   C.R.S. § 37-90-137(11).
37   C.R.S. § 37-92-305(8); C.R.S. § 25-8-202(7).

often an issue when sewage treatment plant effluent is used to replace depletions and there is a municipal water diversion located downstream. The State Engineer has adopted regulations to evaluate the quality of water used in augmentation plans, substitute water supply plans, and water exchange plans and to enforce this requirement.[38]

As with changes of water rights, the water court is required to retain jurisdiction of plans for augmentation for some period of time after the decree is entered to reconsider the question of injury to the vested rights of others.[39] The period of retained jurisdiction is left to the discretion of the water judge, who is required to make specific findings and conclusions on the matter. Retained jurisdiction can be invoked when the actual operation of the plan for augmentation reveals that it may cause injury to other vested water rights. The party seeking to invoke the water court's retained jurisdiction must normally make a *prima facie* showing of injury from the plan's actual operation. Upon such a showing, the burden of showing non-injury shifts to the decree holder.[40]

§ 10.4 WATER SUBSTITUTIONS OR EXCHANGES

In certain circumstances, it is advantageous for a water user to provide a supply of water to a senior appropriator and then to take an equal amount of water at a point upstream to satisfy the water user's needs. This practice is called a water substitution or exchange. For example, a water user may control an amount of water stored in a reservoir below the user's actual place of need. The water user can release the water from the reservoir to the stream at a time when a downstream senior appropriator is diverting water for his or her own needs. The water user can thus supply part or all of the amount of water that is being diverted by the senior appropriator from the stream with the release of the stored water. The water user can then divert an equal amount of water upstream (less any applicable stream transit losses) to his or her own uses without regard to priority.[41] The exchange or substitution must usually be operated simultaneously, meaning that the water user must divert its water upstream at the same time that it is satisfying the needs of the downstream senior appropriator.

Such water substitutions or exchanges can only be operated with the approval of the State Engineer. The State Engineer (or the water court) can only approve the

---

38   The Rules & Regs. For Implementation of Subsection 25-8-202(7) (S.B. 181 R.) (codified as amended at 2 CCR 402-8.) *available at* http://water.state.co.us/pubs/rule_reg/sb181.pdf.

39   C.R.S. 37-92-304(6).

40   *City of Thornton v. City & County of Denver*, 44 P.3d 1019 (Colo. 2002).

41   C.R.S. § 37-83-104.

practice if it does not impair the availability of water lawfully divertible by others and the substituted water is of a quality and continuity to meet the requirements of the purpose for which the senior appropriation has normally been used.[42]

Substitutions and exchanges do not require prior approval of a water court decree. However, a practice of substitution or exchange may constitute an appropriative water right, and may be adjudicated as any other water right.[43] When an existing exchange is adjudicated the original priority date is recognized and preserved, unless it would be contrary to the manner in which the exchange has been administered. It is often advantageous to obtain a decree for a substitution or exchange because the practice only works if there is sufficient water in the stream between the senior appropriator's point of diversion and the water user's point of diversion to satisfy all water rights being diverted in that reach. This amount of water is often referred as the "exchange potential" of that stream reach. The effect of a water court decree for a water substitution or exchange is to make the water between the two points of diversion unavailable for diversion by junior appropriators if the junior diversions would have the effect of stopping the exchange. As with plans for augmentation, water court decrees for exchanges are required to contain a retained jurisdiction provision.

The primary difference between an exchange and a plan for augmentation is that an exchange operates by providing replacement water for the diversions of a senior appropriator to allow an equal amount of water to be diverted by the junior appropriator. In contrast, a plan for augmentation operates to replace depletions to the stream system caused by a junior diversion, usually with historic depletions from a senior water right, and allows the junior diversion to operate outside of the priority system by preventing injury to all other water users.[44]

Finally, by statute, the State Engineer may permit an upstream junior reservoir to store water out of priority with regard to a downstream senior reservoir, if the water so stored can later be released to the downstream senior reservoir in the event that the downstream reservoir does not fill due to insufficient water supply.[45] This practice allows efficient reservoir filling without injury to the senior appropriators.

---

[42] C.R.S. § 37-80-120.
[43] C.R.S. § 37-80-120(4); C.R.S. § 37-92-305(10).
[44] *Empire Lodge Homeowners' Ass'n v. Moyer*, 39 P.3d 1139 (Colo. 2001).
[45] C.R.S. § 37-80-120(1).

§ 10.5   TIME AND COST CONSIDERATIONS

While changes of water rights, plans for augmentation, exchanges, and other procedures for using water rights in new and more productive ways are enormously advantageous to water users and Colorado, they can come with a high cost. Change of water right and plan for augmentation cases routinely take two to three years or longer to adjudicate in water court, and have been known to take more than 20 years. They often involve numerous parties, numerous attorneys, and numerous engineers. The cost to adjudicate a complex change of water right or plan for augmentation can easily exceed $100,000 or more, and has been known to exceed $1,000,000. Such applications are usually only undertaken by water suppliers with significant resources, and are usually opposed by water suppliers and other parties with large resources. Even the temporary change of use procedures involving the State Engineer can take many months depending upon the complexity of the case and the number of parties involved.

The various administrative procedures recently enacted by the Colorado General Assembly providing the State and Division Engineers with authority to approve temporary changes of water rights and other temporary measures to change water rights are due, in part, to the fact that water court proceedings cannot be conducted quickly enough to allow water to be moved to new uses in times of severe drought. They represent an attempt to provide streamlined procedures for temporary situations while continuing to provide adequate due process and protection of other water rights from injury.

CHAPTER 11 REGULATORY CONCERNS

In today's world, the acquisition, use, and protection of water rights are no longer solely a matter of compliance with Colorado water law. Rather, the exercise of water rights is increasingly restricted by an overlay of federal, state, and local laws and regulations designed to protect environmental values, including those related to water quality, endangered species, and land use. This chapter addresses some of the key regulatory concerns that may impact water project planning and the development and use of water rights in Colorado.

Federal, state, and local environmental regulations are primarily a function of statutes and regulations adopted by legislative bodies and regulatory agencies. This is in contrast to the state's water law, which primarily developed through the common law, that is, judicial decisions. Environmental laws and regulations are much more detailed and consequently extensive than water laws. For instance, there are literally thousands of pages of environmental laws and regulations that affect the the use of water in Colorado. The authors have attempted to facilitate navigation of this complex and confusing body of law with additional citations to relevant regulations and other useful materials.

§ 11.1   WATER QUALITY

Colorado generally has excellent water quality, particularly in comparison to other states. Part of this is luck; Colorado is the source of seven major rivers, so we start out with essentially pristine waters, rather than water that has been used several times. Out of Colorado's 107,463 miles of streams and rivers, approximately seven percent are designated as "impaired" waters that do not meet water quality standards or designated uses under the Clean Water Act (discussed below).

§ 11.1.1 Federal Clean Water Act

The federal Clean Water Act (CWA)—enacted "to restore and maintain the chemical, physical, and biological integrity of the Nation's waters"—is the primary basis for water quality management in Colorado.[1] In addition, the state has its own water quality laws that both implement and expand upon the CWA. The centerpiece of this state legislation is the Colorado Water Quality Control Act.[2]

While the U.S. Environmental Protection Agency (EPA) has the final responsibility for assuring compliance with the CWA, implementation of the federal and state water quality statutes in Colorado is primarily the role of the Water Quality Control Commission of the Colorado Department of Public Health and Environment. The Water Quality Control Division (WQCD) administers the state's water quality programs pursuant to rules and policies adopted by the Commission and federal requirements.

---

1   33 U.S.C. §§ 1251 to 1387.
2   C.R.S. §§ 25-8-101 to 25-8-703.

Jurisdiction

The federal CWA applies to "navigable waters," defined as "waters of the United States."[3] This definition generally includes all surface waters, although the U.S. Supreme Court has held it does not reach isolated wetlands.[4] Federal jurisdiction does not extend to groundwater. In contrast, Colorado regulates water quality in "state waters," which include both surface and groundwater.[5] The state, however, does not directly regulate water quality in conveyance structures, such as irrigation ditches (discussed below). See Section 11.1.3 discussion of "navigable waters" under the CWA.

Federal and state water quality laws also differ in their deference to state water rights. "It is the policy of Congress that the authority of each State to allocate quantities of water within its jurisdiction shall not be superseded, abrogated or otherwise impaired by [the Clean Water] Act. It is the further policy of Congress that nothing in [the Clean Water] Act shall be construed to supersede or abrogate rights to quantities of water that have been established by any State."[6] Exactly how much protection this provides the exercise of state water rights is subject to ongoing litigation.[7] In contrast, the Colorado statute is clear: no provisions of the Colorado Water Quality Control Act "shall be interpreted so as to supersede, abrogate, or impair rights to divert water and apply water to beneficial uses" in accordance with the state constitution.[8]

§ 11.1.2 Colorado Water Quality Control Act

Colorado's water quality program is based on three main components:

(1) Use classifications.[9]

(2) Water quality standards.[10]

(3) Antidegradation provisions.[11]

---

3   33 U.S.C. § 1362(7).

4   *Solid Waste Agency of N. Cook County v. United States Army Corps of Engineers*, 531 U.S. 159 (2001).

5   C.R.S. §§ 25-8-103(19), 25-8-503(5).

6   33 U.S.C. § 1251(g).

7   *Riverside Irrigation Dist. v. Andrews*, 758 F.2d 508 (10th Cir. 1985); *P.U.D. No. 1 of Jefferson County v. Washington Dept. of Ecology*, 511 U.S. 700 (1994); *South Fla. Water Mgmt. Dist. v. Miccosukee Tribe*, ___ U.S. ____, 124 S. Ct. 1537, 158 L. Ed.2d 264, 2004 U.S. LEXIS 2376 (Mar. 23, 2004).

8   C.R.S. § 25-8-104(1).

9   5 C.C.R. 1002-31 at §§ 31.6, 31.13.

10   5 C.C.R. 1002-31 at §§ 31.7, 31.11, 31.12.

11   5 C.C.R. 1002-31 at § 31.8.

Use Classifications

The Water Quality Control Commission establishes use classifications to protect current and future uses, including aquatic life, recreation, agriculture, domestic water supply, and wetlands.[12] There are over 700 separate segments of classified water bodies in the state, covering the state's 100,000 plus miles of rivers and streams, lakes, and reservoirs.

Water Quality Standards

The Commission establishes water quality standards for each pollutant and each classified use.[13] Standards may be either numeric or narrative, *e.g.*, "harmful to the beneficial uses or toxic to humans, animals, plants or aquatic life."[14] Numeric standards set the maximum acceptable concentration of a specific pollutant in the water. Standards are often based on EPA criteria, taking into account scientific research; these are referred to as "table value standards."[15] The Commission may adopt "site-specific standards" based on site-specific studies of the water quality necessary to protect the classified uses in a particular segment.[16] The Commission may also adopt temporary modifications for segments that do not currently meet their stated water quality goals where it is recognized that it will take several years to reach the desired standard.[17]

Antidegradation

Special rules apply to waters with quality better than that required by water quality standards. The EPA interprets the CWA to prohibit the degradation of water better than necessary to protect designated uses. The agency further suggests that this "antidegradation requirement" is not technology based (like NPDES permits, discussed below), but is based on actual water quality on a parameter by parameter basis.[18] Most waters in Colorado are subject to antidegradation requirements because the overall water quality is better than required for the segment's use designation. Antidegradation applies differently to the three classes of designations.

---

12 5 C.C.R. 1002-31 at §§ 31.6 to 31.13.

13 5 C.C.R. 1002-31 at § 31.7.

14 5 C.C.R. 1002-31 at § 31.11(1)(a)(iv).

15 5 C.C.R. 1002-31 at § 31.16.

16 5 C.C.R. 1002-31 at §§ 31.7(1)(b)(iii), 31.7(1)(c).

17 5 C.C.R. 1002-31 at § 31.7(3).

18 40 C.F.R. § 131.12.

No degradation is allowed for "outstanding waters," high quality waters that constitute an outstanding natural resource.[19] Degradation of "reviewable waters" is allowed if there are no reasonable alternatives available and the underlying water quality standards are met.[20] Degradation is allowed for "use protected waters," segments not capable of sustaining a wide variety of aquatic life or exhibiting poor water quality, so long as the classified uses and underlying water quality standards are still met.[21]

Triennial Review

The Commission reviews and revises water quality use classifications and standards on a three-year cycle.[22] These reviews include both statewide basic standards, and individual river basin standards and classifications, and are scheduled on a rotating basis several years in advance. The triennial review process seeks to involve the public and regulated community from beginning to end, so anyone wishing to propose changes to the use designations or standards has an opportunity to make his or her case.

Wetlands

Narrative standards generally apply to wetlands to protect the ambient water quality or the quality of the most hydrologically connected surface waters.[23] Site-specific water quality classifications and standards may also be adopted to protect wetlands functions.[24] Created and compensatory wetlands, including isolated wetlands, are typically subject to statewide narrative standards, but not numeric standards.[25]

---

19   5 C.C.R. 1002-31 at § 31.8(1)(a).

20   5 C.C.R. 1002-31 at § 31.8(1)(c).

21   5 C.C.R. 1002-31 at § 31.8(1)(b).

22   Colo. Water Quality Control Comm'n. Policy #98-2, Colo. Water Quality Mgmt. and Drinking Water Protection Handbook, at 28 (updated October 15, 2002) *available at* http://www.cdphe.state.co.us/op/wqcc/GeneralINfo/ StatutesRegsPolicies/Policies/cppfinal2002.pdf.

23   5 C.C.R. 1002-31 at § 31.11(1)(b).

24   5 C.C.R. 1002-31 at §§ 31.13(1)(e)(v), 31.7(b)(iv).

25   5 C.C.R. 1002-31 at § 31.7(1)(b)(iv).

Ground Water Standards

The Commission has established statewide ground water quality standards for some pollutants, namely radioactive materials and organic chemicals, which are usually the same as those applied to surface waters.[26] However, the primary mechanism to protect ground water is site-specific standards.[27] Site-specific standards exist for some 50 specific areas, primarily to protect public water supply systems.[28] Interim narrative standards apply outside site-specific areas to maintain water quality at the less restrictive of two water quality standards: ambient water quality as of January 1, 1994, or the table value standards for surface waters.[29]

Point Sources

The key regulatory program established in the CWA for protecting water quality is the National Pollution Discharge Elimination System (NPDES). The NPDES permit system requires each discharger from a point source—"any discernable, confined and discrete conveyance, including but not limited to any pipe, ditch, channel, tunnel, conduit, well, discrete fissure, container...."[30]—to meet technology-based effluent standards nationally promulgated by EPA for each category of discharge.[31] Tighter water quality-based effluent standards are imposed on discharges where necessary to meet water quality standards.[32] The Water Quality Control Division issues permits for most point sources in Colorado.[33] The EPA can veto individual permits and may enforce state-issued permits.[34] The EPA issues permits for discharges from federal facilities[35] and on Indian reservations,[36] although the state must certify such permits under Section 401 of the CWA.[37] See Section 11.1.4.

---

26   5 C.C.R. 1002-41 at § 41.5(C).

27   5 C.C.R. 1002-42.

28   5 C.C.R. 1002-42 at § 42.7.

29   5 C.C.R. 1002-41 at § 42.5(C)(6).

30   33 U.S.C. § 1362(14).

31   33 U.S.C. § 1311(b).

32   33 U.S.C. §§ 1311(b)(1)(C), 1313(e)(3)(A).

33   5 C.C.R. 1002-61 at § 61.3(1).

34   33 U.S.C. §§ 1342(d)(2), 1319(a).

35   Environmental Protection Agency Gen. Couns. Mem., State Regulation of Federal Facilities Under the Federal Water Pollution Control Act Amendments of 1977 (Clean Water Act) – Policy Guidance Memorandum (Mar. 10, 1978).

36   33 U.S.C. § 1377(e) (2004); 40 CFR 123.1(h).

37   33. U.S.C. § 1341 (2004); 5 C.C.R. 1002-82 at § 82.4(B).

> Anyone with a potential point source discharge should contact the Division of Water Quality for permitting information well in advance of potential discharges because an application must be submitted 180 days prior to a discharge.[38] The Water Quality Control Division is located at 4300 Cherry Creek Drive South, Denver, CO 80246-1530; Phone: (303) 692-3500; Web site: http://www.cdphe.state.co.us/wq/wqhom.asp

Although the Colorado attorney general once opined that waters of irrigation ditches are "waters of the state,"[39] by Colorado statute "[a]ctivities such as diversion, carriage, and exchange of water from or into streams, lakes, reservoirs, or conveyance structures, or storage of water in or the release of water from lakes, reservoirs, or conveyance structures, in the exercise of water rights shall not be considered to be point source discharges of pollution...."[40] The Water Quality Control Commission may, however, apply water quality standards to such activities by adopting an appropriate control regulation, which it has not done. No person may discharge into a ditch or man-made conveyance for the purpose of evading the requirement to obtain a discharge permit.[41]

Whether the diversion and delivery, from one stream or waterbody to another, of water that contains pollutants requires a point source permit under the CWA is an issue recently litigated before the U.S. Supreme Court.[42] Although the court ruled that transbasin diversions are point sources, it did not hold that such diversions require NPDES permits. This issue may be addressed in pending litigation in New York or Florida, and/or the subject of new litigation, likely in California. If a permit is ultimately required for a transbasin diversion, hundreds or thousands of water diversions in Colorado would be affected. Not only would such trans-waterbody diversions require permits, they would have to comply with related requirements, including water quality standards and antidegradation—a difficult challenge given Colorado's extreme precipitation events.

---

38 5 C.C.R. 1002-61 at § 61.4(1)(c).
39 Hon. John P. Moore, Colo. Attorney General, Opinion of August 26, 1974, at 1, 6.
40 C.R.S. § 25-8-503(5).
41 C.R.S. § 25-8-501(1).
42 *South Fla. Water Mgmt. Dist. v. Miccosukee Tribe*, 124 S. Ct. 1537, 158 L. Ed.2d 264, 2004 U.S. LEXIS 2376 (Mar. 23, 2004).

Domestic Wastewater Treatment Works

Domestic wastewater treatment works are subject to additional permit requirements to ensure timely plant expansion to meet population growth. Specifically, domestic wastewater treatment works must initiate engineering and financial planning for expansion whenever the throughput and treatment reaches 80 percent of design capacity.[43] Expansion construction must begin when throughput and treatment reaches 95 percent of design capacity.[44] In addition, if a municipality fails to commence plant expansion at 95 percent of design capacity, it must normally cease issuing building permits.

The federal Water Pollution Control Revolving Fund is a low-interest loan program for publicly owned treatment works.[45] The state Domestic Wastewater Treatment Grant Program assists areas of less than 5,000 people with wastewater treatment needs. The Domestic Wastewater Treatment Grant Funding System,[46] and the Wastewater Treatment Grant Program: Intended Use Plan[47] describe the planning and design requirements for grants.

> Additional information on wastewater financial assistance programs is available on the Water Quality Control Division Web site: http://www.cdphe.state.co.us/wq/OA/OAhom.html

Stormwater

Stormwater runoff from rainfall or snowmelt is subject to different, special permitting requirements. Colorado's Phase I stormwater program applies to municipalities with more than 100,000 residents.[48] The more recently effective Phase II applies to municipalities with more than 10,000 residents, smaller municipalities within a metropolitan area, and construction activities that disturb at least one acre.[49] A small municipality must develop a stormwater management plan to reduce the discharge of pollutants to the maximum extent practicable (MEP). This plan must include best

---

43   C.R.S. § 25-8-501(d).
44   C.R.S. § 25-8-501(e).
45   5 C.C.R. 1002-51 at §§ 51 to 52.
46   5 C.C.R. 1002-53.
47   5 C.C.R. 1002-54.
48   5 C.C.R. 1002-61 at §§ 61.3(2), 61.4(3), 61.8(4)(n)-(o).
49   5 C.C.R. 1002-61 at §§ 61.3(2)(f), (h), 61.4(3)(d), 61.8 (11), (12).

management practices (BMPs).[50] Industrial stormwater dischargers must develop individual stormwater management plans under a general permit.[51] The principal elements of such plans are best management practices (BMPs) to eliminate or reduce the amount of pollutants that enter state waters. Industrial activities requiring permits include construction sites larger than one acre, mining operations, transportation facilities, and other industrial operations.[52] A permit application generally must be submitted 180 days in advance of stormwater discharge, except that a construction activity must submit an application 90 days before commencing construction.[53] Thus, potential stormwater dischargers should contact the WQCD well in advance of expected discharges.

> Additional information about Colorado's stormwater program, including permit applications and guidance documents, is available on the Water Quality Control Division's Web site, "Water Quality Permitting," at http://www.cdphe.state.co.us/wq/PermitsUnit/wqcdpmt.html.

Nonpoint Sources

Nonpoint source water pollution results from pollutants transported by rainfall and snowmelt moving over and through the ground, and includes agricultural stormwater discharges and return flows from irrigated agriculture.[54] Colorado has adopted nonpoint source control regulations applicable to limited geographic areas, *i.e.*, Dillon Reservoir, Cherry Creek Reservoir, Chatfield Reservoir, the Bear Creek watershed, and Cheraw Lake.[55] The state also has a general nonpoint source management program, which identifies best management practices for categories of nonpoint source pollution.[56] Colorado has adopted BMPs for agriculture, silviculture, urban runoff, construction runoff, mining, and hydrologic modifications. The management program relies on voluntary efforts to implement needed actions.

---

[50] 5 C.C.R. 1002-61 at § 61.8(11)(1)(i).

[51] "Stormwater Fact Sheet," 1.C, available at http://www.cdphe.state.co.us/wq/PermitsUnit/SWFactsheet.pdf.

[52] 5 C.C.R. 1002-61 at § 61.3(2)(e)(ii).

[53] 5 C.C.R. 1002-61 at § 61.4(3)(a)(i).

[54] 33 U.S.C. § 1362(14).

[55] 5 C.C.R. 1002-71 at §§ 71 to 75.

[56] Colorado's Nonpoint Source Management Program (2000), *available at* http://www.cdphe.state.co.us/op/wqcc/Other/NPS/cnpsmpfin.pdf.

So-called "section 319 funding"[57] is available from the Water Quality Control Division to demonstrate water quality improvement through nonpoint source controls, including pollutant load reductions, changes in pollutant concentrations, or increases in the numbers or age classes of fish species. See "Colorado Nonpoint Source Program, FY 2004 Grant Opportunities, Guidance for Prospective Project Sponsors," available at http://www.cdphe.state.co.us/wq/nps/2004grantlinks/FY2004ColoradoGrantGuidance.pdf.

Individual Sewage Disposal Systems (Septic Tanks), a.k.a. Onsite Wastewater Systems

The State Board of Health is responsible for adopting guidelines on individual sewage disposal systems.[58] These guidelines establish minimum standards for the location, construction, performance, installation, alteration, and use of such systems.[59] Local boards of health implement the guidelines through the adoption of rules and regulations. Thus, counties and other local governments have primary regulatory responsibility for onsite wastewater systems. The Water Quality Control Division, however, regulates onsite systems with a capacity greater than 2,000 gallons per day.[60] These larger systems require site approval and discharge permits.[61]

Section 208 Regional Plans

Section 208 of the CWA requires a state to identify areas that have substantial water quality issues.[62] The Governor may designate regional planning agencies to conduct water quality management planning for these areas. Five regional water planning agencies conduct planning in their respective regions. The five regional planning agencies are: Denver Regional Council of Governments (State Management Region Three); the Pikes Peak Area Council of Governments (Region Four); the Pueblo area (Region Seven); the North Front Range Water Quality Planning Association (Region

---

57   33 U.S.C. § 1329.

58   C.R.S. § 25-10-104(1).

59   Colo. St. Bd. of Health, Guidelines on Individual Sewage Disposal Systems, Revised 2000, (2000), *available at* http://www.cdphe.state.co.us/op/regs/waterregs/100306individualsewagedisposalsystems.pdf.

60   C.R.S. §§ 25-8-103(5), 25-10-104(20).

61   Colo. St. Bd. of Health, Guidelines on Individual Sewage Disposal Systems, Revised 2000, at II.A (2000), *available at* http://www.cdphe.state.co.us/op/regs/waterregs/100306individualsewagedisposalsystems.pdf.

62   33 U.S.C. § 1288.

Two); and the Northwest Colorado Council of Governments (Region 12, except Routt County). The Water Quality Control Division coordinates regional planning in the balance of the state, in cooperation with local governments. The principal import of 208 plans is to identify priorities for improving or constructing wastewater facilities. An approved plan is a key eligibility requirement for federal and state financial assistance. The Water Quality Control Division administers both programs.

Impaired Waters and Total Maximum Daily Loads (TMDLs)

Section 303(d) of the Clean Water Act requires the identification, every two years, of stream segments that do not meet water quality standards, the "303(d) List."[63] The Water Quality Control Commission prepares this list from recommendations from the Water Quality Control Division and the public. In addition, Colorado must prepare a biennial report ("305(b) Report") on the water quality of all navigable waters in the state, the extent to which such waters provide for the protection and propagation of shellfish, fish, and wildlife and allow recreational activities, and an estimate of the extent to which such uses will be met through implementation of the CWA.[64]

For updated information on the current and proposed 303(d) List, check the Water Quality Control Division's Web site, http://www.cdphe.state.co.us/op/wqcc

---

For every segment on the 303(d) List, the state must develop total maximum daily loads (TMDL).[65] A TMDL refers to the maximum amount of pollution a body of water can assimilate from all sources combined before it begins to exceed the water quality standards.[66] The water quality standards, in turn, define how clean the water must be in the river (as opposed to the end of the discharge pipe) in order to protect various uses, such as drinking, fishing, or swimming.[67] Preparation of a TMDL requires a calculation of pollutants from all existing sources (including pollutants from nonpoint sources, such as forests, farms and roads, and natural sources), and an assessment of the assimilative capacity of the stream segment. More importantly from a political and economic standpoint, this work results in a pollutant allocation plan

---

63   33 U.S.C. § 1313 (d)(1)(A).
64   33 U.S.C. § 1315(b).
65   33 U.S.C. § 1313(d).
66   33 U.S.C. § 1313(c).
67   33 U.S.C. § 1313(c).

that authorizes certain parties to make specific levels of discharges consistent with the assimilative capacity of the water body. To achieve necessary reductions in pollutant loading, point source discharges of pollutants are reduced through enforceable NPDES permits, discussed above. Nonpoint sources may be reduced through voluntary, non-regulatory programs.[68] In practice, point sources are almost invariably responsible for any required reduction in pollutant loading.

Enforcement

The CWA is a significant piece of environmental legislation with teeth. The EPA can issue civil penalties for negligent violations of the CWA of up to $25,000 per day.[69] The state can impose penalties up to $10,000 per day for permit violations.[70] In addition, citizens have the right to bring suit against a discharger who is not meeting applicable requirements,[71] and may recover the costs of litigation if they prevail.[72]

§ 11.1.3 CWA Section 404, Dredge and Fill Permitting

Introduction

As noted above, the goal of the CWA is "to restore and maintain the chemical, physical, and biological integrity of the Nation's waters."[73] Section 404 of the CWA requires anyone proposing to discharge dredged or fill material into waters of the United States to obtain a permit from the Army Corps of Engineers (Corps) before proceeding with the activity as one mechanism to implement this goal.[74]

Discharge of Dredged or Fill Material

Section 404 of the CWA regulates the discharge of "dredged or fill material" into jurisdictional waters. Dredged material is material that is excavated or dredged from waters; fill material refers to any material used for the primary purpose of replacing an aquatic area with dry land or of changing the bottom elevation of a water body.[75] The "discharge" of such materials refers to their addition or placement into

---

68 33 U.S.C. § 1329.
69 33 U.S.C. § 1319.
70 C.R.S. § 25-8-608(1).
71 33 U.S.C. § 1365(a).
72 33 U.S.C. § 1365(d).
73 33 U.S.C. § 1251(a).
74 33 U.S.C. § 1344.
75 33 C.F.R. § 323.2(c)-(f).

jurisdictional waters. Regulable discharges into jurisdictional areas include a wide range of activities, such as:

- Site-development and roadway fills.
- The building of any structure or impoundment requiring rock, sand, or dirt.
- The placement of fill necessary for the construction of headgates and diversion structures.
- The construction of dams and dikes.
- Property protection and/or reclamation devices such as riprap.
- The placement of fill for structures such as sewage treatment facilities, intake and outfall pipes, and utility lines.

A traditional reading of Section 404 was that it did not apply to excavation work unless there was an associated "discharge" or deposit of the scooped out material into jurisdictional waters. Today it is evident that there is no such bright line between what is and is not a regulable discharge associated with excavation activities. Under the regulations, Section 404's permitting requirements do not apply to what is referred to as mere "incidental fallback"—the redeposit of small volumes of dredged material that is incidental to excavation activity in waters of the United States when such material falls back to substantially the same place as before the initial removal.[76] An example of incidental fallback is the soil that is disturbed when dirt is shoveled. Under current Corps' regulations, however, the Corps and the Environmental Protection Agency regard the use of mechanized earth-moving equipment to conduct land clearing, ditching, channelization, in-stream mining, or other earth-moving activity in waters of the United States as resulting in a regulable discharge of dredged material unless project-specific evidence shows that the activity results in only incidental fallback.[77]

Jurisdictional Waters

The placement of dredged or fill material must occur in jurisdictional waters to qualify as a regulated discharge requiring a permit under Section 404. The types of water subject to the Corps' 404 jurisdiction, however, is very broad.

---

[76] 40 C.F.R. § 323.2(d)(2)(ii) (2004).

[77] 40 C.F.R. § 323.2(d)(2)(i); *American Mining Cong. v. United States Army Corps of Engineers*, 951 F. Supp. 267 (D.D.C. 1997), *aff'd sub nom*; *National Mining Ass'n v. United States Army Corps of Engineers*, 145 F.3d 1339 (D.C. Cir. 1998); Further Revisions to the Clean Water Act Regulatory Definition of Discharge of Dredged Material, Final Rule, 66 Fed. Reg. 4549, 4550 (Jan. 17, 2001) (codified at 33 C.F.R. pt. 323 and 40 C.F.R. pt. 232).

Section 404 grants the Corps authority to issue permits for the discharge of dredged or fill material into the "navigable waters" at specified disposal sites.[78] Navigable waters are defined by the CWA as "the waters of the United States, including the territorial seas."[79] By regulation, the Corps has defined such "waters of the United States" to include "waters such as intrastate lakes, rivers, streams (including intermittent streams), mudflats, sandflats, wetlands, sloughs, prairie potholes, wet meadows, playa lakes, or natural ponds, the use, degradation or destruction of which could affect interstate or foreign commerce...."[80] Thus, jurisdictional waters extend to waters that the federal government can constitutionally regulate under the Commerce Clause.[81] These waters include an almost exhaustive array of water bodies beyond traditional navigable waters, including non-navigable streams and creeks that are part of the tributary system[82] and their adjacent wetlands, intrastate lakes and their contiguous wetlands,[83] intermittent streams,[84] constructed irrigation ditches that receive water from natural streams and lakes and function as a connected tributary to other waters,[85] and man-made roadside drainage ditches that drain into tributary waters.[86]

404 Permits

Section 404 authorizes the Corps to issue two types of permits—general permits and individual permits. General permits are issued for categories of activities that have only minor impacts to waters and wetlands. Because of their minimal impacts, activities covered under general permits undergo an abbreviated review process (in contrast to an individual permit) and may go forward with reduced paperwork and delay. Such permits may be issued nationwide (NWPs) or for specific Corps districts

---

[78] 33 U.S.C. § 1344(a).

[79] 33 U.S.C. § 1362(7).

[80] 33 C.F.R. § 328.3(a)(3).

[81] *Leslie Salt Co. v. Froehlke*, 578 F.2d 742 (9th Cir. 1978); *Natural Res. Def. Council, Inc. v. Callaway*, 392 F. Supp. 685 (D.D.C. 1975).

[82] *United States v. Ashland Oil & Transp. Co.*, 364 F. Supp. 349 (W.D. Ky. 1973), *aff'd*, 504 F.2d 1317 (6th Cir. 1974); *United States v. Riverside Bayview Homes, Inc.*, 474 U.S. 121 (1985).

[83] *United States v. Byrd*, 609 F.2d 1204 (7th Cir. 1979); *Solid Waste Agency of N. Cook County v. United States Army Corps of Engineers*, 531 U.S. 159 (2001).

[84] *North Carolina Shellfish Growers Ass'n v. Holly Ridge Assoc. LLC*, 278 F. Supp. 2d 654 (E.D.N.C. 2003).

[85] *Headwaters, Inc. v. Talent Irr. Dist.*, 243 F.3d 526 (9th Cir. 2001)(NPDES permit at issue); *United States v. Holland*, 373 F. Supp. 665 (M.D. Fla. 1974).

[86] *United States v. Deaton*, 332 F.3d 698 (4th Cir. 2003); *Treacy v. Newdunn Assocs.*, 344 F.3d 407 (4th Cir. 2003).

or regions, for a period of five years. About 80 percent of the activities permitted annually under Section 404 are done through NWPs.

The current NWPs cover 44 categories of activities.[87] The trends in recent years have been toward (1) restrictions on the scope of activities covered by NWPs; (2) imposition of additional "pre-construction" notification requirements before one can proceed with covered activities; (3) applicability of "add-on" regional conditions for NWPs; and (4) the retention of Corps' discretion to require that an applicant obtain an individual permit when it is in the public interest. It is prudent to seek advance concurrence from the Corps that a particular activity is in fact covered by a given general permit. If the requirements for a general permit are not met, or should the Corps determine that fuller permit processing is warranted, an individual permit is required. An individual permit involves a more rigorous review of the project and a public notice and hearing process.

> Additional information on 404 Permits can be found (with some perseverance) on the U.S. Army Corps of Engineers Web site: http://www.usace.army.mil/ (Click on "where we are," click on "Division/District Boundaries," click on "Engineer Division/District map," click the map where your project is located, click on "Permits," then click on "Colorado Regulatory office, home page.")

In considering an individual permit application, the Corps evaluates the probable impacts, including cumulative effects, of the proposed activity and its intended use on the "public interest."[88] The Corps must engage in a general balancing test of the benefits and detriments that may reasonably be expected to accrue from the proposed project. Its decision must reflect consideration of factors related to the public and private need for the proposed project, availability of alternatives to the undertaking, and its benefits and detriments to land use. In addition, the Corps must consider such factors as conservation, economics, aesthetics, general environmental concerns, wetlands, historic properties, fish and wildlife values, floodplain values, land use, property ownership, recreation, safety, and water supply. Under this review, the Corps is directed to grant the permit unless the District Engineer determines that it would be contrary to the public interest.

An individual permit application must also comply with the EPA's CWA 404(b)(1) Guidelines, which contain substantive criteria governing the evaluation

---

87   33 C.F.R. § 330; 67 Fed. Reg. 2020, 2077 (2002).
88   33 C.F.R. § 320.4(a).

and approval of 404 permits.[89] Under these criteria, "no discharge of dredged or fill material shall be permitted if there is a practicable alternative to the proposed discharge which would have less adverse impact on the aquatic ecosystem, so long as the alternative does not have other significant adverse environmental consequences." An alternative is deemed "practicable" if it is capable of being done after taking into consideration cost, existing technology, and logistics in light of overall project purposes. Where the proposed activity is not "water dependent" (*i.e.*, does not require access or proximity to wetlands or special aquatic sites to fulfill its basic purpose), practicable alternatives outside of such areas are presumed to be available unless clearly demonstrated otherwise. An example of a non-water dependent activity would be a proposed building that could be constructed on uplands, rather than involving site-development fills in a wetland area. A defensible project purpose should shape the evaluation of whether there are alternatives to an undertaking. Passing the "practicable alternatives" test is a crucial component of any successful 404 permitting process and should be taken seriously.

The 404(b)(1) Guidelines also contain other substantive criteria, including the requirements: (1) that the discharge not cause or contribute to violations of applicable state water quality standards or toxic effluent standards; (2) that it not jeopardize the continued existence of federally listed species or destroy or adversely modify designated critical habitat protected under the Endangered Species Act; (3) that it not "cause or contribute to significant degradation of the waters of the United States;" and (4) that appropriate and practicable steps are taken to minimize potential adverse impacts of the discharge on the aquatic ecosystem. The regulatory preference is first to avoid wetlands if possible, then minimize the impact, and finally to mitigate or compensate for any unavoidable impact so as to result in no net loss of wetland resources.

The EPA may veto any permit issued by the Corps that, in its opinion, will have "an unacceptable adverse effect on municipal water supplies, shellfish beds and fishery areas (including spawning and breeding areas), wildlife, or recreational areas."[90] The EPA defines an "unacceptable adverse effect" as an "impact on an aquatic or wetland ecosystem which is likely to result in significant degradation of municipal water supplies (including surface or ground water) or significant loss of or damage to fisheries, shell fishing, or wildlife habitat or recreation areas."[91] To date, the EPA has exercised its veto authority sparingly, having vetoed less than a dozen Corps-approved

---

89 40 C.F.R. § 230.10.

90 33 U.S.C. § 1344(c).

91 40 C.F.R. § 231.2(e).

wetlands permits in its history. One such veto, of the permit for the Two Forks Reservoir proposed by Denver and a group of suburban water providers, occurred in 1990.

Many water projects will trigger the need for a Section 404 permit. In water project planning, it is important to proceed with an awareness of potential Section 404 considerations and requirements, particularly those related to the scope of the project and its purpose and need, the existence or absence of practicable alternatives to the proposed undertaking, and the regulatory preference of avoiding impacts to jurisdictional waters and wetlands to the extent possible. It is also important to acknowledge in project planning that, in addition to the requirements of Section 404 itself, the permit process may trigger Section 7 consultation under the Endangered Species Act and may require review under the National Environmental Policy Act, discussed in Sections 11.2 and 11.4.

§ 11.1.4 CWA Section 401, State Certification

Section 401 of the CWA requires that an applicant for a federal license or permit to conduct an activity that may result in a discharge of a pollutant into waters of the United States obtain a "certification" from the state in which the discharge will originate that the discharge will comply with state water quality requirements.[92]

The state agency certification may contain limitations on the pollutants or "effluent" discharged by a project and may impose monitoring requirements "necessary to assure that any applicant…will comply with any applicable effluent limitations and other limitations…and with any other appropriate requirement of State law set forth in such certification…."[93] Limitations contained in the state certification are incorporated as conditions in the federal license or permit.

The authority to issue these certifications has been delegated in Colorado to the Colorado WQCD. By statute,[94] the division is required to certify general and nationwide permits under Section 404 of the CWA without the imposition of any additional state conditions. In addition, under the statute the division can only attach conditions to such certifications to implement rules that the Colorado Water Quality Control Commission has made applicable to Section 401 certifications. The Water Quality Control Commission has adopted an implementing regulation.[95] After

---

92   33 U.S.C. § 1341.
93   33 U.S.C. § 1341(d).
94   C.R.S. § 25-8-302(1)(f).
95   5 C.C.R. 1002-82.

considering water quality standards, use classifications, antidegradation, storm water discharge, best management practices (BMPs), and public comments, the Water Quality Control Division may issue an unconditional certification, a conditional certification, or deny certification.[96] Certification of nonexempt activities requires implementation of BMPs.[97]

State certification conditions may impact water quantity as well as water quality. In *PUD No. 1 of Jefferson County v. Washington Dep't of Ecology*,[98] the U.S. Supreme Court upheld the state of Washington's imposition of bypass flow requirements on a hydropower project as a condition of its Section 401 water quality certification in order to protect fishery values. The Court held that Section 401 allows a state to impose conditions consistent with "any other appropriate requirement of State law," not just numeric water pollution standards and limitations.

§ 11.2 ENDANGERED SPECIES ACT

§ 11.2.1 Introduction

The Endangered Species Act (ESA)[99] has been referred to as the "crown jewel" of the environmental laws due to its seemingly uncompromising standards for species' protection. The Act was intended by Congress to afford listed species "the highest of priorities" among competing public interests.[100]

The ESA requires the Secretary of Interior to identify those species that qualify for protection as "endangered" or "threatened" pursuant to the listing procedures and criteria in Section 4 of the Act.[101] "Critical habitat" may also be designated for such species and thereby afforded protection.

> For a list of threatened and endangered species, visit the Fish and Wildlife Service Web site: http://endangered.fws.gov (Region 6)

ESA compliance has been an important planning consideration for water use activities in Colorado for more than two decades. This is due to several factors. First, federally listed species are found in and near rivers both within the state and down-

---

96 5 C.C.R. 1002-82 at § 82.5(A).
97 5 C.C.R. 1002-82 at § 82.6(B).
98 511 U.S. 700 (1994).
99 16 U.S.C. §§ 1531 to 1543.
100 *Tennessee Valley Auth. v. Hill*, 437 U.S. 153, 174 (1978).
101 16 U.S.C. § 1535.

stream. Federally listed fish species (such as the Colorado pikeminnow, bonytail chub, humpback chub, and razorback sucker) are native to the Upper Colorado River Basin. Federally listed birds, including the whooping crane, the interior least tern, and the northern great plains population of the piping plover, use portions of the Central Platte River area in Nebraska for roosting, foraging, and nesting habitat. Federally listed plant and terrestrial species (such as the Ute ladies' tresses orchid and Colorado butterfly plant) also inhabit riparian zones in Colorado.

Second, habitat alteration is widely regarded as a major threat to federally listed species. The U.S. Fish and Wildlife Service (FWS) has asserted that water use activities cause jeopardy to threatened and endangered species due in part to the direct impact of the siting and construction of water facilities in or across species' habitat. In the agency's view, listed species may also be jeopardized by the indirect effects of water diversion and storage that may result in depletions to the stream, reduction of peak flows, alteration of return flow patterns, and changes in sediment transport rates, dissolved oxygen levels, temperature, and the like. Third, water use activities that require federal permits or are otherwise connected with federal agency action frequently trigger ESA compliance requirements under Section 7 of the Act, as discussed below.

§ 11.2.2 ESA Section 7, Agency Consultation

ESA Section 7(a)(2) requires each federal agency to "insure that any action authorized, funded, or carried out by such agency…is not likely to jeopardize the continued existence of any endangered species or threatened species or result in the destruction or adverse modification of habitat of such species which is determined by the Secretary …to be critical…."[102] To comply with Section 7(a)(2), a federal agency considering action that may affect a protected species or critical habitat is required to engage in a consultation process with the FWS.[103] Formal consultation typically concludes with issuance of a "biological opinion" by the FWS that includes a description of the proposed action; a summary of the current status of the species; an analysis of the direct, indirect, and cumulative effects of the action; and a determination by the FWS as to whether the project is likely or not likely to jeopardize listed species or adversely modify critical habitat.

If the determination is that the activity is likely to cause jeopardy or adverse habitat modification, the FWS biological opinion must identify "reasonable and prudent alternatives" (RPAs) if available to avoid or offset that project's prohibited effects.[104]

---

[102] 16 U.S.C. § 1536(a)(2).
[103] 50 C.F.R. § 402.01(b).
[104] 16 U.S.C. § 1536(b)(3)(A).

The RPAs must be consistent with the purpose of the project, be consistent with the federal agency's legal authority and jurisdiction, be economically and technically feasible, and—in the FWS's opinion—avoid jeopardy and adverse modification.[105]

It is key that the scope of the "federal action" that is the subject of consultation be properly defined. The FWS has often sought to treat the entirety of a project as the federal action for consultation purposes, even where there is no discretionary federal involvement or control beyond the issuance of a specific permit for a discrete aspect of the undertaking. This agency position could effectively "federalize" an otherwise private project and broaden the scope of impacts subjected to scrutiny under Section 7.

During consultation, the FWS must use "the best scientific and commercial data available" in making its required findings.[106] Where the "available data" is imperfect, the FWS is not obligated to supplement it or to defer issuance of its biological opinion until better information is available. Rather, the FWS must develop its biological opinion based upon the best scientific and commercial data available regardless of the "sufficiency" of that data."[107]

Construction and operation of water projects in Colorado frequently involve one or more federal authorizations, such as a CWA Section 404 permit from the Corps, a Federal Land Policy and Management Act (FLPMA) special use authorization from the Forest Service or Bureau of Land Management, a hydropower license from the Federal Energy Regulatory Commission, or a water contract with the U.S. Bureau of Reclamation. The requested federal approvals may imbue these activities with a federal nexus sufficient to constitute federal agency action for purposes of triggering Section 7 consultation requirements. Since the late 1970s, the FWS has required formal ESA consultation for virtually all water-depletive projects with a federal nexus in the Colorado and Platte River Basins. The FWS has, over the objections of certain water users, applied these requirements not only to new water projects undergoing Section 7 consultation, but also has applied them to, and required water-offset mitigation for, existing water-related activities at such time as they develop a federal nexus and come under Section 7 scrutiny.

In Colorado, this predicament has given rise to species Recovery Implementation Programs that are designed to offer an alternative to the traditional Section 7 regulatory approach. Instead of imposing project-specific measures to offset depletive

---

[105] 50 C.F.R. § 402.02.

[106] 16 U.S.C. § 1536(a)(2).

[107] Interagency Cooperation – Endangered Species Act of 1973, as amended; Final Rule, 51 Fed. Reg. 19926, 19951 (June 3, 1986) (codified at 50 C.F.R. pt. 402).

impacts, these programs take a cooperative, basin-wide approach to attain the recovery goals of the ESA and programmatically satisfy the substantive regulatory requirements of Sections 7 and 9 of the Act. An example is the "Recovery Implementation Program for Endangered Fish Species in the Upper Colorado River Basin," created in 1988 as the result of a cooperative agreement between the Secretary of Interior, Administrator of the Western Area Power Administration, and the Governors of the States of Colorado, Wyoming, and Utah.

§ 11.2.3 ESA Section 9, Take Prohibition

Section 9 of the ESA and the implementing regulations make it unlawful for any person subject to the jurisdiction of the United States to "take" any member of an endangered or threatened species of fish or wildlife.[108] The ESA defines "take" as "to harass, harm, pursue, hunt, wound, kill, trap, capture, or collect, or to attempt to engage in any such conduct."[109] "Harm" is further defined by regulation to include killing or injuring a protected species through "significant habitat modification or degradation" where it actually kills or injures wildlife by significantly impairing essential behavioral patterns, including breeding, feeding, or sheltering.[110] The causation requirement under Section 9's take prohibition has been the subject of significant litigation.[111]

Section 9's broad prohibition on take is limited by several exceptions identified in Section 10 of the Act. Most important here, Section 10 allows the Secretary of Interior to issue an incidental take permit (ITP), which authorizes its holder to take certain members of protected species when the taking is incidental to the carrying out an otherwise lawful activity.[112] The permittee is not liable for takings that are covered by the permit.

To obtain an ITP, an applicant must develop and submit a habitat conservation plan (HCP), which specifies (1) the likely impact from the proposed taking; (2) the steps the applicant will take to minimize and mitigate such impact and the funding available for such mitigation; (3) alternative actions considered, and the reasons for not selecting them; and (4) such other measures as the Secretary may require as

---

[108] 16 U.S.C. §§ 1538(a)(1), 1533(d); 50 C.F.R. 17.31(a).

[109] 16 U.S.C. § 1532(19).

[110] 50 C.F.R. § 17.3.

[111] *Defenders of Wildlife v. EPA*, 688 F. Supp. 1334 (D. Minn. 1988), *aff'd in part and rev'd in part*, 882 F.2d 1294 (8th Cir. 1989); *Sierra Club v. Lujan*, 1993 U.S. Dist. LEXIS 3361 (W.D. Tex. 1993).

[112] 16 U.S.C. § 1539(a).

necessary or appropriate for the purposes of the plan. Upon submission of a permit application and related conservation plan, "the Secretary shall issue the permit," if he or she finds, after opportunity for public comment, that:

(1) The taking will be incidental.

(2) The applicant will, to the maximum extent practicable, minimize and mitigate the impacts of such taking.

(3) The applicant will ensure that adequate funding for the plan will be provided.

(4) The taking will not appreciably reduce the likelihood of the survival and recovery of the species in the wild.

(5) Other measures required by the Secretary will be met.[113]

The permit will also contain other appropriate provisions including reporting requirements deemed necessary to confirm compliance with permit terms and conditions. Because the decision to issue an ITP is itself discretionary federal agency action, the FWS must also comply with the dictates of Section 7 of the ESA. This means that the FWS may engage in an internal consultation under Section 7 and issue a permit only upon a finding that it is not likely to jeopardize the continued existence of protected species or result in the destruction or adverse modification of critical habitat.[114] In contrast to the somewhat lengthy history of ESA Section 7 compliance in Colorado, the Section 10 HCP experience is still relatively new in our state. To date, the majority of HCPs have been developed to address incidental take of the Preble's meadow jumping mouse by land-use activities along the Colorado Front Range.

For federal-nexus projects already undergoing Section 7 consultation, a written "incidental take statement" may be included in the biological opinion where the FWS concludes that such taking will not jeopardize the continued existence of the species or adversely modify its critical habitat. The incidental take statement must specify: (1) the allowable amount or extent of take; (2) reasonable and prudent measures that are necessary or appropriate to minimize that impact; (3) terms and conditions, including reporting requirements, to implement the above measures; and (4) procedures to be used to handle or dispose of any individuals of a species actually taken.[115] Actions undertaken in compliance with the terms and conditions of the incidental

---

[113] 16 U.S.C. § 1539(a)(2)(B).

[114] 50 C.F.R. § 402.01(b).

[115] 50 C.F.R. § 402.14 (i).

take statement are shielded from liability as takings under the ESA.[116] Securing ESA Section 9 compliance in this manner may offer procedural streamlining for water projects undergoing federal permitting.

§ 11.3   FEDERAL LAND USE AUTHORITY

§ 11.3.1 Federal Land Policy Management Act (FLPMA)

Many water use facilities originate on or traverse lands that are under public ownership. The construction, operation, and maintenance of such facilities may, accordingly, require federal land-use authorizations under the Federal Land Policy Management Act of 1976 (FLPMA).[117] FLPMA establishes a comprehensive scheme for management of public lands. FLPMA requires that public lands be managed under principles of multiple use and sustained yield in a manner that (1) will protect the quality of scientific, scenic, historical, ecological, environmental, air and atmospheric, water resource, and archaeological values; (2) where appropriate, will preserve and protect certain public lands in their natural condition; (3) will provide food and habitat for fish and wildlife and domestic animals; and (4) will provide for outdoor recreation and human occupancy and use.

The U.S. Bureau of Land Management (BLM) implements FLPMA's policies in accordance with land-use plans developed by BLM under Section 202 of FLPMA.[118] The BLM's land-use plans are termed Resource Management Plans, which define broad, long-term multiple use objectives and resource uses for public lands. These plans inventory resources within geographic management areas, determine whether areas are open or closed to certain land uses, and define the terms and conditions applicable to such uses.[119] Project-specific land-use decisions must be made in conformity with the plan.

FLPMA requires project proponents to obtain federal permission to use, occupy, or traverse Forest Service or BLM lands. FLPMA authorizations are routinely required for the siting and operation of facilities on or across such lands for the impoundment, storage, transportation, or distribution of water, such as ditches, canals, laterals, pipelines, and reservoirs.[120] The agencies may permit, permit with

---

116   16 U.S.C. § 1536(o)(2).
117   43 U.S.C. §§ 1701 to 1785.
118   43 U.S.C. §§ 1712, 1732(a).
119   43 C.F.R. pt. 1600.
120   43 U.S.C. § 1761(a)(1).

conditions, or deny the requested use of public lands pursuant to their federal land use authorities after balancing a number of competing interests under the FLPMA.

Controversy has arisen in recent years concerning each agency's authority to regulate or modify existing water use when renewing land use authorizations for existing water supply facilities located on federal land.[121] All federal actions under FLPMA are "subject to valid existing rights."[122] The Forest Service, however, maintains that it has the authority to require the owner of an existing water right to forego the diversion of some water under the right as a condition of re-issuance of FLPMA authorizations. This is the case notwithstanding assertions that the Forest Service lacks legal authority to impose such a "bypass flow" requirement. Such a condition arguably deprives water users of part of their decreed water rights and interferes with state water allocation systems in violation of a "savings clause" in the statute. The question also arises as to whether bypass flow requirements are effectively federal claims to water that are inconsistent with traditional federal deference to state water law. The traditional practice is for federal claims to the use of water be asserted, quantified, and adjudicated in McCarran Act proceedings in Colorado. See Section 1.5.2. To date, two reported cases have sided with the Forest Service on this issue.[123]

A significant number of water facilities predate enactment of FLPMA and may operate pursuant to vested rights-of-way or special-use permit entitlements that are not subject to cancellation, modification, or updating pursuant to FLPMA considerations. A recent federal court decision in Idaho, however, wrongly held that the BLM's decision not to attempt to re-open such vested rights-of-way was discretionary agency action under Section 7 of the ESA.[124] It is also possible that an activity traversing Forest Service lands has qualified under the so-called Ditch Bill for a permanent easement in instances where the originally constructed facilities comprising the water system were constructed and in operation prior to October 21, 1976, have been in substantially continuous operation since that time, and are used for agricultural irrigation or livestock watering purposes.[125] Water users should assess the nature of

---

[121]   43 U.S.C. § 1765.

[122]   43 U.S.C. § 1765; *City and County of Denver Bd. of Water Com'rs v. Bergland*, 695 F.2d 465 (10th Cir. 1982).

[123]   *Okanogan County v. Nat'l Marine Fisheries Serv.*, 347 F.3d 1081 (9th Cir. 2003) *cert. denied* 124 S. Ct. 2094 (May 3, 2004); *Trout Unlimited v. U.S. Dept. of Agric.*, 2004 U.S. Dist. LEXIS 14436, C.A. No. 96-WY-2686-WD (D. Colo. Apr. 30, 2004).

[124]   Memorandum of Decision and Order, *Western Watersheds Project v. Matejko*, ___ U.S. Dist. LEXIS ___, Civ. No. 01-0259-E-BLM (D. Idaho Mar. 23, 2004).

[125]   43 U.S.C. § 1761(c).

the specific authorization under which a water facility operates and the federal act pursuant to which it vested to determine the nature of the public lands entitlement at hand and the potential authority or continued jurisdiction of the Forest Service or BLM over such activities.[126]

§ 11.3.2 National Forest Management Act (NFMA)

National Forest System Lands are also managed under Congressional mandates for multiple use and sustained yield.[127] The National Forest Management Act (NFMA)[128] requires the Forest Service to use a "systematic, interdisciplinary approach" to forest planning, reflecting consideration of physical, biological, economic, and other sciences. Pursuant to NFMA, the Forest Service develops and revises land and resource management plans (Forest Plans) to guide and coordinate multiple uses and the availability of lands for resource management in each administrative unit of the National Forest System. Forest Plans must satisfy the principles and goals of the Multiple Use Sustained Yield Act of 1960 (MUSYA), which contains broad and competing goals and allows the Forest Service discretion in balancing various interests.[129] Accordingly, the Forest Service manages forests for a multitude of competing interests including outdoor recreation, range, timber, watershed, and wildlife and fish purposes, and to provide a sustained yield of various renewable resources. These plans guide decisions on site-specific actions, including project decisions for particular uses such as water use development. Forest Plans are adjusted periodically to conform to changing needs and conditions. Depending upon their wording, special-use permits for water facilities may be "updated" to incorporate new conditions and restrictions to address consistency with changes in Forest Plans. Whether such new conditions may lawfully impose bypass flow requirements remains an open question.

---

126 Depending on the circumstances related to each specific case, rights-of-way might have been granted under R.S. 2339 (Act of July 26, 1866, ch. 262, § 9, 14 Stat. 253) or R.S. 2340 (Act of July 9, 1870, ch. 235, § 17, 16 Stat. 218), both codified as amended at 43 U.S.C. § 661 (2004); Act of March 3, 1891, ch. 561, § 18, 26 Stat. 1101, codified as amended at 43 U.S.C. § 946 (2004); Act of May 11, 1898, ch. 292, § 2, 30 Stat. 404, codified as amended at 43 U.S.C. § 951 (2004); or Act of February 1, 1905, ch. 288, § 4, 33 Stat. 628, codified as amended at 16 U.S.C. § 524 (2004).

127 Forest Service Organic Act of 1897, codified as amended at 16 U.S.C. §§ 473 to 482, 551; Multiple Use and Sustained Yield Act of 1960, 16 U.S.C. §§ 528 to 531. Forest and Rangeland Renewable Resources Planning Act of 1974, 16 U.S.C. §§ 1600 to 1614. National Forest Management Act of 1976, 16 U.S.C. §§ 1600 to 1614; 16 U.S.C. §§ 1604(e), 1607, 1609.

128 16 U.S.C. §§ 1600 to 1614.

129 16 U.S.C. §§ 528 to 531.

§ 11.4   NATIONAL ENVIRONMENTAL POLICY ACT

The National Environmental Policy Act (NEPA)[130] was passed by Congress in 1969. It embraces a national environmental policy implemented through "action forcing" procedures designed to fully inform agency decision-makers of the environmental impact of their decisions. NEPA requires the preparation of an Environmental Impact Statement (EIS) for all "major Federal actions significantly affecting the quality of the human environment."[131] An EIS is a "detailed statement" examining in depth the environmental impact of the proposed action and alternatives to the proposed action.

NEPA exists to ensure a process, not a result. Thus, NEPA does not forbid harm to the environment but rather requires government decision-makers to evaluate that harm and explain why the action is justified despite the harm:

> NEPA is not designed to prevent all possible harm to the environment; it foresees that decision-makers may choose to inflict such harm, for perfectly good reasons. Rather, NEPA is designed to influence the decision making process; its aim is to make government officials notice environmental considerations and take them into account.[132]

NEPA's EIS procedures apply to federal agency "actions" involving the exercise of discretionary authority. NEPA thus does not apply to ministerial duties and does not apply if legislative mandates compel a single course of action.[133] Common "triggering" actions related to water projects include requested federal agency approvals for CWA Section 404 dredge and fill permits and for FLPMA special use authorizations, and construction of or contracting related to U.S. Bureau of Reclamation water facilities.

Agencies can by regulation adopt "Categorical Exclusions" (CEs) for categories of activities that are excluded from NEPA documentation requirements because the actions have been determined in a public process to have no significant effect individually or cumulatively on the environment nor to involve unresolved conflicts concerning alternative uses of available resources.[134] A CE can only be used for actions specifically defined by the regulatory exclusion category.

An agency considering whether an action requires preparation of an EIS will normally prepare a preliminary evaluation, called an environmental assessment (EA). EAs are intended to be concise documents that "briefly provide sufficient evidence

---

[130]   42 U.S.C. § 4321 to 4361.
[131]   42 U.S.C. § 4332(2)(C).
[132]   *Massachusetts v. Watt*, 716 F.2d 946 (1st Cir. 1983).
[133]   *Flint Ridge Dev. Co. v. Scenic Rivers Ass'n*, 426 U.S. 776 (1976).
[134]   40 C.F.R. § 1508.4.

and analysis for determining whether to prepare either an EIS or a 'finding of no significant impact' (FONSI)."[135] If the federal agency makes a FONSI based upon the EA, then no EIS is required. An agency's decision to issue a FONSI, and not to prepare an EIS, may be reviewed by the courts.[136]

NEPA requires that an EIS be prepared before taking action that may significantly affect the quality of the human environment.[137] An EIS must be prepared if substantial questions are raised as to whether a project may cause significant degradation of some human environmental factor. "The plaintiff need not show that significant effects will in fact occur, but if the plaintiff raises substantial questions whether a project may have a significant effect, an EIS must be prepared."[138] In assessing the significance of a project's impact, NEPA regulations require the agency to consider a variety of factors related to the "context" and "intensity" of project effects. Relevant considerations include: the scope of the affected area and region, the severity of the impact, whether public health may be affected, whether unique resources may be affected, the degree to which the effects are likely to be controversial or uncertain, the precedential nature of the action, the impact of other related actions, the degree to which the action may affect an endangered or threatened species or critical habitat, and whether the action threatens a violation of federal, state, or local law.[139]

The EIS itself is a detailed statement addressing the environmental impacts of the proposed action, any adverse environmental effects that cannot be avoided should the proposal be implemented, alternatives to the proposed action, the relationship between local short-term uses of the environment and the maintenance and enhancement of long-term productivity, and any irreversible and irretrievable commitments of resources that would be involved in the proposed action should it be implemented.[140] The EIS should disclose and analyze relevant direct, indirect, and cumulative effects. The federal agency must rigorously explore these issues with good-faith objectivity.[141] The reality is that an EIS may ultimately comprise several hundred pages or more of text and take over two years to prepare pursuant to the required public scoping process and notice and comment procedures. As the EIS must be completed

---

135   40 C.F.R. § 1508.9.

136   *March v. Oregon Natural Res. Council*, 490 U.S. 360 (1989); *Morongo Band of Mission Indians v. FAA*, 161 F.3d 569 (9th Cir. 1998); *Oregon Natural Res. Council v. Lowe*, 109 F.3d 521 (9th Cir. 1997).

137   42 U.S.C. § 4332.

138   42 U.S.C. § 4332.

139   40 C.F.R. pts. 1502 (Environmental Impact Statement), 1508 (Terminology and Index).

140   42 U.S.C. § 4332(2)(c).

141   *Coalition for Canyon Pres. v. Bowers*, 632 F.2d 774 (9th Cir. 1980).

before the agency authorizes or undertakes proposed action, it is critical to factor potential NEPA compliance into water project planning schedules.

§ 11.5   LOCAL GOVERNMENT LAND USE AUTHORITY

Counties are not independent governmental entities existing by virtue of any inherent sovereign authority. They are political subdivisions of the state, existing only for the convenient administration of state government and created to carry out the will of the state. Thus, county power over water development is limited to that expressly granted by the General Assembly and such power reasonably necessary to exercise the granted power. Several statutes grant counties land-use authority that can affect water facilities, as discussed below.

§ 11.5.1 County Planning and Zoning

The County Planning Code grants counties the power to provide for the physical development of the unincorporated territory within the county and for the zoning of all or any part thereof.[142] Under this statute, counties have the power to regulate the uses of land for trade, industry, recreation, and other purposes,[143] and may create districts or zones to regulate such uses.[144]

Counties may (and many do) condition subdivision approval upon the availability of an adequate water supply. State statute in fact requires developers to submit adequate evidence that a water supply is sufficient in terms of quantity, quality, and dependability to serve the proposed subdivision.[145]

> Information on individual county subdivision requirements, county water supply requirements, and city location and extent review is available from county planning and zoning departments, and sometimes online through the county Web site.

Douglas County Water Supply – Overlay District

Douglas County has adopted a zoning overlay district to ensure that development in all areas of the county provides an adequate water supply.[146] This is a supplemental

---

142 C.R.S. §§ 30-28-101 to 30-28-139.
143 C.R.S. § 30-28-111(1).
144 C.R.S. § 30-28-113(1).
145 C.R.S. § 30-28-133(3)(d).
146 Douglas County Zoning Resolution, § 18A (Mar. 13, 2002).

regulation that applies to rezoning, use by special review, subdivision, the issuance of building permits, and the formation of special districts. The regulation establishes minimum water supply requirements for various locations and land uses within the county. It is likely that additional counties will adopt similar requirements in the future to ensure future development has adequate water supplies.

County Location and Extent Review

Whenever a county or regional planning commission has adopted a master plan for the county, no public facility or private utility may be constructed in the unincorporated area of the county without first submitting the "proposed location and extent thereof" to the planning commission for approval.[147] The board of county commissioners may overrule a planning commission disapproval. In addition, the governing body or official with the power to authorize or finance the facility or utility may also overrule a disapproval. It is incumbent upon the entity having jurisdiction over a project to submit the proposal to the planning commission before commencing the project, even though it has authority to later override a disapproval.[148]

§ 11.5.2 County H.B. 1041 Permitting Authority

In 1974, the General Assembly enacted H.B. 1041 to permit each local government to regulate certain areas and activities by designating them as matters of state interest.[149] H.B. 1041 grants counties, among other things, the power to designate as "matters of state interest" the site selection and construction of major new domestic water treatment systems, major extensions of existing domestic water treatment systems, and the efficient utilization of municipal and industrial water projects.[150] The essence of so-called county "1041 powers" is the ability to require a county permit for any activity designated as a matter of state interest.[151] Therefore, a county may designate a water project as a matter of state interest and require a county permit, even from municipalities and water districts.

Of particular importance to water development, the Colorado Supreme Court has held that H.B. 1041 "does not completely exempt local governments from the regulatory schemes of [other] local governments which impact the developer's

---

147 C.R.S. § 30-28-110(1)(a).

148 *Blue River Defense Comm. v. Town of Silverthorne*, 33 Colo. App. 10, 516 P.2d 452 (1973).

149 C.R.S. §§ 24-65.1-101 to 24-65.1-502.

150 C.R.S. § 24-65.1-203.

151 C.R.S. § 24-65.1-501.

established water rights."[152] The Colorado Court of Appeals has similarly held "[t]he existence of previously decreed water rights does not provide an exemption for the developer from regulation."[153] However, a county may not unduly interfere with the exercise of water rights as decreed. In sum, a county may regulate but not prohibit proposed water development projects, although the scope of county regulation is unclear.

§ 11.5.3 Local Government Land Use Control Enabling Act

The "Local Government Land Use Control Enabling Act" confers broad authority to plan for and regulate the use of land within the local government's jurisdiction.[154] This scheme authorizes counties to, among other things, (1) regulate development and activities in hazardous areas; (2) protect land from activities that would cause immediate or foreseeable material damage to wildlife habitat; (3) regulate the use of land on the basis of the impacts on the community or surrounding area; and (4) otherwise regulate land use so as to provide planned and orderly use on land and protection of the environment.[155]

The statute also confers the specific power to impose development impact fees subject to certain limitations and procedural requirements.[156] First, the county must quantify the reasonable impacts of the proposed development on existing capital facilities. Second, the county cannot impose a fee that exceeds the cost of the impacts directly related to the development. In short, impact fees are limited to the cost to defray the impacts to existing capital facilities caused by the development.

---

[152] *Denver Bd. of Water Comm'rs v. Grand County*, 782 P.2d 753, 765 (Colo. 1989).

[153] *City of Colo. Springs v. County Comm'rs of the County of Eagle*, 895 P.2d 1105 (Colo. App. 1994).

[154] C.R.S. §§ 29-20-101 to 29-20-205.

[155] C.R.S. § 29-20-104.

[156] C.R.S. § 29-20-104(1)(g).

CHAPTER 12 MUNICIPAL WATER CONSERVATION PROGRAMS

Water Recycling

Water recycling involves the additional treatment of municipal wastewater to make it suitable for reuse for industrial and outdoor irrigation purposes. Water leaving a wastewater treatment plant must meet certain water quality standards established under the federal Clean Water Act. To recycle this water, it must be treated again to meet the higher water quality standards for recycled water established by Water Quality Control Commission of the Colorado Department of Public Health and Environment.[1]

By recycling water, municipalities can augment their water supply and reduce the need to pursue additional water sources. Recycled water is commonly used to irrigate city parks, landscaping, and municipal golf courses. Although the water is not safe for drinking, it is safe for incidental contact by adults, children, and pets. The water is dechlorinated to reduce potential harm to wildlife and is considered safer than water at most beaches. The cities of Aurora, Westminster, and Colorado Springs, and the City and County of Denver either recycle water now or are in the process of initiating such programs; others are considering recycling programs.

Mandatory Conservation Measures

> For current municipal water restrictions, visit the Colorado State University's drought Web site, http://www.drought.colostate.edu

In response to municipal water shortages brought on by drought, municipalities across Colorado have adopted or are considering a variety of mandatory water conservation measures for their water shortage response plans or as part of their routine water conservation programs. These mandatory measures include:

- Water-efficient landscape and lawn sprinkling systems and their maintenance.

- Sprinkler inspections and audits.

---

[1]   Declaimed Domestic Wastewater Control Regulation; 5 C.C.R. 1002-84), *available at* http://www.cdphe.state.co.us and http://www.water.denver.co.gov/recycle/recycleframe.html.

- Landscape and lawn watering restrictions.

- Restrictions on special water features, such as fountains, ponds, and swimming pools.

- Moratoria on, or regulation of, new lawn and/or garden installations.

- Restrictions on car-washing and the cleaning of impervious surfaces.

- Prohibitions on wasting water through poorly maintained irrigation systems, excessive watering, or other wasteful practices.

- Mandating water-saving fixtures in homes.

- Water system leak detection programs.

- Regulating distribution system water pressure to deliver water only at needed pressures and rates.

- Restrictions on the serving and use of water at restaurants and lodging establishments.

- Water metering and increased water service fees.

- Ordinance provisions suspending restrictive covenants on property that discourage water conservation measures, *e.g.*, homeowners' association covenants.

Voluntary Conservation Measures

A number of the mandatory water conservation measures listed above are only promoted as voluntary measures in some communities. In many communities, the following water conservation measures remain entirely voluntary:

- Xeriscaping—a form of landscaping using plants and materials that require less water to maintain.

- Incentive-based turf conversion programs that convert lawns to xeriscapes.

- Water-wise lawn care.

- Water-saving fixtures and appliances in the home.

- Home, commercial, and industrial water-use audits.

Colorado law encourages and, in some instances, requires the implementation of water conservation measures by private water users and public agencies. All new construction and renovation of residential structures or facilities for human use within office, commercial, or industrial buildings, except structures or facilities served by a septic system, are required to install low-flow plumbing fixtures that comply with specific statutory requirements.[2] Any state agency or local governmental entity completing state or federally-funded construction or renovation projects must use the best available approved devices for the purpose of conserving water.[3] State-owned buildings, however, are subject to specific statutory standards for water-efficient plumbing fixtures.[4] In addition, certain public projects or facilities receiving state funding and involving new construction or renovation must develop landscaping plans that seek to conserve water in the landscaping of the public project or facility.[5]

An office of water conservation has also been established under the Colorado Water Conservation Board (CWCB) to promote and fund water use efficiency measures by state agencies and municipal and other urban water providers.[6] The CWCB is authorized to fund pilot programs by public agencies demonstrating the benefits of water efficiency measures.[7] Colorado law also ties the state's financial assistance to certain urban water providers to their development of water use efficiency plans that consider many of the water-saving measures discussed in this chapter.[8]

---

2   C.R.S. §§ 9-1.3-101 to 9-1.3-105.
3   C.R.S. § 9-1.3-105.
4   C.R.S. § 37-96-103(7).
5   C.R.S. §§ 37-96-101 to 37-96-103.
6   C.R.S. § 37-60-124.
7   C.R.S. § 37-60-125.
8   C.R.S. § 37-60-126.

CHAPTER 13 COLORADO WATER CONSERVATION BOARD

The Colorado Water Conservation Board (CWCB) was created by the state legislature in 1937.[1] Its purpose is to aid and protect the development of water for the benefit of the present and future inhabitants of the state. The CWCB has 15 members including the Executive Director of the Department of Natural Resources, the Attorney General, the Commissioner of Agriculture, the State Engineer, the Director of the Division of Wildlife, and the CWCB director. Nine members are appointed by the Governor to serve three-year terms. The members are geographically split with four members from the western slope and five members from the eastern slope, one being required to be from the Rio Grande basin. Members appointed to the CWCB should have experience and expertise in water resource management, water project financing, engineering, planning and development of water projects, water law, or irrigated farming and ranching.

Throughout its history, the CWCB has played a key role in the development of water projects within the state of Colorado. Some notable projects include Stage Coach and Elkhead Reservoirs near Steamboat Springs, Platoro Reservoir near Alamosa, and McPhee Reservoir near Cortez. The CWCB is also very active in providing small loans to a host of towns and small entities, which may not be great in dollar expenditure but are key to the use of water rights. These include ditch, headgate, and dam repair and replacement. The specific loan sources and their individual requirements are discussed in Section 7.1.

The CWCB administers the reserved rights litigation fund, which provides for the Attorney General to protect Colorado's water from claims by other states and the federal government.

The CWCB has also been developing a Colorado Decision Support System. It is an information system, including computer river models, to assist in making decisions about water development and use. As of this writing, the Colorado River, its tributaries, and the Rio Grande have been completed. The South Platte River is under development and the Arkansas River is scheduled for future development.

Floodplain mapping and flood information are also created and managed by the CWCB. The flood protection program's staff review and approve floodplain designations prior to adoption by local government entities and provide local jurisdictions with technical assistance and other floodplain information.

---

[1]   C.R.S. §§ 37-60-101 to 37-60-210.

An increasingly important and somewhat controversial program within the CWCB is the instream flow and natural lake level protection program, discussed in Section 3.4.1. In 1973, the legislature created the instream flow program, which has been criticized and amended substantially in the last few years. For decades, the CWCB was the only entity that could adjudicate an instream flow water right to preserve the natural environment of the state of Colorado to a reasonable degree. The CWCB now holds instream flow water rights in approximately 8,000 miles of streams and 475 lakes throughout the state. Recent amendments to the original instream flow legislation allow the CWCB to lease water rights, obtain other interests in water rights to protect instream flows, and accept donations.

A new role for the CWCB is to review and recommend to the water court findings for claims to recreational in-channel diversions by third parties, discussed in Section 3.4.2. The CWCB has adopted rules and regulations to guide its decisions on these claims. Hearings are held before the CWCB on these applications for this new category of instream flows.

The CWCB also provides services in conservation and drought planning through the Office of Water Conservation, which was established in 1991. It is a voluntary program that develops and approves water efficiency plans, monitors water use, and provides technical assistance, public information and other planning and policy development to conserve water and also plan for drought.

CHAPTER 14 U.S. BUREAU OF RECLAMATION

The U.S. Bureau of Reclamation (Reclamation), an agency of the U.S. Department of the Interior, was formed in 1902 under the Reclamation Act of June 17, 1902.[1] Reclamation was formed at a time when local and private development of irrigation projects in the West had become increasingly difficult, and federal participation and assistance was necessary to construct larger projects. Reclamation has constructed a number of water development projects in Colorado, including the Uncompaghre Project near Montrose, the Animas-La Plata Project near Durango (construction in progress), the Grand Valley Project near Grand Junction, the Trinidad Project near Trinidad, the Colorado-Big Thompson Project in northeastern Colorado, and the Frying Pan-Arkansas Project in southeastern Colorado. The water from the projects is used primarily for irrigation, although in some projects, such as those on the Front Range of Colorado, the water is increasingly being used for municipal purposes. Except for the Animas-La Plata Project, no new Reclamation projects are now planned or being constructed in Colorado.

Generally, for a Reclamation project to be constructed, a local water user organization was formed to contract with Reclamation to use the water from the project, to repay all or a portion of the costs of the project, and to operate and maintain all or a portion of the project works. Project costs were allocated among the different project purposes, and only the portion of the project costs allocated to local water uses were required to be repaid under contracts ranging from 40 years up to 100 years. Project costs allocated to power generation, or fish and wildlife benefits, for instance, were not necessarily repaid by the local water users. Costs allocated to power generation were repaid through the sale of electric power and energy. At times, subsidies have been provided to the local water users from power revenues, or through low interest rates on the repayment obligation.

With only a few minor exceptions, water from Reclamation projects is allocated to water users under contracts with the local repayment entity. The local repayment entity in Colorado has usually been a water conservancy district, although early projects have different types of repayment entities. Title to the water rights and works of the Reclamation projects remains in Reclamation, and ultimately in the United States

---

[1]   Act of June 17, 1902, ch. 1093, 32 Stat. 388 (codified as amended in scattered sections of 43 U.S.C.).

government. Beneficial title to the water rights is considered to be in the repayment entity for the benefit of the local water users.

Reclamation projects are important to water users in Colorado for two reasons. First, they provide water for beneficial uses. The use of water from Reclamation projects is controlled by both Colorado water law and by Reclamation law. For instance, under Colorado water law, water from the Colorado-Big Thompson Project, which is imported from the Colorado River basin to the South Platte River basin, may be used and reused to extinction as imported water (although under the applicable contracts the person or entity making the first use of the water can only make one use), and the use may be changed without water court proceedings both because the water is imported and because the right to use the water is represented by a contract and not a water right. In addition, the water can only be used for the purposes of the project that were authorized by Congress. Reclamation projects are generally authorized by congressional legislation, and the authorization usually specifies the purposes of the project, including the uses that may be made of the water from the project. These permissible uses cannot be changed without further action by Congress.

Second, Reclamation projects often consist of extensive works that may have excess physical capacity to carry or store water for third parties. However, since the works are owned by the United States, they can only be used for these additional purposes under a contract with the United States, usually acting through Reclamation, and with the local repayment entity for the project. Whether or not Reclamation will enter into such a contract will depend upon the facts of each proposed use, and the legal authority that Reclamation may have to authorize such use. Reclamation does not have general authority to authorize the use of excess capacity in Reclamation projects for any purpose or with any entity. In some cases, it has been necessary to obtain specific authorization by an act of Congress to allow new uses of Reclamation project facilities. For example, the City of Loveland found it necessary to obtain an act of Congress in 2000 to authorize Reclamation to enter into a contract to carry Loveland's municipal water in the Colorado-Big Thompson Project from the Big Thompson River to Loveland's water storage and treatment facilities.

If Reclamation has the legal authority to authorize a new use of particular Reclamation project facilities, and is willing to enter into a contract, the new user will be required to pay the full cost of using the facilities, including a pro rata share of operation and maintenance costs and the original capital costs of constructing the facilities. Contracts for the use of excess capacity in Reclamation project facilities can be as long as 40 years. Reclamation's decision to enter into such a contract is a discretionary action subject to compliance with the National Environmental Policy Act, the Endangered Species Act, and other similar federal legislation. See Chapter 11 for a discussion of the issues that these statutes raise. Obtaining a decision from Reclamation that it has the authority to authorize use of excess capacity and negotiating the necessary contract can take a number of years. The prospective contractor will be expected to pay all of Reclamation's costs of the process, including all environmental compliance costs. The City of Aurora is currently in the process of negotiating such a contract with Reclamation for the use of facilities of the Frying Pan-Arkansas Project, after Reclamation determined that it has the legal authority to contract with Aurora for the use of excess capacity in the facilities.

CHAPTER 15 WATER ORGANIZATIONS

§ 15.1 INTRODUCTION

Water organizations arose in Colorado as a means for water users to pool their resources in a collective effort to divert and transport water to its various locations of use, which were frequently at great distances from the water sources. The first water organizations consisted of groups of neighboring landowners agreeing to jointly bear the responsibilities and costs for the construction, operation, and maintenance of irrigation ditches and reservoirs servicing their properties. The agreements creating these "joint" or "common" ditches and reservoirs are generally governed by common law principles of contract and property law, though certain statutory duties have also been imposed on all owners of ditches and reservoirs.[1] Some statutory remedies for certain disputes among ditch owners have also been adopted, such as statutory liens against ditch co-owners delinquent in the payment of their proportion of a ditch's costs and expenses.[2]

As the demand for water grew and water supply systems became more complex, private water companies were formed. Some companies incorporated under Colorado's general corporation laws[3] and incorporation statutes specifically applicable to ditch and reservoir companies.[4] For instance, for-profit carrier ditch companies

---

1   C.R.S. §§ 37-84-101 to 38-84-121.
2   C.R.S. §§ 38-23-101 to 38-23-110.
3   C.R.S. §§ 7-101-101 to 7-117-105.
4   C.R.S. §§ 7-42-101 to 7-42-118.

were formed to attract capital for new water development projects by promising investors returns through rates charged for the companies' water delivery services. Nonprofit water companies, known as mutual ditch companies, were incorporated under nonprofit incorporation statutes[5] and the incorporation statutes specifically applicable to ditch and reservoir companies. In some respects, a mutual ditch company can be considered the corporate form of a joint ditch, though there are important differences in the laws controlling each.

Another type of private incorporated water organization, the water users association, arose in response to the federal funding of reservoir and irrigation works under the Reclamation Act of June 17, 1902.[6] This type of water users association was incorporated in conformity with both federal and state requirements in order to repay the costs of the federal water works and, upon doing so, to assume management and operation of those works. It should not be confused with other water users associations that are formed for networking, educational, and/or advocacy purposes. Finally, the most recent addition to the array of private organizations participating in the water arena, the homeowners association,[7] is playing an expanding role in water management and water rights adjudications.

All of the incorporated water organizations are vested with corporate powers and are subject to the statutory rules and common law applicable to corporate governance. Although each type of private water organization described above continues to operate today, private organizations alone proved inadequate to meet the public's continually increasing demands for water for irrigation, industry, and the diverse needs of Colorado's growing communities.

Beginning with irrigation districts, the Colorado General Assembly has provided statutory authority for the citizen-initiated creation of a variety of public or quasi-public water organizations to meet the evolving needs of a rapidly growing state. These organizations, with varying powers to levy taxes and/or assessments and to sell bonds to fund water projects, include water conservancy districts, water conservation districts, water and sanitation districts, and other special districts. The General Assembly has also authorized specific public water organizations or special districts with powers affecting water matters, such as the Colorado River Water Conservation District.

---

5   Colorado Revised Nonprofit Corporation Act, C.R.S. §§ 7-121-101 to 7-137-301; originally enacted as Nonprofit Corporation Act, C.R.S. §§ 7-20-101 to 7-20-108 (repealed 1998).

6   Act of June 17, 1902, ch. 1093, 32 Stat. 388 (codified as amended in scattered sections of 43 U.S.C.).

7   C.R.S. §§ 38-33.3-101 to 38-33.3-319.

Municipalities in Colorado also enjoy broad powers over water matters. The Colorado Constitution vests home rule cities and towns with broad authority over their local water matters. Home rule municipalities like the City and County of Denver were among the first to enter the water supply field. Statutory cities and towns, which are authorized by the General Assembly, also have broad statutory power to develop municipal water supply and treatment systems.

Finally, municipalities, districts, and political subdivisions of the state can pool their resources to form larger water organizations. These organizational entities may be water or drainage authorities, regional authorities, or metropolitan water districts, although none of the latter have been formed.

All of these private, quasi-public, and public water organizations play important roles in the development, distribution, and conservation of Colorado's water resources. Most of these organizations are active participants in Colorado's water rights adjudication and administration systems and compete for an increasingly scarce resource while exploring new ways to conserve, reuse, and increase the efficiency of their water use.

The following sections of this book touch on the purposes, formation, governance, funding, powers, statutory authority, and other important institutional features of Colorado's private and public water organizations. These sections are also intended to familiarize the reader with some of the key water conservation and water supply programs being implemented by many of the public water organizations.

> Formation of any entity to deal with water and water rights will probably require the services of an attorney with relevant experience.

§ 15.2 JOINT DITCHES

A joint ditch, also known as a common ditch, is a water transport ditch owned and used by two or more parties. The ownership rights in the ditch are real property rights that may be conveyed or reserved separately from the land or water right(s) associated with the ditch. In the absence of any contract establishing the owners' interests in the ditch, they are assumed to own the ditch as tenants in common, with all the legal rights and liabilities such co-ownership entails. Each ditch owner has an equal right to use the ditch and can transfer his or her interest in the ditch separately from the other owners' interests.

In regard to joint ditches, it is important to keep in mind the distinction between the exercise of a water right and the ownership of the water upon its diversion into a ditch. A water right is a real property right established by the diversion of water from a natural stream for a beneficial use. Once water is lawfully diverted from a natural stream, however, it takes on characteristics as if it were the personal property of the party who diverted the water for a beneficial use. As a result, changing the point of diversion for a water right diverting to a joint ditch will not necessarily cause legal injury to other ditch water rights through reduced ditch flows.[8] Even though the reduction in ditch flows may increase the ditch loss and evaporation borne by the remaining ditch water, the water impacted is personal property unprotected by the water statutes governing changes in water rights. The other ditch users normally would have no claim to reliance on water that was the personal property of another ditch user. The law in this area is different, however, for stockholders in mutual ditch companies, discussed in the following section, because such stockholders have an obligation to avoid injury to the company and other stockholders without their consent.[9]

Finally, all joint ditch owners and users are subject to Colorado statutes that establish ditch construction, maintenance, and operation responsibilities and impose penalties for failure to comply with statutory requirements.[10] Other statutes provide ditch owners with the means to extract contributions from other ditch co-owners who are delinquent in their payments for their share of ditch expenses.[11] Under such circumstances, any co-owner can attach and seek judicial enforcement of a lien on the delinquent co-owner's interest in the ditch.[12]

§ 15.3 DITCH AND RESERVOIR COMPANIES

Statutory Authority: Ditch and Reservoir Companies, C.R.S. §§ 7-42-101 to 7-42-118.
Colorado Business Corporation Act, C.R.S. §§ 7-101-101 to 7-117-105.
Colorado Revised Nonprofit Corporation Act, C.R.S. §§ 7-121-101 to 7-137-301.

§ 15.3.1 Introduction

Ditch and reservoir companies exist in two forms in Colorado, as mutual ditch companies and as carrier ditch companies. Their primary differences have been described by Colorado courts as follows:

---

8   *Brighton Ditch Co. v. City of Englewood*, 124 Colo. 366, 237 P.2d 116 (1951).
9   *Wadsworth Ditch Co. v. Brown*, 39 Colo. 57, 88 P. 1060 (1907).
10 C.R.S. §§ 37-84-101 to 37-84-125.
11 C.R.S. §§ 38-23-101 to 38-23-110.
12 C.R.S. §§ 38-23-101 to 38-23-110.

A mutual ditch company is one not organized for profit or hire, but existing primarily for the benefit of the shareholders. It is engaged in the business of storing and transporting water to its shareholders, who own the right to use the water. Delivery of the water is conditioned on payment of an annual assessment levied to meet operating expenses of the company. A carrier ditch owns the legal title to a decreed appropriation of water from a natural stream. Carrier ditches carry water for sale to consumers who have contracted with the company. Charges for water delivered by carrier ditches are fixed by the board of county commissioners. Mutual ditches are distinguished from carrier ditches in that the shareholders of mutual ditch companies are the sole owners of the ditch and diversion works. They share the costs of operation without profit, while the carrier ditch is entitled to a reasonable return on its investment over and above costs.[13]

§ 15.3.2   Formation

Although there is no mandate that a ditch company incorporate, most will do so to limit the exposure of their shareholders to potential personal liability from their activities. Today, carrier ditch companies operating for profit may incorporate under the Colorado Business Corporation Act, while mutual ditch companies, which tend to be nonprofit, may also incorporate under the Colorado Revised Nonprofit Corporation Act.[14] In either case, these companies are also subject to the Ditch and Reservoir Companies Statute as well as other statutes generally applicable to all corporations.[15]

In some instances, disputes may arise over whether a ditch company should be considered a mutual ditch company or a carrier ditch company, especially when articles of incorporation are lacking or unclear. Such disputes have arisen when assessments or water delivery charges are at issue and a party asserts that an assessment be treated as a water delivery charge or vice versa. In such cases, the courts look not only to the formation documents of the company but also consider the

---

13   *Nelson v. Lake Canal Co. of Colo.*, 644 P.2d 55, 57-58 (Colo. App. 1981) (citations omitted).
14   Colorado Business Corporation Act, C.R.S. §§ 7-101-101 to 7-117-105; Colorado Revised Nonprofit Corporation Act, C.R.S. §§ 7-121-101 to 7-137-301.
15   Ditch and Reservoir Companies, C.R.S. §§ 7-42-101 to 7-42-118; Colorado Corporations and Associations Act, C.R.S. §§ 7-90-101 to 7-90-1005.

company's historic practices, policies, and operations.[16] The status of a ditch company, therefore, is still a matter for the common law of the courts.

§ 15.3.3 Governance

Both the Colorado Business Corporation Act and the Colorado Revised Nonprofit Corporation Act provide for associations incorporated under their provisions to be governed by a board of directors. The board can vary in size and is typically vested with the power to adopt, repeal, and amend bylaws, which guide the business affairs of the corporation. As a private corporation, a ditch company has the same powers as an individual to do all things necessary or convenient to carry out its affairs consistent with the company's articles of incorporation, bylaws, and laws applicable to corporate governance.

The articles of incorporation may also vest stockholders with special, conditional, or limited voting rights based on the class of their shares and, for nonprofit corporations, may establish classes of members or directors with certain voting rights. Therefore, stockholders and members may participate in the governance of companies to varying extents. In any event, the actions of the board of directors remain subject to other statutes and common law applicable to corporate governance. It is advisable, whenever conducting a transaction involving a mutual ditch company, to review its articles of incorporation and bylaws to ensure that the transaction is completed in conformity with their provisions. In particular, a mutual ditch company's bylaws commonly include provisions governing the sale of stock or any change in a stockholder's water rights. For instance, the bylaws may include a right of first refusal for the ditch company for any sale of stock or may require that an application for a change of a stockholder's water right first be approved by the ditch company to ensure that appropriate conditions are imposed to prevent injury to other ditch shareholders.[17]

§ 15.3.4 Funding

A mutual ditch company is generally funded through pro rata assessments on the corporation's capital stock for the maintenance and operation of the company's ditches, reservoirs, or other works, for the payment of any indebtedness, or for other

---

16 *Billings Ditch Co. v. Indus. Com'n*, 127 Colo. 69, 253 P.2d 1058 (1953).

17 *Fort Lyon Canal Co. v. Catlin Canal Co.*, 642 P.2d 501, 508-09 (Colo. 1982); *Model Land & Irr. Co. v. Madsen*, 285 P. 1100, 1101-02 (Colo. 1930).

expenses of the company. No assessment can be made, however, unless it is first submitted to the stockholders for a vote at an annual or special meeting.

A carrier ditch company is generally funded through the sale of water to consumers who have contracted with the ditch company for the delivery of water. Charges for water delivered by a ditch company are fixed by the board of county commissioners as provided by Section 8 of Article XVI of the Colorado Constitution and by statute.[18]

§ 15.3.5   Shareholders' Rights

The shares of stock in a mutual ditch company represent the stockholder's ownership interest in the company's facilities and water rights. The stockholders own the water rights and each has the right to the exclusive use of the water his or her shares of stock represent. The stockholders also have the right to change the type and place of use of their water if other users will not be injured by the change. They also have the right to sell their shares of stock subject to any right-of-refusal or other requirements or limitations in the company's bylaws or articles of incorporation. Although the Ditch and Reservoir Companies Statute declares the shares of stock to be personal property, case law indicates that they have real property aspects as well and are frequently treated as such, especially when they are purchased and sold.

The relationship between the stockholders and the mutual ditch company is basically a contractual relationship implied by the company's articles of incorporations, bylaws, and the issuance of shares. A trust relationship springs from this contract, in which the company is required to conduct business in the interest of the stockholders. As the stockholders' trustee, the company is bound to protect their interests.[19]

As for carrier ditch companies, the courts have recognized that they are quasi-public entities with quasi-fiduciary duties to their contract consumers in setting rates and in permitting such consumers to exercise their constitutionally protected rights to continue to put water to beneficial use on an annual basis.[20] "The extent to which the consumer is entitled to protection is measured in part by the terms of the contract defining the conditions of purchase and delivery of the water."[21]

---

[18]   C.R.S. § 7-42-107.
[19]   *Jacobucci v. Dist. Court*, 189 Colo. 380, 541 P.2d 667 (1975).
[20]   *City of Westminster v. City of Broomfield*, 769 P.2d 490 (Colo. 1989).
[21]   *Id.* at 493.

For More Information: *See* J. Kahn, *Ownership of Mutual Ditch Company Assets*, 20 COLO. LAW No. 10, P. 2081 (1991).

§ 15.4   WATER USERS ASSOCIATIONS

Statutory Authority: Water users Associations, C.R.S. §§ 7-44-101 to 7-44-107.
Colorado Business Corporation Act, C.R.S. §§ 7-101-101 to 7-117-105.
Colorado Revised Nonprofit Corporation Act, C.R.S. §§ 7-121-101 to 7-137-301.
Reclamation Act of June 17, 1902, 32 Stat. 388 (1902).

Water users associations in Colorado were originally organized as private corporations authorized by the General Assembly for the primary purpose of dealing, contracting, or cooperating with the United States under the Reclamation Act of June 17, 1902[22] to secure a water supply or irrigation works, or both.

Water conservancy districts and water conservation districts have largely supplanted the role of the early water users association in contracting for federal irrigation projects, but some of the original water users associations still exist. In fact, the first such association in Colorado and the second in the nation, the Uncompahgre Valley Water Users Association, recently paid off its 100-year contract with the U.S. Bureau of Reclamation for the original completion of its irrigation works, which the association took control of in 1932.

A water users association is governed by a board of directors consistent with the association's articles of incorporation and duly enacted bylaws. The articles of incorporation, however, may vest stockholders with special, conditional, or limited voting rights based on the class of their shares and, for nonprofit corporations, may establish classes of members or directors with certain voting rights. In addition to the traditional corporate powers and its own statutory powers, these associations are vested with the powers conferred by law upon ditch, canal, or irrigation companies.

Water users associations have the power to levy assessments upon the stock of the association for the purpose of raising funds to accomplish the purposes for which they formed. Such assessments constitute liens upon the lands of the stockholders. In

---

22   Act of June 17, 1902, ch. 1093, 32 Stat. 388 (codified as amended in scattered sections of 43 U.S.C.).

its articles of incorporation, a water users association will prescribe classes of shares and the number of shares of each class that the corporation is authorized to issue. The preferences, limitations, and relative rights of the shares in each class are also described in the articles of incorporation. Generally, these shares represent certain rights and preferences to the use of water secured by the water users association for the use of its stockholders and, as with ditch companies, may be bought and sold consistent with the association's articles of incorporation and by-laws and any contracts with the United States.

More recently, other types of private water users associations have been formed in Colorado and they vary from loosely-formed associations with little formal organization to well-organized incorporated or unincorporated associations. The purposes and powers of these organizations vary as much as Colorado's terrain. Many are formed as advocacy groups to keep their members informed and involved in issues important to their water rights, water quality, and other water-related matters.

§ 15.5   HOMEOWNERS ASSOCIATIONS

> Statutory Authority: Colorado Common Interest Ownership Act, C.R.S. §§ 38-33.3-101 to 38-33.3-319.
> Condominium Ownership Act, C.R.S. §§ 38-33-101 to 38-33-113.

Homeowners associations are organizations responsible for the management of common interest communities, such as condominiums, cooperatives, and planned communities. They are commonly incorporated as nonprofit organizations governed by a board of directors under the organization's articles of incorporation and bylaws. Increasingly, homeowners associations find themselves on the front line of water disputes and, for many people, they are the first point of contact when it comes to water matters.

A common interest community is typically created by the developer of the community in consultation with local governments as part of the land use approval process. The community is created when the developer, or declarant, drafts a declaration that is executed and recorded in the same manner as a deed. Such a declaration is akin to a community charter and, in addition to other provisions, commonly imposes restrictive covenants on real estate in the community, such as covenants requiring a certain type of landscape or exterior building architecture. When a developer completes the construction of a common interest community, it is turned over to the homeowners association for management of its common elements, for the collection of association dues, and for the enforcement of the community's restrictive covenants.

Of particular importance in terms of water are landscape covenants that require landowners to maintain green lawns through irrigation, which can present a problem during water shortages. It is not uncommon for landowners to be prevented from landscaping their yards with materials and plants that require less water to maintain, a form of landscaping called xeriscaping. Drought conditions and resulting water shortages have forced homeowners associations to reconsider such restrictive covenants that may not make sense in an arid region that is prone to drought. In fact, some municipalities, like the City of Colorado Springs, have adopted measures that take effect during declared water shortages and temporarily rescind restrictive covenants that are not friendly to water conservation. In response to the 2002 drought, the General Assembly passed legislation in 2003 that prohibits any new restrictive covenants that prohibit or limit the installation or use of drought-tolerant vegetative landscapes.[23]

Homeowners associations are also playing a growing role in the management of water resources and the adjudication of water rights. The management and protection of part or all of the community's water supply commonly falls to the homeowners association. Safeguarding the water supply frequently means participating in water court adjudications of water rights that may impact the surface or ground water rights upon which the community may depend. It may also mean seeking out new water sources as existing sources are either depleted or prove inadequate during times of drought. The homeowners associations may also inherit responsibility for the administration of water augmentation plans or substitute water supply plans necessary for the use of their water supply. Indeed, a homeowners association's restrictive covenants relating to water use may impose requirements necessary to allow the association to meet its obligations under an augmentation plan.

Homeowners associations are increasingly operating non-potable water supplies to meet their homeowners outdoor needs for irrigation, fire protection, or other purposes. Frequently, the amount of potable water dedicated to such a community under certain water rights, or dedicated to a municipal water supplier, may be limited to the amount necessary to just meet indoor uses with non-potable supplies providing for outdoor uses. If a community either does not have separate plumbing systems for potable and non-potable systems or fails to enforce limitations on the use of potable water for indoor uses only, a community can end up using more potable water than it is entitled to use under the water rights intended to provide potable water service.

---

23   C.R.S. § 37-60-126(11).

§ 15.6   IRRIGATION DISTRICTS

Statutory Authority: Irrigation District Law of 1905, C.R.S. §§ 37-41-101 to 160. Irrigation District Law of 1921, C.R.S. § 37-42-101 to 140. Irrigation Districts of 1905 and 1921, C.R.S. §§ 37-43-101 to 189.

The first irrigation districts in Colorado were formed under the Irrigation District Law of 1905, which is codified as Article 41 of Title 37 of the Colorado Revised Statutes, and are commonly referred to as "Article 41 irrigation districts." Irrigation districts organized after April 7, 1921, were formed under the Irrigation District Law of 1921, which is codified as Article 42 of Title 37, and are commonly referred to as "Article 42 irrigation districts." Both Article 41 and Article 42 irrigation districts are also subject to the provisions of Article 43 of Title 37. When reviewing the rules governing irrigation districts, Article 43 should be reviewed in concert with either Article 41 or Article 42, as appropriate.

The purpose of irrigation districts is to allow the owners of land in an area to provide for the irrigation and/or drainage of district lands as necessary to maintain their irrigability.[24] Such districts are initiated through landowner petitions to the board of commissioners for the county containing most of the district. After the board considers lands proposed for inclusion or exclusion, the proposed boundaries are fixed and submitted to the qualified electors within the proposed district for a vote on the organization of the district. Although there are 16 active irrigation districts in Colorado, water conservancy districts, water conservation districts, and special districts are now the more common means of fulfilling the functions of irrigation districts.

Irrigation districts are governed by a three- to five-member board of directors representing their respective divisions of the district. Although Articles 41, 42, and 43 prescribe virtually all the rules for a board's transaction of business and for the management of an irrigation district, the board may adopt bylaws, rules, and regulations for the distribution of water in the district.

The districts are funded through special tax levies certified by their board of directors and assessed by the counties on lands in the districts, except those lands that are unsuitable for irrigation or incapable of irrigation except at a financial loss. The levies fund the maintenance, operation, and current expenses of the districts, the

---

24   C.R.S. § 37-41-101(1).

interest and principal of the district's bonds, repayment of indebtedness to the United States for federal irrigation projects, and other purposes. In addition, the board of directors may also levy and assess tolls and charges on the use of a canal and water for irrigation or other purposes.[25] The board of directors may also sell bonds to fund the construction or purchase of canals, reservoir sites, reservoirs, water rights, and works.

Irrigation districts are not governmental entities for purposes of Article X, Section 20, of the Colorado Constitution, which places limitations on the taxation, spending, and revenues of governmental entities.[26] An irrigation district's authority to levy and obtain collection of special assessments does not transform an essentially private entity into a governmental entity for purposes of Section 20.

§ 15.7   WATER CONSERVANCY DISTRICTS

> Statutory Authority: Water Conservancy Act, C.R.S. §§ 37-45-101 to 153.

§ 15.7.1   Purpose

Water conservancy districts are established to finance and construct water works to provide water for domestic, manufacturing, irrigation, power, and other beneficial uses. In addition to directly benefiting lands to be irrigated by the water works, water conservancy districts indirectly benefit lands already under irrigation by stabilizing the flow of water in streams and by increasing the flow and return flow of water to such streams. They also directly benefit municipalities by providing supplies of water for domestic, manufacturing, and other beneficial uses.

These districts should not be confused with flood control conservancy districts authorized under the Conservancy Law of Colorado,[27] which are formed primarily for flood control and only deal with water supply development and use when they are part of a flood control project. There are only four active flood control conservancy districts in the state today.

§ 15.7.2   Formation

Water conservancy districts can include both rural and urban lands. They can be formed either through court or voter approval. Both approval processes are initiated by the filing of a petition with the district court with jurisdiction in a county in which all or part of the lands proposed for the district are located. An election on the

---

25   C.R.S. §§ 37-41-127, 37-43-141.
26   *Campbell v. Orchard Mesa Irr. Dist.*, 972 P.2d 1037 (Colo. 1998).
27   C.R.S. §§ 37-1-101 to 37-8-101.

organization of a district may be triggered by a petition signed by not less than ten percent or two hundred electors of the proposed district, whichever number is smaller. Other requirements apply for petitions submitted to create a district by court order. If formation petitions submitted to the court for approval encounter strong enough opposition, the issue will be submitted for voter approval. Even if a district is approved under these procedures, municipalities have the ability to opt out of a proposed district under certain circumstances.

If a district is ultimately approved by either the court or the voters, a court decree is issued establishing the district as a political subdivision of the state and as a corporate body with all the powers of a public or municipal corporation. Water conservancy districts are, therefore, subject to the Open Meetings Law, the Public (Open) Records Law, and the taxing, spending, revenue, and other limitations of Section 20 of Article X of the Colorado Constitution.[28]

> Compliance with either the Open Records Law or TABOR will probably require the advice of an attorney.

§ 15.7.3 Governance

Water conservancy districts are governed by a court-appointed board of directors consisting of not more than 15 persons who are residents of the counties in which the water conservancy district is situated. The board members must be landowners in the district and knowledgeable in water matters. They are appointed to achieve general geographical representation as provided by statute. There is also a process through which 10 percent of the electors within a county or a portion of a county entitled to a director may petition the court to elect a director to replace the director whose term is about to expire. The board has the power to adopt bylaws and rules and regulations for carrying on the business, objects, and affairs of the board and the district.

§ 15.7.4 Funding

The main source of funding for water conservancy districts is the levying and collection of taxes and special assessments. To fund the maintenance and operation of water works and to pay their obligations and indebtedness, districts have four classes of taxes and assessments, each with its own statutory provisions:[29]

---

28 C.R.S. §§ 24-6-401 to 24-6-402; C.R.S. §§ 24-72-101 to 24-72-502; Colo. Const. art. X, § 20.
29 C.R.S. §§ 37-45-121 to 37-45-125 and 37-45-131.

- Class A: Ad valorem taxes upon all property within the district.

- Class B: Assessments for special benefits accruing to property within municipalities for which use of water or capacity of works is allotted.

- Class C: Assessments for special benefits accruing to property within public corporations for which use of water or capacity of works is allotted.

- Class D: Assessments for special benefits accruing to lands for which use of water or capacity of works is allotted.

The district's board of directors may allot water or capacity of water works through contracts with municipalities, public corporations, and landowners and provide for the levying and collection of Class B, C, and D assessments based on the allotments. Districts may also generate revenue through the sale or lease of water by contract and may sell bonds to fund the acquisition, construction, or completion of any source of water supply, waterworks, or other improvements or facilities.

§ 15.7.5   Key General Powers

Water conservancy districts are granted broad powers to appropriate, acquire, sell, lease, and use water, water rights, sources of water supply, and all real and personal property of any kind within and without the district. They may construct, operate, and maintain waterworks and facilities necessary or convenient for their purposes. They may also contract with the federal government for the construction, preservation, operation, and maintenance of tunnels, reservoirs, regulating basins, diversion canals, works, dams, power plants, and all necessary and incidental works. Districts have the power of eminent domain and dominant eminent domain to achieve their purposes, though these powers cannot be used to acquire water rights intended for transmountain diversion.[30] The term "dominant eminent domain" means that the power of eminent domain is superior to that of other governmental subdivisions of the state, but not the state itself.[31]

The board of directors has the power to make and enforce all reasonable rules and regulations for the management, control, delivery, use, and distribution of water. The board also has the power to approve the transfers of allotment contracts, to withhold water when there is a default or delinquency of payment, to declare forfeiture of rights to use water upon default or failure to comply with allotment contracts, and to

---

30   C.R.S. § 37-45-118(1)(c).
31   *Town of Parker v. Colo. Div. Of Parks & Outdoor Recreation*, 860 P.2d 584, 587-588 (Colo. App. 1993).

allocate and reallocate the use of water to lands within the district. The board must also consent to changes in the district boundary through the inclusion and exclusion of lands.

Subdistricts may be organized upon the petition of real property owners, within or partly within and partly without a water conservancy district under the same procedures for organization of the principal district. If formation is approved, the board of directors of the larger district also acts as the board of the subdistrict. The subdistrict is treated as an independent district when it comes to the appraisal of benefits, the issuance of bonds, the levying of assessments, finances, and all other matters affecting only the subdistrict.

§ 15.7.6   Special Characteristics

Water conservancy districts are subject to a unique mitigation requirement when exporting water from the Colorado River basin:

> Any works or facilities planned and designed for the exportation of water from the natural basin of the Colorado River and its tributaries in Colorado, by any district created under this article, shall be subject to the provisions of the Colorado River Compact and the "Boulder Canyon Project Act." Any such works or facilities shall be designed, constructed, and operated in such manner that the present appropriations of water and, in addition thereto, prospective uses of water for irrigation and other beneficial consumptive use purposes, including consumptive uses for domestic, mining, and industrial purposes, within the natural basin of the Colorado River in the state of Colorado from which water is exported will not be impaired nor increased in cost at the expense of the water users within the natural basin. The facilities and other means for the accomplishment of said purpose shall be incorporated in and made a part of any project plans for the exportation of water from said natural basin in Colorado.[32]

An example of such mitigation is the Green Mountain Reservoir, which was constructed as part of the Colorado-Big Thompson Project that diverts water from the Colorado River basin to the Northern Colorado Water Conservancy District in northeastern Colorado. The Green Mountain Reservoir was constructed with a

---

[32]   C.R.S. § 37-45-118(1)(b)(II).

capacity to store 152,000 acre-feet of water, including 52,000 acre-feet to replace out-of-priority diversions to northeastern Colorado and 100,000 acre-feet of water for power generation and subsequent use by present and future water users in the Colorado river basin.

§ 15.8 WATER CONSERVATION DISTRICTS

> Statutory Authority: Colorado River Water Conservation District, C.R.S. §§ 37-46-101 to 37-46-151.
> Southwestern Water Conservation District, C.R.S. §§ 37-47-101 to 37-47-151.
> Rio Grande Water Conservation District, C.R.S. §§ 37-48-101 to 37-48-195.

Water conservation districts are similar in many ways to water conservancy districts, but their boundaries are predetermined by state statute as opposed to the citizen-initiated petition process. The three water conservation districts are the Colorado River Water Conservation District (CRWCD), the Southwestern Water Conservation District (for the San Juan and Dolores Rivers)(SWWCD), and the Rio Grande Water Conservation District (RGWCD).

§ 15.8.1 Purpose

Water conservation districts are generally intended to provide for the conservation, use, and development of the water resources of their designated river basins. Each district has the power to construct reservoirs, ditches, and other water works for its particular designated purposes and to promote the growth, health, and general welfare of the district and the State of Colorado. Water conservation districts also help safeguard Colorado's water entitlements under interstate river compacts and court decrees equitably apportioning a river's water among the states.

§ 15.8.2 Formation

Two of the three water conservation districts, the CRWCD and the SWWCD, were formed by statute in 1937 and 1941, respectively. The RGWCD, on the other hand, had its boundaries and purposes designated by statute, but its actual formation was approved by voters in 1967. These three districts are considered bodies corporate and politic and are political subdivisions of the State of Colorado. They are, therefore, subject to the Open Meetings Law, the Public (Open) Records Law, and the taxing, spending, revenue, and other limitations of Section 20 of Article X of the Colorado Constitution.[33]

The CRWCD includes Grand County, Routt County, Moffatt County, Rio Blanco County, Ouray County, Mesa County, Garfield County, Pitkin County, Eagle County, Delta County, Gunnison County, Summit County, and those parts of Hinsdale and Saguache counties lying west and north of the continental divide and within the drainage of the Gunnison River, and that part of Montrose County not included in the SWWCD.

The SWWCD includes San Miguel County, Dolores County, Montezuma County, Archuleta County, San Juan County, La Plata County, that part of Mineral County lying south and west of the continental divide and being within the drainage of the San Juan River, and those parts of Hinsdale County and Montrose County not included in the CRWCD.

The RGWCD includes Alamosa County, Conejos County, Rio Grande County, and those portions of Saguache County and Mineral County that are within the drainage basin of the Rio Grande River and its tributaries, including the Rio Grande's "closed basin," the waters of which are isolated from the Rio Grande River.

The landowners in a district and the district's board may pursue the establishment of subdistricts or subdivisions, which are special improvement districts that are considered separate public corporations and political subdivisions of the state. They may be governed solely by the board of directors of the larger district but, in some instances, a board of managers with more limited powers may be established for a subdistrict.

§ 15.8.3 Governance

Each of the water conservation districts is governed by a board of directors, whose members are appointed for three-year, staggered terms by the boards of county commissioners from each county wholly or partially within the respective districts. Each board member must be a resident and landowner within the district and, for the CRWCD and SWWCD, must have resided in the district for two years, and be a landowner that has paid taxes to the county during the calendar year preceding the appointment. Although the statutes authorizing the water conservation districts govern many of their functions and operations, the districts have the power to make

---

[33]   C.R.S. §§ 24-6-401 to 24-6-402; C.R.S. §§ 24-72-101 to 24-72-502; Colo. Const. art X § 20.

general rules and regulations for the conduct of business in the districts and their subdistricts.

§ 15.8.4 Funding

Although there are many similarities, the funding sources for the three water conservation districts are not identical and careful review of each district's statutory authority is required to discern all of their differences. Still, some generalities may be stated. All of these districts may levy ad valorem taxes on the property of the districts to fund the general and incidental operational expenses of the districts, including the construction of water works. In lieu of this general tax, a district's board may choose to levy special assessments upon all real estate within the district. Such assessments are made in proportion to the appraised benefits to each piece of real estate accruing from the organization of the district and its adoption of a comprehensive plan of development. The purposes for which the CRWCD may levy ad valorem taxes are broader than those of the other two water conservation districts.

On behalf of their subdistricts, all three water conservation districts are authorized to issue improvement district bonds, general obligation bonds, and revenue bonds or to otherwise incur a general obligation indebtedness to finance the construction or other acquisition of water works or other improvements for the beneficial use of water. The districts, and some of their public contractors, may also fix and collect rents, rates, fees, tolls, and other charges for connections to and use of their water and/or electrical systems and facilities.

§ 15.8.5 Key General Powers

The other general powers of the three water conservation districts are very similar. They have all the powers necessary or helpful to secure and ensure an adequate supply of water, present and future, for irrigation, mining, manufacturing, and domestic purposes within their boundaries. These powers include the power to investigate, survey and acquire, by eminent domain or otherwise, the property necessary for ditches, irrigation works, and reservoirs to store or use water for the districts' purposes. They may file for water rights and initiate appropriations for the use and benefit of the ultimate appropriators. They may also contract with agencies of the United States for the construction of water works and the repayment of such construction costs. And they are given broad powers to contract or otherwise cooperate with private and public entities in joint ventures, including the formation of separate "joint action entities" with all the powers of a district or subdistrict except those relating to taxes, assessments, service charges, and police power rules and regulations.

§ 15.9   MUNICIPALITIES

Statutory Authority: Colorado Constitution, Article XX, §§ (1) and (6).
Water and Sewage, C.R.S. §§ 31-35-101 to 31-35-514.
Water and Water Systems, C.R.S. § 31-15-708.
Municipal Utilities, C.R.S. § 31-15-707.

Colorado has three types of municipalities: territorial, home rule, and statutory cities and towns. Because the Town of Georgetown is the only territorial municipality that is still active today, only home rule and statutory cities and towns are addressed here. Both of these types of municipalities enjoy broad authority for the acquisition, development, and distribution of water supplies.

§ 15.9.1   Home Rule Cities and Towns

Article XX of the Colorado Constitution grants home rule powers to cities and towns adopting a charter consistent with constitutional and statutory requirements. A home rule municipality's charter is its organic law and may extend to all local and municipal matters. These home rule laws and municipal powers are not subject to repeal, revision, or limitation by the General Assembly. State statutes do apply to home rule municipalities when it comes to matters of state interest. In matters of mixed local and state interest, home rule charter provisions and a state statute may co-exist; but if there is a conflict, the statute supersedes the home rule charter provisions.[34]

Sections 1 and 6 of Article XX of the Colorado Constitution provide that home rule municipalities shall have:

> the power, within or without their territorial limits, to construct, condemn and purchase, purchase, acquire, lease, add to, maintain, conduct and operate water works, light plants, power plants, transportation systems, heating plants, and any other public utilities or works or ways local in use and extent, in whole or in part, and everything required therefore, for the use of said [home rule municipality] and the inhabitants thereof, and any such systems, plants, or works or ways, or any contracts in relation or connection with either, that may exist and which said [home rule municipality]

---

[34]   *City and County of Denver v. Board of County Com'rs of Grand County*, 760 P.2d 656, 661 (Colo. 1988).

may desire to purchase, in whole or in part, the same or any part thereof may be purchased by the [home rule municipality] which may enforce such purchase by proceedings at law as in taking land for public use by right of eminent domain, and shall have the power to issue bonds upon the vote of the taxpaying electors, at any special or general election, in any amount necessary to carry out any of said powers or purposes, as may by the charter be provided.[35]

These broad powers and the power to acquire real and personal property to the extent embraced in a home rule municipality's charter and ordinances can generally provide such municipalities with all the necessary authority to acquire and develop adequate water supplies. They may do so through a water board, a public works board, a utilities department, and/or through contracts with other water providers. Because each home rule municipality has its own charter as well as ordinances and policies adopted pursuant to its charter, it is not possible to summarize their many features. The remainder of this section, therefore, will focus on statutory provisions governing municipalities in regard to water matters.

> Consult the relevant home rule charter and ordinances for specific information on a home rule city.

§ 15.9.2   Statutory Cities and Towns

Statutory cities and towns are those organized under Title 31 of the Colorado Revised Statutes that have not chosen to adopt a home rule charter. They receive all of their powers, mandates, authorizations, and limitations from Colorado statutes.

Cities and towns subject to state statutes may acquire, construct, operate, and maintain water facilities and supply water within and beyond their territorial limits; acquire water and water rights; exercise the power of eminent domain; regulate the supply, distribution, and use of water; levy taxes, assessments, and other charges on water users to fund water improvements and services; and issue bonds to fund the development of water facilities. Cities and towns may exercise these powers through municipal utility departments or by establishing municipal water boards to exercise these powers.

---

35   Colo. Const. art. XX § 1.

Both statutory and home rule cities and towns are subject to the Open Meetings Law, the Public (Open) Records Law, and the taxing, spending, revenue, and other limitations of Section 20 of Article X of the Colorado Constitution.[36]

§ 15.9.3   Municipal Water and Sewer Boards

Any municipality has the power to create by ordinance a non-political local legislative body or board to have complete charge and control of the sewerage and/or water facilities or joint water and sewer system of a city or town.[37] The board is vested with all powers, rights, privileges, and duties vested in the city or town creating the board and pertaining to the type of facilities designated in the ordinance. The city or town also may prescribe by ordinance the number of board members, their qualifications, terms, and other matters concerning the board's conduct of business to the extent not already prescribed by statute. The board also has the power to delegate any and all executive, administrative, and ministerial powers to officials and employees of the city or town.

§ 15.9.4   Raw Water Dedication and Cash-In Lieu of Water Rights

Increasingly, municipalities and water districts condition the approval of any new development, subdivision, or replats within their boundaries, or the annexation of new lands, on the adequate dedication of untreated, raw water to cover anticipated demands on the entity's water supply. The raw water may be surface and/or ground water and is generally provided to the municipalities or water organizations in the form of water rights that, if necessary, are changed for domestic, municipal, or other beneficial uses. It is common for these entities to provide water tap fee credits in exchange for a certain average annual volume of water dedicated. For example, the dedication of one annual acre-foot of water could provide a developer with a credit from the municipality or water service organization for one tap for one single-family home.

Many municipalities have identified specific water rights that are acceptable or criteria that different types of water rights must meet in order to be acceptable, and have established rules for accepting the dedication of raw water from certain well-established water sources like the Colorado-Big Thompson Project. Such policies and/or ordinances also may specify the amount of raw water required per acre and the procedures and other requirements that must be satisfied to complete a dedica-

---

36   C.R.S. §§ 24-6-401 to 24-6-402; C.R.S. §§ 24-702-101 to 24-72-502; COLO. CONST. art. X, § 20.
37   C.R.S. §§ 31-35-501 to 31-35-514.

tion. If a new development is unable to dedicate enough water rights, a developer may be able to pay "cash in lieu" of water rights to help fund the entity's development or acquisition of new water supplies.

§ 15.10   SPECIAL PURPOSE DISTRICTS

Special districts are quasi-municipal corporations that provide one or more services for public and private purposes and include, among others, water districts, water and sanitation districts, multiple-purpose metropolitan districts, metropolitan water districts, regional service authorities, and special statutory districts. Water districts, water and sanitation districts, and multiple-purpose metropolitan districts are all governed by the provisions of the Special District Act, which applies to all special districts that are not necessarily metropolitan or regional in the scope of their services and are not special statutory districts.[38] These three types of special districts are discussed together in Section 15.10.1.

Metropolitan and regional entities are governed by their own separate statutes and are addressed separately in Sections 15.10.2 and 15.10.3. Finally, one special statutory district involved in water matters, the Urban Drainage and Flood Control District, is briefly discussed in Section 15.10.4. It should be noted here that another special statutory district, the Three Lakes Water and Sanitation District, originally created by statute in 1971 to protect the water quality of Grand Lake, Shadow Mountain Lake, and Lake Granby, all in Grand County, is now governed by the provisions of the Special District Act like other water and sanitation districts in the state.

§ 15.10.1   Water Districts, Water and Sanitation Districts, and Metropolitan Districts

> Statutory Authority: Special District Act, C.R.S. §§ 32-1-101 to 32-1-1605. Metropolitan Districts—Additional Powers and Duties, C.R.S. § 32-1-1004. Sanitation, Water and Sanitation, or Water Districts—Additional Powers and Duties, C.R.S. § 32-1-1007.

Water districts, water and sanitation districts, and multiple-purpose metropolitan districts are all governed by the provisions of the Special District Act. As provided in that Act, the purpose of a water district is to supply water for domestic and other

---

38   C.R.S. §§ 32-1-101 to 32-1-1307.

public and private purposes and to provide reservoirs, treatment works, and facilities. Sanitation districts are intended to provide storm and/or sanitary sewers, flood and surface drainage, treatment and disposal works and facilities, or solid waste disposal facilities or waste services. Water and sanitation districts merely provide the services of both water districts and sanitation districts. A metropolitan district provides its inhabitants with two or more services, which may include water and sanitation services. A metropolitan water district, on the other hand, as discussed in Section 15.10.2, only provides water service but is formed of two or more municipalities in the same, adjacent, or nearby counties.

A special district may be formed entirely within or entirely outside, or partly within and partly outside, one or more municipalities or counties, and may consist of non-contiguous tracts of property. Two districts providing the same service are only allowed to overlap under certain circumstances prescribed by statute. The first step in the organization of a special district is to secure resolutions approving a service plan for the district from the county boards of commissioners for each county that has territory within the boundaries of the proposed special district. If the district falls entirely within a municipality or municipalities, their governing bodies must approve the proposed district. Districts are formed through a petition filed with the district court and the approval of the voters within the proposed district.

Special districts are political subdivisions and instrumentalities of the state and are considered local governments. They are, therefore, subject to the Open Meetings Law, the Public (Open) Records Law, and the taxing, spending, revenue, and other limitations of Section 20 of Article X of the Colorado Constitution.[39]

Special districts are governed by a board of directors composed of five or seven members elected for four-year terms from director districts having roughly the same number of eligible electors. The board has management, control, and supervision of all the business and affairs of the special district and all construction, installation, operation, and maintenance of special district improvements. The board may adopt and enforce bylaws, rules, and regulations for carrying on the business objectives and affairs of the board and the special district.

The board of a special district has the power to levy and collect ad valorem taxes on all taxable property within the district, subject to voter approval. The board may also fix fees, rates, tolls, penalties, or charges for services, programs, or facilities

---

[39] C.R.S. §§ 24-6-401 to 24-6-402; C.R.S. §§ 24-72-101 to 24-72-502; Colo. Const. art. X, § 20.

furnished by the special district and pledge those revenues for the payment of any of its indebtedness. The board may borrow money and incur indebtedness and may issue general obligation bonds, negotiable coupon bonds, and revenue bonds, subject to applicable voter approval requirements

Key General Powers

Special districts may exercise the power of eminent domain and dominant eminent domain, but not for the acquisition of water rights. The term "dominant eminent domain" means that the power of eminent domain is superior to that of other governmental subdivisions of the state, but not the state itself.[40] In addition to the general powers granted to all special districts, multi-purpose metropolitan districts, water districts, and water and sanitation districts have specific additional powers. Metropolitan districts providing water and/or sanitation services have all the powers of water districts and water and sanitation districts.

Water districts and water and sanitation districts have the power to fix different rates, fees, tolls, or charges and different rates of levy for tax purposes against all of the taxable property within the different areas of the districts according to the services and facilities furnished or to be furnished within a reasonable time. These districts may also construct, operate, and maintain works and facilities within and outside the district, but not within another special district providing the same services unless certain conditions are met. They may also acquire water rights.

A special district may pursue the formation of subdistricts consistent with the services, programs, and facilities to be furnished within such areas of the special district.[41] Such subdistricts are independent quasi-municipal corporations with all of the rights, privileges, and immunities of the special district. The board of the special district constitutes *ex officio* the board of directors of the subdistrict and the subdistrict must comply with the approved service plan for the special district. Any debt of the subdistrict is not considered the debt of the special district and, if taxes are to be levied or debt is to be created in the subdistrict, the board must seek voter approval for such taxes and debt.

---

40 *Town of Parker v. Colo. Div. of Parks & Outdoor Recreation*, 860 P.2d 584, 587-588 (Colo. App. 1993).
41 C.R.S. §§ 32-1-1101(1)(f) to 32-1-1101(1.5).

§ 15.10.2 Metropolitan Water Districts

> Statutory Authority: Metropolitan Water Districts, C.R.S. §§ 32-4-401 to
> 32-4-416.

Although no metropolitan water districts currently exist in Colorado, such districts were authorized to facilitate more regional cooperation on the development and distribution of water supplies. They may be formed of any two or more municipalities, if such municipalities are located in the same county or in adjacent or nearby counties. When so organized, each such district is a governmental subdivision of the state and a quasi-municipal corporation. They were intended to construct water works to control and use water for domestic, manufacturing, irrigation, power, and other beneficial uses.

The organization of a metropolitan water district is accomplished through a process primarily consisting of the adoption of ordinances or resolutions by the municipalities to be included in the proposed district. The size of the board of directors governing a metropolitan water district would vary with the population within the district. Board members from a participating municipality would be appointed by the governing body of the municipality, while board members from unincorporated areas would be appointed by the board of county commissioners.

Metropolitan water districts may levy and collect ad valorem taxes on all taxable property within the district to fund, along with other revenue, the construction, operation, and maintenance of its works and equipment, and to pay interest and principal of bonds and other obligations of the district. Districts may fix water rates and pledge such revenue for the payment of any indebtedness of the district. They may also sell developed water, as conditioned by its board, for domestic, municipal, irrigation, and industrial uses at fair and reasonable rates. They are also authorized to manufacture and sell electrical power to public and private corporations, as incidental to its purposes.

§ 15.10.3 Regional Service Authorities

> Statutory Authority: Regional Service Authorities, C.R.S. §§ 32-7-101 to
> 32-7-146.

Section 17 of Article XIV of the Colorado Constitution provides for the formation of regional service authorities that may include all or part of one county or all or part of two or more adjoining counties. They may not include only a part of any city or town or any city and county. No service authority can be formed in the metropolitan area composed of the City and County of Denver, and Adams, Arapahoe, and Jefferson Counties without including all of the City and County of Denver and all or a portion of the other counties as detailed by statute. Presently, the Ouray County Regional Service Authority is the only regional service authority in Colorado.

Regional service authorities may be formed to provide a wide array of public services, including domestic water collection, treatment and distribution, and urban drainage and flood control, if the services are approved by the voters as provided by Article XIV of the constitution. These regional authorities are intended to provide those functions, services, and facilities that transcend local government boundaries, thus reducing the duplication, proliferation, and fragmentation of local governments. They may be formed through a special petition process, monitored by the court and culminating in an election on the formation of the authority.

A regional service authority may levy ad valorem taxes on all taxable property within the service authority and may also fix rates, fees, tolls, and other service charges pertaining to the services of the service authority, including service availability charges. A service authority may also levy special assessments on specially benefited property in any improvement district within the service authority, levy ad valorem taxes, and fix fees and other charges within the boundaries of any special taxing district within the service authority. Local improvement districts and special districts may be formed by resolution of the board, subject to review by the district court.

§ 15.10.4 Urban Drainage and Flood Control District

> Statutory Authority: C.R.S. §§ 32-11-101 to 32-11-817.

Certain water users may be impacted by the activities of the Urban Drainage and Flood Control District ("District"), which is a special statutory district formed in 1969 to establish a drainage and flood control system. Its boundaries include lands in the City and County of Denver, the City and County of Broomfield, and Adams, Arapahoe, Boulder, Douglas, and Jefferson Counties. Its main purpose is to alleviate the dangers and risks to property and the health and safety of persons in the District from torrential storms and floods.

The District is governed by a board of directors in part appointed on a biennial basis by the governing bodies of the counties, the cities and counties, and the governor. The mayor of Denver and the mayor of any city located within the District with a population over 100,000 are *ex officio* directors. Each year, the District board also must appoint a director who is a registered professional engineer licensed by the state. As a political subdivision of the state, the District is subject to the Open Meetings Law, the Public (Open) Records Law, and the taxing, spending, revenue, and other limitations of Section 20 of Article X of the Colorado Constitution.[42]

The District may levy taxes on all taxable property in the District, subject to certain limitations in the absence of voter approval. An additional limited tax may be levied on the taxable property within those portions of Adams, Arapahoe, Denver, Douglas, and Jefferson Counties lying within the district to fund maintenance and improvements on that portion of the South Platte River which lies within the District.

The District is active in floodplain management as well as the planning, design, construction, and maintenance of drainage and flood control facilities. The South Platte River receives special attention because it is the receiving body of water for all the other drainageways in the District. Although the District may regulate activities in its floodplains, it has chosen not to do so as long as local governments implement their own regulations. The District's construction and maintenance activities, however, may impact water users within and downstream of the District. These activities include detention pond mucking; trash rack cleaning; tree thinning; local erosion repair; local channel grading, shaping, and stabilization; the rebuilding or replacing of drop structures; building low-flow trickle channels; establishing maintenance access into drainageways; and providing protection for existing channel improvements, box culverts, retaining walls, bridges, and other facilities. A water user seeking to establish a new water use or to change an existing water use within the District may also be affected by local government regulation of the District's floodplains.

§ 15.11 WATER AND DRAINAGE AUTHORITIES

> Statutory Authority: C.R.S. § 29-1-204.2 (Establishment of separate governmental entity to develop water resources, systems, facilities, and drainage facilities.)

§ 15.11.1 Purpose

Water and drainage authorities may be used by any combination of municipalities, special districts, or other political subdivisions of the state that are authorized to own and operate water facilities or drainage facilities. These authorities develop water

---

[42]   C.R.S. §§ 24-6-401 to 24-6-402; C.R.S. §§ 24-72-101 to 24-72-502; COLO. CONST. art. X, § 20.

resources, systems or facilities, or drainage facilities for the benefit of the inhabitants of such entities or others at the discretion of the authorities' boards of directors. There are currently 12 water authorities in Colorado.

§ 15.11.2 Formation

Water and drainage authorities are formed by contract between any combination of municipalities, special districts, or other political subdivisions of the state that are authorized to own and operate water systems or facilities or drainage facilities. Such authorized entities can join an existing water and drainage authority at the discretion of the board of directors, subject to fulfilling any and all conditions or requirements of the contract establishing the authority. Water and drainage authorities are separate governmental entities and are considered political subdivisions and public corporations of the state with all the duties, privileges, immunities, rights, liabilities, and disabilities of a public body politic and corporate. They are, therefore, subject to the Open Meetings Law, the Public (Open) Records Law, and the taxing, spending, revenue, and other limitations of Section 20 of Article X of the Colorado Constitution.[43]

§ 15.11.3 Governance

A water or drainage authority's contract establishes and organizes a board of directors in which all legislative power of the authority is vested. The contract and specific and general statutes applicable to the authority as a political subdivision and public corporation prescribe the composition, management, duties, privileges, immunities, rights, liabilities, and disabilities of the board of directors.

§ 15.11.4 Funding

Water and drainage authorities can fix fees, rates, and charges for functions, services, or facilities provided by the entity. Rates need not be uniform between the authority and the contracting parties. They may also issue bonds, notes, and other obligations that are not considered the debts, liabilities, or obligations of the original contracting entities. The contracting entities may also provide in the contract for payment to the authority of funds from the proprietary revenues for services rendered by the entity, from proprietary revenues or other public funds as contributions to defray the cost of any purpose set forth in the contract, and from

---

43   C.R.S. §§ 24-6-401 to 24-6-402; C.R.S. §§ 24-702-101 to 24-72-502; Colo. Const. art. X, § 20.

proprietary revenues or other public funds as advances for any purpose subject to repayment by the authority.

> For More Information: *See* "Using a Water Authority to Develop And Deliver Water Resources," 19 Colo. Law. 651 (1990).

§ 15.12 DRAINAGE DISTRICTS

First authorized in 1911, the state's 11 drainage districts were formed at the initiation of owners of agricultural lands susceptible to drainage to reclaim their lands for cultivation.[44] If their lands could be drained by the same general system of works, landowners could petition the board of commissioners for the county where the majority of lands are located for an election to approve the organization of the district.

Drainage districts are governed by a three-member board of directors elected from landowners in the district for two-year terms. The board may levy special assessments on the property in the district according to the benefits to each property and may issue bonds with the approval of the electors of the district. Although their primary purpose is the drainage of lands, the district may appropriate, divert, and use waters for beneficial purposes, including any water gathered in or discharged by the works of the district. The districts may also file applications for water rights, changes of water rights, and plans for augmentation.

§ 15.13 WATER ACTIVITY ENTERPRISES

> Statutory Authority: Water Activities – Enterprise Status, C.R.S. §§ 37-45.1-101 to 37-45.1-107.
> Colorado Constitution, Article X, § 20. Compliance with constitutional limitations will probably require the services of an attorney.

§ 15.13.1 Introduction

State and local governmental entities authorized to conduct water activities may form water activity enterprises. Enterprises are government-owned businesses that receive less than ten percent of their annual revenues in grants that are not subject to

---

44   C.R.S. §§ 37-20-101 to 37-33-109.

the limits on spending, revenues, and indebtedness imposed by the Colorado Constitution.[45] Water activity enterprises allow counties, municipalities, water conservancy districts and water conservation districts, water and sanitation districts, other special districts, and water and drainage authorities to fund water activities and projects in a manner that does not require such entities to seek voter approval under the constitution.[46]

§ 15.13.2 Purpose

Water activity enterprises are established for the purpose of pursuing or continuing water activities, including the construction, operation, repair, and replacement of water or wastewater facilities. Water activities also include but are not limited to the diversion, storage, carriage, delivery, distribution, collection, treatment, use, reuse, augmentation, exchange, or discharge of water as well as the provision of wholesale or retail water or wastewater or stormwater services, and the acquisition of water and water rights. Water activity enterprises are intended to supply water for domestic, agricultural, power, milling, manufacturing, mining, metallurgical, fish, wildlife, recreational, and all other beneficial uses. They are also a means for the state and local governments to secure water to which the state is entitled under its interstate water compacts and court decrees equitably apportioning water among the states.

§ 15.13.3 Enterprises

The Colorado Constitution places limits on the power of the state or any local government to increase certain taxes, revenues, spending, or indebtedness without first obtaining voter approval.[47] These limits do not apply, however, to "enterprises," which are expressly excluded from the application of the constitutional limitations. An "enterprise" is defined as a government-owned business authorized to issue its own revenue bonds and receiving under ten percent of annual revenue in grants from all Colorado state and local governments combined. The constitution does not define what constitutes a grant, but the General Assembly has determined that a "grant" is a cash payment that is not required to be repaid. The statute authorizing the formation of water activity enterprises also declares that grants do not include, among other things, public funds paid or advanced to a water activity enterprise in exchange for an

---

45   COLO. CONST. art. X, § 20.
46   COLO. CONST. art. X, § 20.
47   COLO. CONST. art. X, § 20.

agreement to provide services including the provision of water, the capacity of project works, materials, or other water activities. Therefore, while a local government may not be able to incur additional indebtedness to fund a water project without voter approval, it may form a water activity enterprise that may issue revenue bonds to be repaid through payments from the local government for services provided by the water activity enterprise. However, the local government's obligation to the enterprise is governed by applicable constitutional limitations, including the prohibition or multiple-fiscal year debts and other financial obligations without voter approval.

§ 15.13.4 Formation

Water activity enterprises may be formed by "districts," which are state or local governments with existing authority to conduct water activities. Each district may establish a water activity enterprise by resolution or ordinance, as appropriate under the laws governing each district.

A resolution or ordinance establishing a water activity enterprise should: (1) define the water activity for which the enterprise is established; (2) identify the nature of enterprise revenues, including revenues from rates charged by the district for classes of water service; (3) restrict the receipt of grants to under 10 percent of total annual revenues; (4) establish an enterprise fund to account for revenues and expenditures; (5) prohibit the enterprise from levying any tax which is subject to a constitutionally-required vote or entering into any general obligation of the local government without a vote; and (6) authorize the use of all legal authority available to an enterprise under applicable law.[48]

A water activity enterprise must be wholly owned by a single district and cannot be combined with any water activity enterprise owned by another district. This requirement does not limit, however, the ability of an enterprise to contract with any other person or entity, including other districts or water activity enterprises.

§ 15.13.5 Governance

The governing body of a water activity enterprise is the governing body of the district that owns the enterprise or such governing body as may be prescribed by applicable laws, city and county, county, municipal charters, county resolutions, municipal ordinances, or intergovernmental agreements that designate a different governing body for the water activity enterprise.

---

48   G. Hobbs, Jr., Water Activity Enterprises, 22 Colo. Law No. 12, at 2557 (1993).

§ 15.13.6 General Powers

A water activity enterprise's governing body may exercise all of the powers relating to water activities that are authorized for the district owning the enterprise, but no enterprise may levy a tax that is subject to the Colorado Constitution's taxing limitations.

SECTION FOUR: PROTECTING WATER

CHAPTER 16 PROTECTING WATER RIGHTS

---

§ 16.1   WATER USE RECORDS

A water right is a right to use water from a public resource. Accordingly, as explained below in this section, this right can be lost because of lack of use. Obviously, it is advantageous and important to the owner of a water right to keep good records of use. The best evidence of the use of a water right is a record of actual diversions. For a direct flow water right diverted from a stream, diversions are recorded using a measuring device, usually a flume or weir, that measures the amount of water actually diverted. Depending on the technology used, the device may also record the amount of diversions and measure and record the duration of the diversion each day. Installed in a stream or ditch, a flume or weir is a device which has a known geometry, cross-sectional area, and water velocity, so that the rate of water flowing through the device in cfs can be determined by reading the depth of the water on a gauge fixed to the side. This measurement can then be converted into acre-feet per day using the approximate conversion factor of one cfs per 24 hours equals two acre-feet. If a well is involved, a totalizing flow meter should be installed and read periodically to determine the actual amount of water pumped over time.

> Useful Web sites with pictures explaining Parshall flumes are:
> http://www.flowmeterdirectory.com/flowmeter_artc/parshall.html and
> http://www.usbr.gov/pmts/hydraulics_lab/pubs/wmm/chap08_10.html
>
> An explanation of weirs can be found at
> http://www.usbr.gov/pmts/hydraulics_lab/pubs/wmm/chap07_11.html

The State and Division Engineers have the authority to require any owner or user of a water right to install and maintain, at such owner's or user's expense, necessary meters, gauges, or other measuring devices, and to report their readings at reasonable times to the appropriate Division Engineer.[1] Regardless of whether the Division Engineer requests diversion records, the owner of a water right should keep his or her own diversion records as carefully as possible to be able to prove the extent of use of the water right at any time. Such records may be important to refute a claim of abandonment, satisfy a potential purchaser that the water right has been used, or support historical consumptive use calculations if the use of the water right is changed in water court.

For a storage water right, measurements of diversions and use are complicated by the phenomena of evaporation and seepage. Evaporation occurs from any water surface exposed to the air. Its rate depends upon temperature, relative humidity, and wind. Evaporation is either measured directly using an evaporation-pan measuring device, or estimated based on publicly available information. Evaporation from a reservoir must be taken into account in determining how much water may be stored, how much water has been stored, and how much water has been used.

The method by which evaporation is taken into account depends upon the type of reservoir. If the reservoir is an in-channel reservoir, meaning that it is physically located in the channel of the stream from which it stores water (such as Chatfield Reservoir on the South Platte River south of Denver or Dillon Reservoir on the Blue River), the amount of water lost to evaporation must be deducted from the amount of water stored in priority under the water right. In other words, evaporation is charged against the storage water right and reduces the amount of water available for use, even though additional water could physically be diverted to replace the evaporation.

If the reservoir is an off-channel reservoir, meaning that it is not physically located in the channel of the stream from which it stores water (such as Horsetooth Reservoir above Fort Collins), the amount of water lost to evaporation simply reduces the amount of water stored in the reservoir.

Similarly, unless a reservoir is lined with an impervious material (an unusual practice except for gravel pit storage sites) water will usually seep from the reservoir into the surrounding soil and rock. This seepage must also be taken into account in determining the amount of water stored and used, and must be charged against the storage water right, in both in-channel and off-channel reservoirs. Seepage is

---

1   C.R.S. § 37-92-502(5)(a).

extremely difficult to estimate or measure with any accuracy, and is usually estimated based upon experience.

Reservoir water rights are subject to a "one-fill" rule. This means that a reservoir can only fill its available storage capacity once each year, unless the decree or other circumstances indicate otherwise. The reservoir water right can only be used to divert and store the lesser of the decreed storage capacity, or the difference between the decreed storage capacity and the amount of water in the reservoir at the start of the fill season, once each year. Because of this rule, once a reservoir water right has been used to divert and store the amount of water permitted in a given year, it cannot be used to divert additional water to replace evaporation or to replace seepage.

The amount of water diverted and stored in an in-channel reservoir can be measured using at least two different methods. First, flumes or weirs set in the stream just above and below the reservoir can be used, which will measure the amount of water going into and out of the reservoir over time. The difference between the upper and lower measurements, adjusted for evaporation and seepage, will indicate the amount of water stored in the reservoir or used at any given time.

Alternatively, the water level in the reservoir can be measured using a staff gauge, which is a vertical pole set in the bottom of the reservoir, at or near the deepest point, with a vertical scale attached, usually with gradations of feet or inches. The water level in the reservoir can then be determined by reading the staff gauge. For the gauge to be useful in determining the volume of water in the reservoir, a stage-capacity table must be created for the reservoir. A stage-capacity table indicates the volume of water stored in the reservoir at each reservoir elevation, and must be created by a surveyor or engineer using an accurate topographic map of the reservoir basin bottom. Using the topographic information, the volume of water in the reservoir at and below any given reservoir elevation can be calculated using simple geometry and displayed in a stage-capacity table.

The amount of water diverted and stored in an off-channel reservoir can also be measured using a flume, weir, or other measuring device set in the ditch or other conveyance structure used to divert water into the reservoir, or with a staff gauge.

As with measuring flumes or weirs, evaporation and seepage from a reservoir must be taken into account when using a staff gauge. Evaporation and seepage will, over time, reduce the amount of water stored in a reservoir. Once a reservoir has been filled, a reservoir owner or operator must allow the evaporation and seepage to reduce the amount of water stored in the reservoir. The reservoir cannot be kept at a given staff gauge level, since this results in water being diverted from the stream (usually out of priority) to replace evaporation and seepage.

§ 16.2 MONITORING THE ACTIONS OF OTHERS

A water right gives its owner the right to divert water in relation to other water rights, if water is physically available in the stream. Therefore, all owners of water rights must be aware of the water court and administrative activities of other water right owners and users to make sure that applications filed by others do not adversely affect or injure their own water rights. A water right may be adversely affected or injured by the operation of other water rights due to either alteration of water quality or reduced amounts of water being available for diversion or storage in priority.

The primary method of monitoring the activities of other water users is review of the monthly résumé of water right applications published by the clerk of each water division. The résumé contains a summary of all water right applications filed in that water division during any given month. It is published in a newspaper or newspapers of general circulation once in every county affected, as determined by the water judge, at the expense of the applicant. The résumé is also mailed at the end of each month to all persons whom the referee has reason to believe would be affected by the application. Such persons include, at a minimum, the persons listed in the application as the owners or reputed owners of the land upon which any structure is or will be located, upon which water is or will be stored, or upon which water is or will be placed to beneficial use. The résumé is also mailed to each person who has requested a copy of it by submitting his or her name and address to the water clerk.[2]

> The résumé of each water division is now available on the Colorado Judicial System Web site under the Water Courts section:
> http://www.courts.state.co.us/supct/supctwaterctindex.htm

As explained in Section 1.2.6 above, any person may file a statement of opposition to the application within two months after the end of the month in which the application is filed.[3] The statement of opposition must state the grounds for objection, be verified as to its accuracy, and be filed with the water clerk's office. Grounds for objection are generally limited to potential injury to the objector's water rights through a reduction in the amount, place, or timing of water available for diversion, and, in the case of plans for augmentation or exchange, a change in water quality. One need not

---

2   C.R.S. § 37-92-302(3).
3   C.R.S. § 37-92-302(1)(b).

allege injury to one's water right, however, when opposing an application to adjudicate a new water right. Such statements of opposition need only demand that the applicant prove the claimed appropriation according to law. In designated ground water basin, an owner or user of a water right should monitor applications filed with the Colorado Ground Water Commission. Applications filed with the Ground Water Commission are published in a newspaper of general circulation in each county concerned with the application. The publication is once each week for two consecutive weeks. Objections to applications can be filed with the Ground Water Commission within 30 days after the last publication of the notice.[4] As with tributary water rights, any owner of a water right that may be adversely affected or injured as a result of the application may file an objection.

Other actions to be monitored for possible opposition include the State Engineer's administrative approval of certain temporary changes of water rights, substitute water supply plans, and interruptible water supply agreements, and the Division Engineer's administrative authority over loans of agricultural water rights and loans of water rights to the Colorado Water Conservation Board (CWCB). See Section 10.2 for a full discussion of these proceedings. Owners of water rights have 30 days after the date of mailing of the notice to file comments on the plan with the State Engineer. In the case of proposed agricultural loans and loans to the CWCB, comments must be filed with the Division Engineer within 15 days. In either case, the party filing comments should address whether the proposed plan would adversely affect or injure his or her water rights. Adverse decisions of the State Engineer are appealable to the water judge in the applicable water division within 30 days after the date on which the decision of the State Engineer is served on the parties.[5] Adverse decisions of the Division Engineer on proposed agricultural loans and loans to the CWCB are appealable to the water judge in the applicable water division within 15 days after the date on which the decision of the Division Engineer is served on the parties.[6]

---

4   C.R.S. § 37-90-112.
5   C.R.S. §§ 37-92-308(4)(c) and 37-92-308(5)(c).
6   C.R.S. § 37-83-105(2).

See Section 10.2 for a full discussion of these proceedings. The State Engineer is required to maintain a substitute water supply plan notification list for each water division for purposes of notifying interested parties of applications for approval of these types of actions. Individuals must affirmatively request that their names be placed on the list and must pay an annual fee.[7] Persons on the list will be mailed notice of each such application filed with the State Engineer or Division Engineer, or, if desired, will be sent copies of notices by electronic mail. Copies of such applications are also usually available on the office of the State Engineer's Web site.

§ 16.3   ABANDONMENT OF WATER RIGHTS

Abandonment of a water right results in the termination of the water right in whole or in part as a result of the intent of the owner to discontinue permanently the use of all or part of the water available under the water right.[8] When a water right has been partially or wholly abandoned, the abandoned portion of the water right ceases to exist and the amount of water that the abandoned water right could have diverted becomes available to other water rights in order of their priority. The water court has jurisdiction over applications for determination of abandonment of a particular water right (usually filed by the owner of a competing water right), but the résumé notice procedures do not apply to such applications.[9]

Abandonment of a water right occurs when there is non-use of the water right coupled with the owner's intent to permanently abandon the right. An unreasonable period of unexplained non-use creates a rebuttable presumption of intent to abandon a water right. The determination of what constitutes an unreasonable amount of time varies with the facts of each case. Once there is a presumption of intent to abandon, however, the water right owner has the burden of establishing facts or conditions that excuse the non-use or show the owner's intent not to abandon the water right.[10]

In recent cases, abandonment of a water right has been found to occur when the water ditches were in unusable condition and had not been used for the past 20 to 30 years,[11] when no beneficial use of water from a well was made for at least 24

---

7   C.R.S. § 37-92-309(6).
8   C.R.S. § 37-92-103(2).
9   *Gardner v. State of Colo.*, 614 P.2d 357 (Colo. 1980).
10   *Haystack Ranch, LLC. v. Fazzio*, 997 P.2d 548 (Colo. 2000).
11   *Id.*

years,[12] and when water had not been diverted or applied to beneficial use from irrigation water rights for 40 years.[13]

In addition to court proceedings involving individual water rights, every ten years (starting in 1990) each Division Engineer is required to compile a list of water rights that the Division Engineer has determined to be abandoned in whole or in part. For purposes of the abandonment list, the failure for a period of ten years or more to apply the water available to a water right to a beneficial use when needed by the person entitled to use the water right creates a rebuttable presumption of abandonment of the water right with respect to the amount of water available that has not been used.[14] Water rights that meet these criteria are usually placed on the abandonment list, unless the owner can adequately refute or justify the non-use.

> The most recent abandonment list for each water division is available online at
> http://www.water.state.co.us/pubs/abandonment/abandonment.asp

The Division Engineer is required to mail a copy of the abandonment list to the owner of every absolute water right on the list.[15] However, the Division Engineer does not maintain accurate records of the identity of water right owners, so notices are sometimes sent to the wrong people. The respective portion of the abandonment list is also required to be published in the county in which the point of diversion of each listed water right is located. An owner of a water right on the abandonment list has the right to file a written objection with the Division Engineer to the inclusion of his or her water right on the list. The objection should either provide evidence that the water right has been used, or justify non-use. After objections have been received, the Division Engineer is required to consider the objections, revise the abandonment list if the objections justify revisions, and file it with the water court. Notice of the filing of the revised abandonment list is then included in the résumé for the respective water divisions for the month of December of the year after the list was initially compiled (for example, the 2000 abandonment list was published in the December 2001 résumé).

Any person can file a protest to inclusion of a particular water right on the abandonment list on or before June 30 of the year following the year in which the list was

---

12   *Hammel v. Simpson*, 83 P.3d 1122 (Colo. 2004).

13   *Denver Bd. of Water Com'rs v. Middle Park Water Conservancy Dist.*, 925 P.2d 283 (Colo. 1996).

14   C.R.S. § 37-92-402(11).

15   C.R.S. §§ 37-92-401 to 37-92-402.

initially published in the résumé (for example, protests to the abandonment list published in December 2001 were due to be filed on or before June 30, 2002). The protest should also provide evidence that the water right has been used, or evidence that justifies its non-use. The water judge is required to hold hearings on the protests, and eventually enter a judgment and decree incorporating the abandonment list with such changes as determined necessary based on the protests and hearings. Thereafter, the Division and State Engineers are required to administer water rights in accordance with the abandonment list, meaning that water rights determined to have been abandoned in whole or in part can no longer divert water under the abandoned priority to the extent of the abandonment.

§ 16.4   ADVERSE POSSESSION OF WATER RIGHTS

In Colorado, water rights are deemed to be real property for purposes of adverse possession claims.[16] The statutory period of adverse possession of real estate in Colorado is 18 years,[17] unless a person claims ownership under color of title and payment of taxes on the real estate, in which case the period is seven years.[18]

A party seeking to establish ownership of a water right by adverse possession must establish that his possession of the water right is actual, adverse, hostile, and under claim of right, as well as open, notorious, exclusive, and continuous for the prescribed period. Adverse possession claims, by nature, are intensely factual. As a general proposition, an adverse possession claim requires that the claimant establish that he or she has openly, exclusively, continuously, and under a claim of right diverted and used water under a specific decreed water right for at least 18 years. The claim may be based on the conduct of the claimant's predecessors in title to the water right, known as "tacking" in the law. In other words, a predecessor's period of adverse possession can be added to, or tacked onto, the claimant's period of adverse possession to satisfy the required time period.

The use by a co-owner of a ditch or reservoir, or by a shareholder in a mutual ditch company, of more than his or her pro rata share of the available water does not necessarily establish adverse possession. For adverse possession to occur in these circumstances, the co-owner or shareholder must be actually prevented in some way from using his share of the water by the person claiming adverse possession.[19] Persons

---

16   *Bagwell v. V-Heart Ranch, Inc.*, 690 P.2d 1271 (Colo. 1984).

17   C.R.S. § 38-41-101.

18   C.R.S. § 38-41-108.

19   *Fallon v. Davidson*, 320 P.2d 976 (Colo. 1958).

in these circumstances generally have a right to use all of the available water if the other parties do not need it. Therefore, water use in excess of a pro rata share is not usually adverse or hostile to the rights of other co-tenants or shareholders.

An adverse possession claim must be made against a specific decreed water right. A claim of adverse possession cannot be made against the unappropriated water in a stream, which is the property of the public.[20] At most, this activity will result in appropriation of a water right that must be adjudicated in water court before the State and Division Engineers will recognize its priority, which would be junior to water rights that have already been decreed.

§ 16.5 AVOIDING IMPLIED CONSENT

As described in Section 4.4.5, municipal and quasi-municipal (meaning water districts) water suppliers have the authority in certain circumstances to enact an ordinance or resolution that incorporates ground water in the Dawson, Denver, Arapahoe, or Laramie-Fox Hills aquifers underlying all or a portion of the entity's service area into its municipal service plan.[21] The ordinance or resolution can only apply to areas included within the entity's service area as of January 1, 1985, and that the entity was obligated to serve by law or contract in effect prior to January 1, 1985. After adoption of the resolution, the owners of land that overlies the ground water are deemed to have consented to the withdrawal by the water supplier of all such ground water. This is called an "implied consent" ordinance or resolution. It can only be adopted after ten days notice published in the newspapers.[22]

---

20 *Mountain Meadow Ditch & Irr. Co. v. Park Ditch & Reservoir Co.*, 277 P.2d 527 (Colo. 1954).
21 C.R.S. § 37-90-137(8).
22 C.R.S. §§ 24-70-101 to 24-70-109.

Owners of lands that are located within municipalities or water districts that are underlain by non-tributary ground water should consider whether they want the water supplier to obtain the right to use the non-tributary ground water under their land in this fashion. There are at least three defensive measures that such landowners can take to defeat an implied consent ordinance or resolution if the measure is taken before adoption of the ordinance or resolution. First, the landowner can obtain a decree from the water court adjudicating the landowner's rights to the non-tributary ground water. See Section 4.4.1 regarding decrees for non-tributary ground water. Second, the landowner can obtain a permit from the State Engineer's Office to construct a well to use the non-tributary ground water. See Section 4.4.1 regarding ground water well permitting. Third, the landowner can convey, or grant consent for, the right to use the non-tributary ground water to a third party and record the conveyance or other document granting the rights.

Finally, if water service to land included in the ordinance or resolution is not reasonably available from the water supplier, and no plan has been established by the supplier allowing the landowner to obtain an alternate water supply, the implied consent ordinance or resolution will not apply to such land.

§ 16.6   REGULATORY CONCERNS

As discussed in Chapter 11, the protection of water rights is no longer solely a matter of compliance with Colorado water law. Rather, various federal, state, and local laws and regulations may apply to protect environmental values. These laws address water quality, endangered species, and land use. In order to protect your water right, the overriding need is to comply with all existing permit(s), terms, and conditions. However, a water right owner may also encounter changing legal requirements, and proposed changes to them by legislative bodies, regulatory agencies, and the courts. Participation in these fora may be appropriate where changes would have a significant impact on the use of a water right.

Permit Compliance

Most federal, state, and local environmental permits contain one or more terms and conditions. These often involve monitoring and reporting requirements, which may trigger action that the permittee must take if certain thresholds are met. Permit holders must therefore not be lulled into complacency once they obtain the requisite permit, but should be certain that they understand what is required to comply with the permit. It is prudent to create a "tickler" system to review permit requirements and periodically perform a compliance self-audit to anticipate and deal with any compliance issues before they arise. This protects the permit, which in some instances the issuer can unilaterally revoke for violations, and which could lead to a shut-down of the permitted activity. In addition, most environmental laws have hefty penalties for violations, often treating each day of violation as a separate offense subject to heavy fines. This is obviously a situation to avoid through careful planning and compliance.

> If in doubt about permit compliance, it is usually worthwhile to discuss your situation with an appropriate professional—an environmental attorney, engineer, or consultant—as soon as you have concerns, and before talking to the regulatory agency.

Permit Modifications

Some permits are perpetually conditional. Such permits can be reopened and modified by the permitting agency based on significantly changed circumstances or other new information and when deemed in the public interest. Although modifications can be more restrictive, there are usually procedural safeguards to ensure the permittee has an opportunity to participate in any proceedings to modify or amend her permit.

Water Quality

The CWA requires Colorado to review its water quality standards and use classifications on a triennial basis, as discussed in Section 11.1.2. Because of antidegradation requirements, it is unusual for water quality standards and use classifications to become less stringent or restrictive. In fact, the opposite generally occurs incrementally over time because Colorado has taken a conservative approach in adopting water quality standards and use classifications, which are not changed until substantial new data become available, and/or analytical methods become more sensitive. In addition, growth adds pollutants and pollution to state waters, which may lead state waters to become "impaired" and subject to allocation of total maximum daily loads. A discharger may consequently face more stringent discharge limits without changing anything about his or her permitted discharge. Protecting the ability to discharge effluent through a point source without costly treatment improvements therefore requires the discharger to be cognizant of the Water Quality Control Commission's triennial review cycle and 303(d) listing of impaired waters. Where possible or proposed changes are likely to impact a discharger, it is prudent to participate in the work group process that usually precedes any rulemaking, often by a few years.

The Water Quality Control Division's Web site contains information on the Water Quality Control Commission's regulatory schedule several years in advance, as well as links to active work groups: http://www.cdphe.state.co.us/op/wqcc/wqcchom.asp

---

Some technical and/or legal expertise is desirable to participate effectively in both the informal work group and particularly in the formal rule-making processes. Most point source dischargers will have some technical expertise in-house that may be sufficient, at least initially. Legal assistance is normally desirable at the time formal rule-making commences—a couple of years in advance through "informational hearings"—and specialized technical expertise and/or studies are often necessary to influence the Commission's final action on water standards and use classifications. In short, this is an area where you must generally think months or years ahead and anticipate, rather than react.

Endangered Species

The Endangered Species Act (ESA) has two critical provisions that affect the use (and therefore value) of water rights, the Section 7 consultation and jeopardy prohibition and the Section 9 take prohibition, as discussed in Section 11.2. Fundamental events that could affect a water right after project permitting are: changes in a permitted project, significant new information showing different effects on listed species than previously considered, or the listing of new threatened or endangered species or the designation of critical habitat for listed species. These changed circumstances could cause the federal permitting agency to reinitiate consultation with the Fish and Wildlife Service (FWS), as discussed in Section 11.2.2. Consultation could lead to the requirement to implement additional reasonable and prudent alternatives to avoid or offset the project's impact or possibly even stop construction or project operations in an extreme situation.

As discussed in Section 11.2.3, a newly listed species would also be protected by Section 9's prohibition on take. Thus, the permittee might need to obtain a new or modified incidental take statement or permit to cover project impacts on the newly listed species or habitat.

To protect both a permitted or existing water project from the impacts of new listings or other changed circumstances, a permittee should monitor the potential listing of species and habitat that could be impacted by his or her project. Because the FWS must use the best scientific information available in its listing decisions, there is an opportunity for the public, including permittees, to provide information that the FWS must consider when making a listing decision or other biological judgments. As with ESA permitting, this is a complicated area of the law and it is prudent to seek professional assistance if this is an issue that may significantly affect your water rights.

Federal Land Use Authority

When a water right is diverted on or traverses federal lands, a federal permit is often required to operate and maintain the diversion structure and ditch or pipeline, although some may be fully grandfathered. As discussed in Section 11.3, federal agencies assert the power to require bypass flows when issuing or renewing these permits, which can lead to a reduction in the amount of water divertable under a decreed right. This issue has arisen in Colorado in the context of permit renewal. Since federal agency permitting decisions are partly driven by agency management plans for the lands involved, water users should participate in the public process by which those plans are adopted and modified to try to protect their ability to use their water rights.

> If any federal government agency tells you that you must bypass or relinquish part of your water right to renew a permit to use your water, you need experienced legal assistance.

Changes in Law

The possibility of significant changes in federal environmental statutes is remote in the short term. Judicial interpretations of federal environmental laws are, however, not so static. There are examples of both expanding and narrowing interpretations at all levels of the federal judiciary in the recent past, although the Tenth Circuit, which includes Colorado, is generally not inclined toward expansive interpretations. Because any change will require regulatory changes to implement—a multi-year process—they are probably not worth worrying about unless you are engaged in long-range planning.

State environmental statutes based on federal statutes, with respect to issues such as water quality, change at a slow pace, and usually in reaction to some federal change, be it statutory, regulatory, or judicial. Thus, you are likely to hear about proposed changes well in advance of their implementation. State water laws, in contrast, continue to see numerous changes in response to drought and growth issues. These changes both increase the flexibility of using water rights and impose new requirements. As a result, changes can both increase and decrease the value of a water right, primarily by modifying how a water right may be used.

> Monitoring statutory and judicial changes is most easily accomplished through joining the Colorado Water Congress or following activity in the Colorado General Assembly through its Web site. (see Appendix §§ 1.1 and 1.4 for contact information).

Local land use laws can and do change with some regularity, particularly zoning, subdivision regulations, and land use plans. Some of these can affect the water required for development. County H.B. 1041 permitting requirements, discussed in Section 11.5.2, also appear to be on the upswing, including multi-county intergovernmental agreements. These may impact the diversion and use of water, particularly transbasin diversions that are the most likely to be subject to H.B. 1041 permitting. Permit conditions that restrict the use of a water right, or impose additional costs before it can be exercised, may impact both the yield of a right and its value.

> Those holding water rights in anticipation of changing their use in the future may need to get involved in local regulatory decisions to protect their water rights.

CHAPTER 17 WATER RIGHT TAXATION

§ 17.1 REAL PROPERTY TAXATION OF WATER RIGHTS AND WATER INFRASTRUCTURE

Water rights and water infrastructure occupy a rather unique position in the real property taxation scheme used in Colorado. They are generally not directly taxable.

Water rights, and the facilities used to supply the water, including dams, reservoirs, ditches, pipelines, and other infrastructure, and the land on which these facilities are located, that are used or held to produce water to support uses on any item of real estate, are not appraised and valued separately. Instead, they are treated like improvements to the lands on which they are used and are appraised and valued with that item of real estate, as a unit.[1] Their value is taxed to the extent that it increases the value of the real estate on which they are used. For example, water rights and infrastructure used to supply water to irrigated land increase the value of that land, and that increased value is then taxed instead of taxing the water rights and infrastructure separately. This rule even extends to shares of stock in mutual ditch companies, which represent an ownership interest in the water rights of the company.[2]

In rare instances, water rights or water infrastructure may not be used or held to produce water to support uses on other real property, or may not be used on separate real estate. In such cases, the water rights or water infrastructure may be separately taxed.

---

1 COLO. CONST. art. X, § 3(1)(d); C.R.S. §§ 39-3-104, 39-5-105(1.1); *Shaw v. Bond*, 64 Colo. 366, 171 P. 1142 (Colo. 1918).

2 *Beaty v. Bd. of County Com'rs*, 101 Colo. 346, 73 P.2d 982 (1937).

SECTION FIVE: LOOKING TO THE FUTURE

CHAPTER 18 EMERGING ISSUES

§ 18.1   STATE ISSUES

§ 18.1.1   Transfers of Water from Agricultural to Municipal Uses

For decades, the means used by growing cities to meet future water supply needs was to appropriate new water rights and develop them through storage, treatment, and transmission to their place of use. As the rivers and streams of Colorado became over-appropriated throughout the second half of the twentieth century, it became increasingly difficult to obtain substantial new supplies under junior water rights. Even with expensive storage, the ability to reliably develop junior water rights is becoming difficult. Junior rights are simply not in priority frequently enough to yield enough water to meet the demands of the cities.

Rather than develop new water rights, cities and towns increasingly purchase existing senior water rights, including the wholesale purchase of farms and ranches in order to dry-up and retire irrigated lands and transfer the water to municipal water systems. Purchases by the City of Aurora in the Arkansas River basin of massive amounts of the Rocky Ford and other ditches, as well as land purchases by the City of Thornton served by the Water Supply and Storage Company in the Cache la Poudre River basin, provide ready examples of agricultural to municipal transfers of water supplies. These transfers are controversial and lead to hard-fought and expensive water court trials. Because of the growing population in Colorado and the reduction in reliability of junior rights, it is anticipated that the future will bring increasing transfers from rural areas to the cities and towns of Colorado. Dry-year leasing of agricultural water for use intermittently within municipal systems may help stall these permanent transfers. See Section 5.3.3. To date, they have proven ineffective.

§ 18.1.2   Basin of Origin Mitigation

During the 1990s and into the new century, numerous bills have been introduced into the Colorado General Assembly to require mitigation for export of water from one river basin to another. Mitigation is focused on economic, environmental, and even social ills that are said to occur when water is exported. Typically, these bills have required payment to various entities in the river basin of origin for increased cost for water diversion, such as lowering of headgates or deepening of wells, payments for damage to the local economy, and a requirement to leave water in the streams for water quality protection and to support environmental values. Some proponents have even advocated broader mitigation such as stabilization payments for local businesses and counties to be distributed throughout the community. Citizen petitions for ballot initiatives requiring mitigation have also been circulated.

The 2002 drought added intensity to the debate about basin of origin mitigation. The drought both intensified the call for protection of basins of origin as water levels dropped to historic lows while, conversely, increasing plans for water exports from those basins that were developed to meet the needs of urban areas experiencing severe water restrictions. No comprehensive basin of origin mitigation has yet been adopted, either through the ballot box or by the legislature. Narrowly focused mitigation requirements have been imposed that require revegetation of dried-up lands and financial payments for reduced property values to pay bonded indebtedness of public entities. See Section 10.1.2.

Concurrent with these debates, rural areas in both the South Platte River basin and the Arkansas River basin have raised concerns that adoption of basin of origin mitigation will increase pressures on rural areas within the same river basins as Denver and Colorado Springs. These advocates argue for area of origin mitigation protection, which would protect rural economies not only outside the Arkansas and South Platte River basins, but within them as well. We expect this debate to continue in the future.

§ 18.1.3 Increasing Environmental Demand for Water

Advocates for broadening the uses and values of decreed water rights have made their mark, arguing that the highest and best use of water is, sometimes, to leave water in the stream. Water in the stream provides aesthetic and recreational benefits that serve the needs of fish, the growing and important recreational industry of rafting and kayaking, and other uses. These are touted as a unique part of the Colorado environment and part of the region's attractive lifestyle. The expansion of decreed water rights to include recreational in-channel diversions discussed in Section 3.4.2, which expanded not only the type of water right that can be recognized but also the entities that could hold these water rights, was a huge change in Colorado law.

Maintaining water quality by allowing a diluting flow to remain in a stream is also advocated as an environmental value, which has, to date, been rejected. Adding the demands of traditional water rights for agriculture, municipal, and other uses together with the new demands for rafting, kayaking, fishing, and other recreational activities stresses the limits of Colorado streams to meet these demands. This stress causes increasing conflicts. We expect to see an increasing demand for non-traditional uses of water to meet the public's growing desire for recreation and environmental enhancement and protection, not just through the use of junior water rights but through attempted curbs on the diversion of senior water rights.

§ 18.1.4 Conservation, Efficiency, and Reuse

The 1990s through 2000s also saw an increasing number of bills introduced into the General Assembly that require or strongly encourage increased water conservation and efficiency. Bills requiring meters on water use, prohibiting covenants that require blue grass in suburban landscapes, and mandating that municipal water providers reduce system losses by repairing leaking pipes or rebuilding inefficient diversions are on the increase. A surge of conservation legislation was seen after the 2002 drought.

However, the notion that Colorado can conserve its way out of a drought or conserve enough water to meet future demands is naïve. For example, the City of Aurora, which has adopted tough conservation measures including a complete prohibition on outside watering at certain times and limited planting of lawns and gardens, has a current need of 58,000 acre-feet per year and future needs of 120,000 acre-feet per year. Even with aggressive conservation, these needs cannot be met with the city's existing supplies. Development of additional supplies is necessary.

Another method being pursued to keep water rights in their original area of use is the creation of districts that use tax revenues either to purchase water rights or obtain conservation easements through open-market purchase agreements with owners of farms and ranches. The Lower Arkansas Valley Water Conservancy District is one such entity. The district was inspired by a strong desire of residents of the Arkansas Valley to tax themselves in order to allow for purchase and conservation of native water supplies. This district, and others like it, are governed by publicly accountable boards of directors who use funds generated from a mill levy to conserve and protect water supplies for use within the Arkansas basin. Conservation easements on water rights were expressly recognized in legislation adopted in 2003. The models of land based conservation organizations have been successfully adopted for these districts.

Water reuse is also a growing trend. For water supplies that can be used more than once under Colorado's water laws, many entities are looking at building reuse plants also known as recycling plants. Denver, for example, has invested in a large reuse plant just below the Denver Metropolitan area on the South Platte River, which will provide 17,000 acre-feet of recycled water every year after 2004. The cost is $164 million. Denver's reuse plant will serve as the irrigation supply for several city parks, Park Hill, and City Park Golf Courses, and as cooling water for a local power plant. Other recycling facilities are operated by Aurora, Colorado Springs, Westminster, and Louisville.

§ 18.1.5 Education and Awareness Measures

Newcomers to the State of Colorado are often said to believe that water comes from the kitchen tap and food comes from the local supermarket. This is in contrast to Colorado ranchers and farmers who understand the production of food from Colorado's agricultural lands and the development of water through complex and expensive water supply projects. Numerous legislative efforts have sought to educate users, many who have moved to Colorado in the last decade. The Colorado Foundation for Water Education, a non-profit organization, was founded in 2002 to promote a better understanding of water issues. The foundation provides user guides and citizen information through publications, workshops, and other materials. The Colorado legislature initially helped fund the foundation. Federal agencies permitting new water development projects have also required, as permit conditions, water education programs in an effort to heighten awareness of water use and promote conservation efforts.

§ 18.1.6 Resource Development and Planning Requirements

One of the new catch phrases of the water supply world is "integrated resource plans." While not uniform in content, these plans typically involve a detailed evaluation of current water use, future needs (typically over a 20-year period), and alternatives for how those needs will be met. They integrate water conservation and efficiency measures. Generally accepted measures of water demand for certain categories of uses, for example, industrial, domestic, and commercial are used. These plans are largely completed for sophisticated water departments in larger cities and towns. We anticipate that smaller entities that have not had the resources to engage in this type of planning will be required to do so in the future. Public participation through public hearings and written comments is typically a part of the development of these plans, providing an opportunity for interest groups and members of the public to influence the development of future water supplies throughout the State of Colorado.

§ 18.2   FEDERAL ISSUES

§ 18.2.1   Forest Service Bypass Flow Requirements

Since approximately 1990, the Forest Service has attempted to use federal land use permitting authority to require that owners of existing water supply facilities located on National Forest lands relinquish a part of the water supply that would otherwise be provided from these facilities. While the current controversy originated in Colorado, information provided to a congressional task force convened in 1997 revealed that related conflicts with the Forest Service exist in other states in the West, including Montana, Arizona, Idaho, and Nevada.[1] In the closing months of the Clinton Administration, the Forest Service once again announced its intent to require water "bypass flows" for existing water facilities.[2] Most recently, litigation in Colorado and Washington federal courts has considered the issue in varying contexts.

As described in Section 11.3.2, NFMA required the Forest Service to adopt formal land and resource management plans, or forest plans, to guide the management of each individual forest. Standards and guidelines in those forest plans include direction concerning the issuance of land-use authorizations by the Forest Service for a variety of uses, including water facilities. Some of the forest plans issued by the agency assert a right to require the owners of water facilities to bypass, or not divert into the facility, a portion of the water historically diverted.

---

[1]   Report of the Federal Water Rights Task Force Created Pursuant to Section 389(d)(3) of P.L. 104-127 at I-1 to I-2 (1997), *available at* http://www.fs.fed.us/land/water.

[2]   USDA Forest Service, WATER FOR THE NATIONAL FORESTS AND GRASSLANDS: INSTREAM FLOW PROTECTION STRATEGIES FOR THE 21ST CENTURY at 2 (2000).

A recent decision in the Ninth Circuit Court, which upheld the agency's imposition of bypass flows in renewed special-use authorizations in order to avoid jeopardizing the continued existence of endangered fish in the area, likely will prompt the Forest Service to seek such flows from many other water users.[3]

Water users whose facilities divert water on or across federal lands should review the nature of the land-use authorization for their facility, as some of the oldest such authorizations should insulate the facility from the loss of water yield that typically attends a bypass flow requirement.[4] For those authorizations that are subject to renewal, a facility owner should consider alternatives to bypass flow requirements, such as donation agreements with the CWCB or reservoir release agreements with other water users that an owner could offer in lieu of such requirements.[5]

§ 18.2.2 Federal Reserved Water Right Claims

The federal/state conflict over federal claims to water within the state of Colorado has a long and tumultuous history. The basis for Federal claims is discussed in Section 3.4.8. The breadth and priority of those claims have been played out in long and hard-fought trials regarding both the Colorado River and the South Platte River, and a complicated settlement concerning the Rio Grande basin. The federal government has been joined in general adjudications of water rights in Colorado's seven river basins, and most claims have been resolved. The few that remain in dispute are Forest Service claims in Water Division 7, involving the Las Animas, La Plata, San Juan, Rio Piedra, Los Pinos, Rio Mancos, and portions of the Dolores Rivers. A claim for the Colorado National Monument has been asserted but is not as controversial as prior federal claims as it is not on the main stem of the Colorado River.

Claims to flows in the Black Canyon of the Gunnison National Monument were also recently settled, although litigation challenging the settlement followed closely

---

3   *Okanogan County v. Nat'l Marine Fisheries Serv.*, 347 F.3d 1081 (9th Cir. 2003). *See also, Trout Unlimited v. U.S. Dept. of Agric.*, ____ U.S. Dist. LEXIS ____, C.A. No. 96-WY-2686-WD (Colo. Apr. 30, 2004).

4   Michael Browning, *The Ditch Bill Deadline Approaches*, 24 COLO. LAW. No. 7, p. 1569 (1995); James Witwer, *The Renewal of Authorizations to Divert Water on National Forests*, 24 COLO. LAW. No. 10, p. 2363 (1995); Peter Fleming, *Vested Pre-FLPMA Rights of Way for Water Conveyance Facilities*, 25 COLO. LAW. No. 2, p. 83 (1996); *but see Western Watersheds Project v. Matejko*, ____ U.S. Dist. LEXIS ____, Civ. No. 01-0259-E-BLW (D. Idaho Mar. 23, 2004) (agency decision-making concerning pre-FLPMA rights-of-way subject to ESA Section 7 consultation requirement).

5   USDA Forest Service, WATER FOR THE NATIONAL FORESTS AND GRASSLANDS: INSTREAM FLOW PROTECTION STRATEGIES FOR THE 21ST CENTURY at 2 (2000).

thereafter. In that litigation, environmental advocates argue that the U.S. Department of Interior did not adequately protect the characteristics of the monument by claiming too little water in resolving these claims.

Colorado and other western states are highly impacted by these federal claims due to the large amount of land ownership and connected water right claims within the western states. Approximately one-third of the state of Colorado is owned by the United States through its various departments.

§ 18.2.3 Endangered Species Act

Scores of articles have been written on highly controversial impacts of the ESA on water use throughout the West. For example, the clash between farmers and federal authorities on the Klamath River in Oregon during the summer of 2002, and the impact of ESA requirements in the Middle Rio Grande for the benefit of a desert fish, the silvery minnow, in the summer of 2003, have been widely analyzed and discussed. While future ESA impacts are not known, it is our opinion that there will be many.

ESA requirements that impact water development are described in Section 11.2. As a result of those requirements, we expect increased activity both with regard to designation of critical habitat in Colorado, as well as future efforts to develop habitat conservation plans (as discussed in Section 11.2.3 of this book). The reason we expect these activities is that endangered species compliance and obligations will go hand-in-hand with the desire to develop new water projects that are vitally necessary to sustain the growing population in Colorado. The scientific side of the ESA, which comes into play as federal biologists and other scientists determine the impacts of water development actions or the extent of critical habitat needed to sustain the species, will also continue to be highly controversial. A call for peer-reviewed science to support the opinions of the FWS that affect water rights has been advocated by members of Congress as well as in the published journal writing of many ESA critiques. The National Academy of Science and other highly regarded scientific groups have been requested, in some instances by Congress, to review the opinions and bases for the actions of the FWS when making these critical determinations of limitations on water rights and water development in order to protect listed species.

Colorado has developed its own recovery implementation program, which seeks to protect and recover species at the state level.[6] In developing this expertise, Colorado will have more tools at its disposal to critically review the work of federal biologists and other scientists engaged by the FWS as they carry out their mission

---

6   C.R.S. §§ 33-2-101 to 33-2-107.

under the ESA. In 1998, Colorado created the Species Conservation Trust Fund and appropriated $10,000,000 to the fund.[7] The fund is under the authority of the Division of Wildlife to develop programs to conserve species that could become endangered or threatened under state or federal law. Unfortunately, due to Colorado's budget crisis, the fund has now been emptied.

As this book goes to print, the ESA is being celebrated for 30 years of existence with both acclaim from the environmental community and calls for reform to alleviate the recent clashes seen as a result of the Act. One area of potential reform is for compensation to be paid to parties whose settled expectations to water rights and water use are sometimes severely impacted by protections to species. The Federal Court of Claims recently issued an opinion[8] concluding that water users whose water was taken for benefit of endangered species were entitled to compensation under the Fifth Amendment of the Constitution. The court reasoned that the water right was a property right that rose to the level for which compensation is required. We expect to see increasing claims for compensation as a result of this decision. Some commentators have opined that if the courts award compensation, federal agencies will temper their desire for protection of species due to budgetary constraints.

§ 18.2.4   U.S. Department of Interior—Water 2025

Colorado and the entire West are facing a serious water crisis. In the long run, we will not have enough water to meet the fast-growing needs of city residents, farmers, ranchers, Native Americans, recreational users, and wildlife. The demand is increasing; the supply is not. In the face of this realization, the U.S. Department of Interior launched its Water 2025 effort with a press conference in Denver in the summer of 2003.

Water 2025 is a problem-solving initiative that seeks to manage scarce water resources and develop partnerships to both protect the environment and sustain the economy. Water 2025 encourages voluntary water banks and other market-based measures, improvements in technology for water conservation and efficiency, and removal of institutional barriers to increased cooperation in the use of water and water facilities among federal, state, local, tribal, and private organizations.

The Denver meeting was the first of a series of conferences aimed at developing a dialogue on means of preventing the chronic water supply problems facing many

---

[7]   C.R.S. § 24-33-111.

[8]   *Tulare Lake Basin Water Storage Dist. v. United States*, 49 Fed. Cl. 313 (2001) *judgment entered*, 59 Fed. Cl. 246 (2003).

communities in the coming decades. The goal is to identify the watersheds facing the greatest potential risk in the next 25 years, evaluate the most effective ways of addressing water supply challenges, and recommend cooperative planning approaches and tools that have the most likelihood of success. President Bush's 2004 budget contained an initial investment of $11 million for such efforts, and the 2005 budget allocates $20 million for this effort.

Significant amounts of water can be conserved by modernizing water storage and delivery systems, working with state and local partners to improve water management with new technology, and targeting technical and financial assistance to help farmers, ranchers, and municipalities make more efficient use of their irrigation and drinking water. Water 2025 also proposes spurring research and concentrating investment in critically needed areas, such as reducing the cost of desalinating sea water and impaired inland water, and providing a more affordable water source for some coastal communities and rural and tribal communities.

§ 18.2.5 Wilderness Water Rights

In creating the Wilderness Act of 1964 and designating wilderness in Colorado and other western states, Congress left a huge ambiguity in the law—did the wilderness reservation include water rights or did it not?[9] This is critical to water users, because if they are reserved, no reservoirs or diversions can be constructed in these areas. Those parties holding conditional water rights in these areas are doubly concerned about this possibility.

Congress did not provide for water rights on the wilderness lands but courts thereafter were left to ponder if the Act included water reservations by implication.[10] Due to the disputes brought about by the vague language of the Wilderness Act, all wilderness designated after these fights over implied reservations in Colorado have carried express language carefully negotiated to address water rights. For example, Congress in the Holy Cross Wilderness designation stated that:

> *Provided,* That no right, or claim of right, to the diversion and use of existing conditional water rights for the Homestake Water Development project by the cities of Aurora and Colorado Springs shall be prejudiced, expanded, diminished, altered, or affected by this

---

9   78 Stat. 890, 16 U.S.C. §§ 1131 to 1136.

10   National Wilderness Preservation System, 16 U.S.C. 1131 (1964); *Sierra Club v. Block,* 622 F. Supp. 842 (D. Colo. 1985).

Act. Nothing in this Act shall be construed to expand, abate, impair, impede, or interfere with the construction, maintenance or repair of said project, nor the operation thereof, or any exchange or modification of the same agreed to by the cities and the United States, acting through any appropriate agency thereof.[11]

Of more current concern are lands nominated as wilderness but not designated. The managing agency is administratively charged with management of the nominated lands to protect wilderness characteristics until a decision is made by Congress. Decisions are not made for decades as the political process drags. No water rights development occurs on these lands during this time.

---

[11]   Public Law 96-560 § 102(a)(5) (Dec. 22, 1980).

APPENDIX

When landowners, lenders, and government officials are confronted with issues concerning water, people often ask from whom, where, when, how much, and how long it will take to acquire water or water rights. Knowing who to contact and what is required in the early stages of acquiring water or water rights or resolving issues concerning water can often save time and money. Most federal, state, and local agencies now have very informative Web sites to assist those in need of this kind of information. These resources are not a substitute for sound legal advice. However, these Web sites can be useful to locate the correct government agency or court, narrow issues, and develop a plan to acquire water.

§ 1   ADDITIONAL RESOURCES

This section contains contact information for various state, federal, and local agencies that are important in water issues:

§ 1.1   STATE AGENCIES

Finding the Appropriate State Agency

State of Colorado – http://www.colorado.gov

The State of Colorado Web site includes links to all state agencies and regulatory divisions. Each division and agency has its own Web site. The sites below are particularly useful when acquiring or securing water rights and can be accessed through the State of Colorado Web site or each individual agency Web site. In addition, this Web site provides links to county and local government Web sites.

Water Court Information

Colorado Judicial Branch – http://www.courts.state.co.us

A link to the seven Colorado Water Courts can be found on this Web site. Each water division provides the names and addresses of the Judges and Court Clerks for each division. The individual water court Web sites usually post the abandonment list and also have the most recent water résumés, and an archive of résumés dating back to 1999.

Many of the divisions of the water court will post significant decisions from that court. Decisions from the Colorado Supreme Court and the Court of Appeals are posted weekly, and can be accessed through this Web site.

Finding Current Legislation

Colorado General Assembly Home Page – http://www.leg.state.co.us

This Web site includes links to the Colorado House and Senate, bills, legislative directory and general legislative resources. The Colorado Revised Statutes are available on this Web site.

Locating Water Records and Water Forms

Colorado Division of Water Resources – http://www.water.state.co.us
1313 Sherman Street
Room 818
Denver, Colorado 80203
(303) 866-3581

The Division of Water Resources, also known as the Office of the State Engineer, is the agency of the State of Colorado that operates under the direction of specific state statutes to administer water rights pursuant to court decrees and interstate compacts. The State Engineer records section has copies of all water right decrees, well permits, and ditch diversion records. The records section is generally open to the public on weekdays between 10:00 a.m. and 3:00 p.m. Between the hours of 9:00 a.m. and 4:00 p.m. the State Engineer staffs a ground water information telephone line at (303) 866-3587 and a records information telephone line at (303) 866-3447. In addition, the State Engineer has a Web site that includes links to water right application forms from the water court and well permit forms from the State Engineer. Standardized forms with instructions on this Web site:

(1) Application for Water Right (Surface) (JDF 296W).

(2) Application for Water Storage Right (JDF 297W).

(3) Application for Underground Water Right (JDF 298W).

(4) Application for Change of Water Right (JDF 299W).

(5) Application for Finding of Diligence or to Make Absolute (JDF 300W).

(6) Application for Approval of Plan for Augmentation (JDF 301W).

(7) Pleading In Protest/In Support (JDF302W).

(8) Statement of Opposition (JDF303W).

(9) Protest to Revised Abandonment List (JDF304W).

Well permit forms that are filed directly with the State Engineer are also on this Web site. Forms that are frequently used include:

(1) Registration of Existing Well (GWS-12 used for wells constructed prior to 1965).

(2) Application for Well Location Amendment (GWS-42).

(3) Residential Water Well Permit Application (GWS 44 for "exempt" wells; see Section 4.2.4).

(4) General Purpose Water Well Permit Application (GWS 45 used for construction of new well or enlargement of use of existing well).

This Web site also provides information on surface flow data and river calls, and briefly explains the priority system in Colorado. Guidelines on filing substitute water supply plans, lining of storage ponds, and ground water well permitting are also available.

To find the names and telephone numbers of the Division Engineers, click on the Colorado Division of Water Resources Web site at the "About DWR" icon and a list of "Contacts" for the Division Engineers appears.

Keeping Current with Water Quality Developments

Colorado Water Quality Control Commission –
http://www.cdphe.state.co.us/op/wqcc/wqcchom.asp
4300 Cherry Creek Drive South
Denver, CO 80246
(303) 692-3469

The Colorado Water Quality Control Commission develops state water quality policies and sets water quality standards and regulations for surface and ground waters. The Commission Web site has a multi-year schedule of meetings and hearings, water quality classifications and standards review, and notices of rulemaking hearings on water quality rules and basic standards.

Finding the Right Water Quality Permitting Instructions and Forms

Colorado Water Quality Control Division – http://www.cdphe.state.co.us/wq
4300 Cherry Creek Drive South
Denver, CO 80246
(303) 692-3500

The Water Quality Control Division regulates the discharge of pollutants into the state's surface and ground waters and enforces the Colorado Primary Drinking Water

Regulations. See Section 11.1.2. Water quality regulations and permitting instructions and forms are available on this Web site. Schedules and notices of upcoming Water Quality Control Commission meetings and hearings are also available.

Source of Information on Water Supply Conservation and Drought Planning

Colorado Water Conservation Board – http://www.cwcb.state.co.us
1313 Sherman Street
Room 721
Denver, Colorado 80203
(303) 866-3441

The Colorado Water Conservation Board is the state executive branch agency responsible for state water policy and planning that oversees programs including water supply protection, water supply planning and finance, conservation, and drought planning. See Section 3.4.1. Information on the various programs is on the CWCB Web site. The Board meets every other month and posts the meeting agendas on its Web site.

Finding Corporate and Partnership Entities

Colorado Secretary of State – http://www.sos.state.co.us
1560 Broadway
Suite 200
Denver, Colorado 80202
(303) 894-2200 (Business Division)

This Web site can be useful when trying to locate the articles of incorporation of ditch companies, and the officers and directors of these companies. However, ditch companies are not required to file annual reports, and much of the information on file is dated. If you cannot find the name of the current secretary of a particular ditch company on this Web site, try contacting the Division Engineer or water commissioner in the respective water district where the ditch is located.

§ 1.2   FEDERAL AGENCIES

Public Lands and Federal Jurisdiction

U.S. Department of Interior – http://www.doi.gov

The following agencies are managed under the Department of Interior: Bureau of Reclamation, Mineral Management Service, National Park Service, Fish and Wildlife

Service, Bureau of Indian Affairs, Bureau of Land Management, Geological Survey, and the Office of Surface Mining. Links to each agency can be accessed through the Department of Interior Web site.

Federal Water Projects

U.S. Bureau of Reclamation – http://www.usbr.gov
Upper Colorado Regional Office
125 South State Street, Room 6107
Salt Lake City, Utah 84138
(801) 524-3600 (Regional Director Office)

Great Plains Regional Office
P.O. Box 36900
Billings, Montana 59107
(406) 247-7600 (Regional Director Office)

The U.S. Bureau of Reclamation manages the delivery of water in the West and the generation of electricity. See Chapter 14. Information on water operations within Reclamation is generally divided by regions within the West. Two regional offices, the Great Plains Region and the Upper Colorado Region, oversee water operations in Colorado. The links to the regional Web sites provide current reservoir data, snow-pack measurements, stream gage information, and other water supply information.

Determining Federal Land Status, Information Regarding Public Lands

U.S. Bureau of Land Management – http://www.blm.gov
BLM Colorado State Office
2850 Youngfield Street
Lakewood, Colorado 80215
(303) 239-3600

The U.S. Bureau of Land Management (BLM) administers 261 million surface acres and about 300 million additional acres of subsurface mineral resources of public lands located primarily in the 12 western states. The Web site has links to each state BLM office and contains information on recreation, resource management, NEPA review status, and resource management plans. Each BLM state office includes microfilm copies of master title plats, oil and gas plats, and land and mineral patents. Initial transfer of land titles from the federal government to individuals is currently being added to the Web site: http://www.glorecords.blm.gov. This site does not currently contain every federal land title record issued, but is a good starting point prior to researching the records at the state BLM office.

Answering Questions About Endangered Species

U.S. Fish and Wildlife Service – http://www.fws.gov
Mountain-Prairie Region Office
134 Union Boulevard
Lakewood, CO 80228
(303) 236-7920 (Office of the Regional Director)

Often other regulatory issues, such as endangered species mitigation (see Section 11.2), must be addressed when acquiring or securing water rights. This Web site has extensive information regarding endangered species, habitat protection, and permitting. Information on the status of the Preble's meadow jumping mouse habitat protection can be found at http://www.r6.fws.gov/preble/.

Information on Current Water Conditions

U.S. Geological Survey – http://www.usgs.gov
Water Resources Division
Colorado District
Denver Federal Center, MS-415
Building 53
Lakewood, CO 80225
(303) 236-4882

The U.S. Geological Survey (USGS) provides information on floods, drought, daily stream flow, and ground water data. Water information by state is summarized on the USGS Web site. Current and historical water information, including real-time surface water conditions, ground water and water-quality data, hydrologic studies, and map-based orientation to water resource studies and data collection sites are on the USGS Web site.

Information on the National Forests

U.S. Department of Agriculture
U.S. Forest Service – http://www.fs.fed.us
Rocky Mountain Region – http://www.fs.fed.us/r2/
P.O. Box 25127
Lakewood, Colorado 80225-0125
(303) 275-5350

The U.S. Forest Service, Rocky Mountain Region, manages 17 national forests and seven national grasslands throughout Colorado, Kansas, Nebraska, South Dakota, and Wyoming. Information regarding forest plans, current and proposed projects for watershed restoration, habitat improvement, recreation sites, and roads within the national forests is summarized on this Web site.

Information on Discharges of Dredge and Fill Material (404 Permits)

U.S. Army Corps of Engineers – http://www.usace.army.mil

In Colorado, there are five different U.S. Army Corps of Engineers (Corps) District regulatory field offices:

Denver Regulatory Office
Omaha District
9307 South Wadsworth Boulevard
Littleton, Colorado 80128
(303) 979-0602

Includes the following counties: Adams, Arapahoe, Boulder, Clear Creek, Denver, Douglas, Elbert, Gilpin, Jackson, Jefferson, Kit Carson, Larimer, Logan, Morgan, Park, Phillips, Sedgwick, Washington, Weld, Yuma, East ½ of Cheyenne, North ¼ of Lincoln, North ½ of Teller.

Southern Colorado Regulatory Office
Albuquerque District
720 Main Street, Suite 205
Pueblo, CO 81003
(719) 543-9459

Includes the following counties: Alamosa, Baca, Bent, Chaffee, West ½ of Cheyenne, Costilla, Crowley, Custer, Elbert, El Paso, Fremont, Huerfano, Kiowa, Lake, Lincoln, Las Animas, Otero, Prowers, Pueblo, South ½ of Teller.

Western Colorado Regulatory Office
Sacramento District
402 Rood Avenue, Room 142
Grand Junction, CO 81501
(970) 243-1199

Includes the following counties: Delta, Eagle, Garfield, Gunnison, Hinsdale, Mesa, Moffat, Montrose, Ouray, Pitkin, Rio Blanco, San Miguel, Northwest ¼ of Saguache.

Frisco Regulatory Office
Sacramento District
301 West Main, Suite 202
P.O. Box 607
Frisco, CO 80443-0606
(970) 668-9676

Includes the following counties: Grand, Routt and Summit.

Durango Regulatory Office
Sacramento/Albuquerque Districts
278 Sawyer Drive, Suite 1
Durango, CO 81303
(970) 375-9452 (Sacramento District)
(970) 375-9509 (Albuquerque District)

Counties within the Sacramento District:

Archuleta, Dolores, La Plata, South ½ of Hinsdale, South ½ of Mineral, Montezuma, San Juan.

Counties within the Albuquerque District: Conejos, Hinsdale, Mineral, Rio Grande, Saguache.

Anyone proposing to discharge dredged or fill material into waters of the United States is required to obtain a permit from the Corps under Section 404 of the Clean Water Act. See Section 11.1.3. The Corps' Web site provides links to wetlands and waterway regulations and permitting procedures, current regulatory guidance letters, applicable Code of Federal Regulations sections, and presidential directives and executive orders.

§ 1.3   LOCAL WATER AGENCIES

Know Your Local Water Agency

Colorado River Water Conservation District – http://www.crwcd.gov
P.O. Box 1120
Glenwood Springs, CO 81602
(970) 945-8522

The Colorado River Water Conservation District (River District) is a public water policy agency chartered by the Colorado General Assembly in 1937 for the conservation, use, and development of the water resources of the Colorado River and its principal tributaries. The River District is comprised of 15 West Slope Counties.

The River District Web site features current hydrologic/drought conditions, and reports and summaries of issues affecting west slope water interests.

Southwestern Water Conservation District – http://www.waterinfo.org
841 Second Avenue
Durango, Colorado 81301
(303) 247-1302

The Southwestern Water Conservation District (Southwestern District) was created in 1941. The Southwestern District serves La Plata, Montezuma, Archuleta, San Juan, San Miguel, Dolores, and parts of Montrose, Hinsdale, and Mineral counties. Among the tasks that the Southwestern District oversees is surveying existing water resources and basin rivers, constructing water reservoirs, entering into contracts with other water agencies, and organizing special assessment districts (water conservancy districts) for purposes of storing, managing and allocating water for various rivers in southwest Colorado.

Rio Grande Water Conservation District – (Web site currently not available)
10900 Highway 160 East
Alamosa, Colorado 81101
(719) 589-6301

The Rio Grande Water Conservation District (Rio Grand District) was created in 1967 to promote the conservation of the water of the Rio Grande and its tributaries for beneficial use and the construction of reservoirs, ditches, and works for the conservation, use, and development of the water resources of the Rio Grande and its tributaries. The Rio Grande District covers Alamosa, Conejos, Rio Grande, and portions of Mineral and Saguache counties.

Northern Colorado Water Conservancy District – http://www.ncwcd.org
220 Water Avenue
Berthoud, Colorado 80513
(970) 532-7700

The Northern Colorado Water Conservancy District (Northern) is a public agency created in 1937 that provides water for agricultural, municipal, and domestic uses in northeastern Colorado. Northern was established as the local agency to contract with the United States to build the Colorado-Big Thompson (C-BT) Project. The Northern Web site features water projects, precipitation reports, irrigation management data, and C-BT Project rental water information.

Southeastern Colorado Water Conservancy District – http://www.secwcd.org
31717 United Avenue
Pueblo, Colorado 81001
(719) 948-2400

The Southeastern Colorado Water Conservancy District (Southeastern District) was created in 1958 for the purpose of developing and administering the Frying Pan-Arkansas Project. The Southeastern District extends along the Arkansas River from Buena Vista to Lamar, and along Fountain Creek from Colorado Springs to Pueblo, Colorado. The Southeastern District Web site provides information on water supply within the district, description of facilities, meeting notices, and a link to the Arkansas River Water Bank Program.

Answering Other Questions

§ 1.4   OTHER RESOURCES

Colorado Foundation for Water Education – http://www.cfwe.org
1580 Logan Street, Suite 410
Denver CO 80203
(303) 377-4433

This is a non-profit organization providing water resource information and educational opportunities regarding water. The Web site posts upcoming seminars and conferences regarding water issues, recent published articles regarding water, and links to state water agencies.

Colorado Water Congress – http://www.cowatercongress.org
1580 Logan Street, Suite 400
Denver, Colorado 80203
(303) 837-0812

Established in 1958 to protect, conserve, and develop Colorado's water resources, the Colorado Water Congress promotes the wise management and stewardship of the State of Colorado's water resources. The Colorado Water Congress advocates positions on water policy in state and federal water-related legislation.

Colorado Bar Association – http://www.cobar.org
600 17th Street, Suite 520-S
Denver, CO 80202
(303) 893-8094.

This Web site is useful to locate a lawyer who is identified as practicing water law, and to gain access to recent Colorado Supreme Court and Colorado Court of Appeals decisions.

Colorado Water Trust – http://www.coloradowatertrust.org
P.O. Box 9386
Denver, CO 80209
(720) 570-2897

The Colorado Water Trust is "a private, non-profit conservation organization, which acquires, or assists others in acquiring, water rights or interests in water rights, using voluntary approaches from willing owners, for conservation benefits."

Ditch and Reservoir Company Alliance – http://www.darca.org
4307 Highway 66
Longmont, CO, 80504
(970) 535-0690

This organization was formed to serve Colorado's mutual ditch and reservoir companies, irrigation districts, incorporated laterals, and private ditches. The Web site includes information regarding current regulatory developments, legislative information, and issues important to ditch and reservoir companies.

National Water Resources Association – http://www.nwra.org
3800 North Fairfax Drive, Suite 4
Arlington, VA 22203
(703) 524-1544

NWRA is a nonprofit federation of state organizations whose membership includes rural water districts, municipal water entities, commercial companies, and individuals. The National Water Resources Association promotes the protection, management, development, and beneficial use of water resources on a national scale.

PACER (Public Access to Court Electronic Records) –
http://www.pacer.psc.uscourts.gov

Although most federal courts are on the Internet, this is an electronic public access database that allows users to obtain case and docket information from federal appellate, district, and bankruptcy courts and from the U.S. Party/Case index. Registration and a small fee are required.

§ 1.5   PROFESSIONAL RESOURCES

Finding a Water Attorney

The Colorado Bar Association (CBA) Web site (http://www.cobar.org) at the "Find a Lawyer" icon is a quick and easy way to locate a lawyer. By limiting the practice area to water law in the search engine, the results will provide a list of attorneys who are members of the CBA and who identify themselves as practicing water law. Similarly, the Martindale-Hubbell Web site (http://www.martindale.com) provides a private lawyer locator/search engine. Unfortunately, the searchable areas of practice do not include water law. On the other hand, Martindale-Hubbell does provide a lawyer rating service (based upon confidential opinions of other lawyers and judges). To evaluate the expertise of an attorney thus may require visiting both Web sites, checking client references, or other methods. Members of the public may also wish to review a CBA brochure entitled "How to Choose a Lawyer," which is available on the Web site.

Finding a Water Engineer

Usually most water attorneys can recommend a qualified hydrologist or water engineer. The American Council of Engineering Companies of Colorado, (303) 832-2200 or http://www.acec-co.org, is an organization of professional consulting engineering firms engaged in the private practice of engineering. Click on the "firm search" icon and select the search by discipline menu.

§ 2   BIBLIOGRAPHY

Citizen's Guide to Colorado Water Law, by Justice Gregory J. Hobbs, Jr. (2004).
Well written overview of Colorado water and water law at a much more general level than this book, by a sitting Supreme Court Justice. Available from the Colorado Foundation for Water Education.

Citizen's Guide to Colorado Water Quality Protection, by Paul D. Frohardt (2003).
Useful and generally more detailed summary of federal and state water quality laws than this book, by attorney and long-time Administrator of the Water Quality Control Commission. Available from the Colorado Foundation for Water Education.

Vranesh's Colorado Water Law, James N. Corbridge, Teresa A. Rice, Stuart B. Corbridge (2001).
The legal treatise on Colorado water law by C.U. law professor emeritus and water law textbook author. Updated annually. University Press of Colorado.

Water Law in a Nutshell, David H. Getches (1997).
One of West's nutshell series for lawyers and law students, providing an overview of the black letter law by C.U. law school dean, water law professor, and water law textbook author. Last update 1996. West Publishing.

GLOSSARY

Abandonment. Loss of whole or part of a water right by intent to permanently discontinue use. By statute, a period of non-use for ten years raises a rebuttable presumption of abandonment. A conditional water right is conclusively presumed to be abandoned if an application for finding of reasonable diligence is not made within six years of the entry of the conditional decree or the most recent diligence decree. The State Engineer prepares a periodic abandonment list. Water rights are declared abandoned through a water court proceeding.

Absolute Water Right. A term often used to describe a water right under which water has been fully diverted and applied to beneficial use so that the water right is no longer a conditional water right, to distinguish it from a conditional water right.

Acre-Foot. Volumetric measurement of water used for quantifying reservoir storage capacity and historic consumptive use and for other purposes. This is the amount of water that will cover an acre of land at a depth of one foot, or 325,851 gallons of water.

Adjudication. The process for obtaining a water court decree for an absolute water right, a conditional water right, a finding of reasonable diligence, an exchange, an augmentation plan, a change of water right, or a right to withdraw non-tributary water or Denver Basin ground water that is outside of a designated ground water basin.

Alluvial Water. Ground water that is hydrologically part of a natural surface stream system.

Ambient Water Quality. The existing quality of water in the environment, such as in a stream, lake, or reservoir.

Antidegradation. Provisions intended to protect the existing quality of a water body.

Appropriate (verb). To take the legal actions necessary to create a right to take water from a natural stream or aquifer for application to beneficial use.

Appropriation. Placement of a specified portion of the waters of the state to a beneficial use pursuant to the procedures prescribed by law. Only previously unappropriated surface water or tributary ground water can be appropriated. The appropriator must have a plan to divert, store, or otherwise capture, possess, and control the water for beneficial use.

Aquifer. A subsurface water-bearing geological structure capable of storing and yielding water to streams, springs, or wells.

Augmentation. Replacing the quantity of water depleted from the stream system by an out-of-priority diversion. When adjudicated and operated to replace depletions to the stream system, the out-of-priority diversion may continue even though a call has been placed on the stream by senior decreed rights.

Augmentation Plan. A court-approved plan that allows a water user to divert water out of priority so long as adequate replacement is made to the affected stream system and water rights in quantities and at times so as to prevent injury to the water rights of other users.

Augmentation Source. The supply of water used to replace depletions in an augmentation plan.

Beneficial Use. Beneficial use is the basis, measure, and limit of a water right. Colorado law broadly defines beneficial use of water as a lawful appropriation that uses reasonably efficient practices to put that water to use without waste.

Best Management Practices or BMP. Structural and/or management techniques determined to be the most effective practices for controlling nonpoint sources of pollution.

Bureau of Land Management or BLM. Federal agency within the U.S. Department of Interior that manages most public lands in Colorado that are not national forests.

Bureau of Reclamation/USBR/BOR/BurRec. Federal water development agency within the U.S. Department of Interior.

Bypass Flow. Water that is allowed to flow past a diversion structure or storage facility.

Call. Demand for administration of water rights. In times of water shortage, the owner of a decreed water right will make a "call" for water. The call results in shut down orders against undecreed water uses and decreed junior water rights as necessary to fill the beneficial use need of the decreed senior calling right.

Clean Water Act or CWA. Federal law enacted in 1972 to restore and maintain the chemical, physical, and biological integrity of the nation's waters.

Colorado Department of Natural Resources or DNR. State department with overall responsibility for water resources development and administration.

Colorado Department of Public Health and Environment or CDPHE. State department with overall responsibility for water quality, including drinking water and wastewater.

Colorado Revised Statutes or C.R.S. The annual compilation of Colorado statutes and court rules published by the Colorado General Assembly.

Colorado Water Conservation Board or CWCB. State agency created to aid and protect the development of water for the benefit of present and future residents.

Colorado Water and Power Development Authority or CWPDA. State agency created to fund water development, including water projects, drinking water treatment plants, and wastewater treatment plants.

Compact. A formal agreement between states and approved by the United States Congress concerning the use of water in a river or stream that flows across state boundaries.

Compact Call. The requirement that an upstream state cease or curtail diversions of water from the river system that is the subject of the compact to satisfy the downstream state's compact entitlements.

Conditional Water Right. A right to perfect a water right with a certain priority upon the completion, with reasonable diligence, of the appropriation upon which such water right is to be based.

Conjunctive Use. Coordinated use of surface and ground water supplies to meet demand so that both sources are used more efficiently.

Conservation. Obtaining the benefits of water more efficiently, resulting in reduced demand for water. Sometimes called "end-use efficiency" or "demand management."

Consumptive Use. The amount of water used up by application of that water to beneficial use. Examples include: water for drinking and water taken up by growing crops.

Continental Divide. An imaginary boundary line that runs north to south through the Rocky Mountains, separating rivers that flow west to the Pacific Ocean from those that flow south and east toward the Gulf of Mexico and the Atlantic Ocean.

Cubic Feet Per Second (cfs). Measurement of flow rate of water in a running stream or taken as a direct diversion from the stream. Water flowing at one cfs will deliver 448.8 gallons per minute or 648,000 gallons per day.

Cumulative Impact Analysis. A review of the cumulative environmental, social, and economic impacts of proposed water projects and activities associated with development within an ecosystem or drainage area.

Denver Basin. The geographic area overlying the base of the Laramie-Fox Hills Aquifer, the deepest of the Denver Basin Aquifers, as shown in the Denver Basin Atlas contained in The Denver Basin Rules, 2 C.C.R. 402-6, adopted by the Colorado Division of Water Resources. The Denver Basin generally includes the Denver metropolitan area, extending to the foothills in the west, almost to Greeley in the north, almost to Colorado Springs in the south, and close to Limon in the east.

Denver Basin Aquifers. In descending order, the Upper Dawson, Lower Dawson, Denver, Upper Arapahoe, Lower Arapahoe, and Laramie-Fox Hills Aquifers underlying the Denver Basin.

Denver Basin Ground Water. Ground water of the Dawson, Denver, Arapahoe, and Laramie-Fox Hills aquifers underlying the Denver Basin outside of any designated ground water basin. This water is allocated to the overlying landowner by statute, administered by rules of the State Engineer, allowing pumping at a rate of one percent per year, assuming a 100-year life of the aquifer and requiring some of the pumped water to be put back into the stream system.

Designated Ground Water. Ground water which in its natural course would not be available to and required for the fulfillment of decreed surface rights, or ground water in areas not adjacent to a continuously flowing natural stream wherein ground water withdrawals have constituted the principal water usage for at least 15 years preceding the date of the first hearing on the proposed designation of the basin, and which in both cases is within the geographic boundaries of a designated ground water basin.

Designated Ground Water Basin. An area established by the Colorado Ground Water Commission as containing designated ground water, which is assumed not to affect the major surface river basin to which the designated basin would otherwise be tributary. Much of eastern Colorado is located within designated basins.

Developed or Imported Water. Water brought into a stream system from another unconnected source, for example, transmountain diversion water or non-tributary well water. This type of water can be reused and successively used to extinction, and is often used in augmentation or exchange plans. In contrast, native basin water is subject to one use, and the return flow belongs to the stream system to fill other appropriations, unless a decree was obtained for the right to reuse and successively use return flows.

Diligence. Reasonable progress toward making a conditional water right absolute by putting unappropriated water to a beneficial use. Must be proved in a water court proceeding through an application initiated every six years after entry of the conditional decree or most recent diligence decree. Acts demonstrating diligence include engineering, permitting, financing, and construction of water facilities needed to complete water diversion and delivery to the place of use.

Direct Flow or Direct Right. Water diverted from a river or stream for use without interruption between diversion and use except for incidental purposes, such as settling or filtration.

Diversion or Divert. Removing water from its natural course or location, or controlling water in its natural course or location, by means of a water structure such as a ditch, pipeline, pump, reservoir, or well. The Colorado Water Conservation Board may appropriate instream flows without diversion, and local governmental agencies may make recreational in-channel diversions, under specified statutory procedures.

Division Engineer. Official appointed by the State Engineer to administer water rights within one of the state's seven water divisions, which generally correspond to major river basins.

Drought. A long period of below-average precipitation.

Duty of Water. The amount of water that through careful management and use, without wastage, is reasonably required to be applied to a tract of land for a length of time that is adequate to produce the maximum amount of the crops that are ordinarily grown there.

Effluent. The water leaving a water or wastewater treatment plant.

Effluent Limits. Limitations on the concentration and/or mass of specific pollutants that a facility is allowed to discharge.

Effluent Exchange. The practice of using wastewater effluent as a replacement source for diversion of water upstream.

Endangered Species Act or ESA. Federal law enacted in 1973 to conserve endangered and threatened species and the ecosystems on which they depend.

Environmental Impact Statement or EIS. Detailed analysis of the impacts of a project on all aspects of the natural environment required by federal National Environmental Policy Act for federal permitting or use of federal lands.

Exchange. A process by which water, under certain conditions, may be diverted out of priority at one point by replacing a like amount of water at a downstream location.

Federal Land Policy Management Act of 1976 or FLPMA. Federal law that requires that public lands be managed under principles of multiple use and sustained yield.

Firm Annual Yield. The yearly amount of water that can be dependably supplied from the raw water sources of a given water supply system for some period of years, usually 50 to 100.

Fish and Wildlife Service or FWS. Federal agency within the U.S. Department of Interior responsible for the protection of threatened and endangered species.

Forest Service or USFS. Federal agency within the U.S. Department of Agriculture that manages the national forests.

Futile Call. Determination made by the State or Division Engineer to lift a shut down order if cessation of diversions by junior decreed water rights will not result in making water available to the senior calling right.

Ground Water. Water located beneath the surface of the earth, typically withdrawn for use through wells.

Headwaters. The small streams, generally in the mountains, that are the sources of a river; the first and smallest tributaries of a river.

Hydrologic Cycle. The movement of water from the atmosphere to the Earth and back again to the atmosphere. The three stages are precipitation, runoff or infiltration, and evaporation.

Injury. The action of another that causes or may cause the holders of decreed water rights to suffer loss of water at the time, place, and amount they would be entitled to use under their water rights if the action had not occurred. Injury is a significant issue in any water court proceeding and in determinations of the State and Division Engineer.

Junior Rights. Water rights that were obtained more recently and therefore are junior in priority to older or more senior rights.

Miner's Inch or Statutory Inch. A measurement of water flow. In Colorado, 38.4 miner's inches is considered equivalent to one cubic foot per second.

National Pollution Discharge Elimination System (NPDES) Permit. A permit required under Section 402 of the Clean Water Act regulating discharge of pollutants into the nation's waterways.

National Environmental Policy Act or NEPA. Federal procedural law enacted in 1969 to ensure federal agencies consider environmental impacts in their decision making.

National Forest Management Act of 1976 or NFMA. Federal law that requires the Forest Service to develop land and resource management plans to provide for multiple use and sustained yield in the national forests.

Non-Consumptive Use. Water drawn for use that is not consumed, such as water diverted for hydroelectric generation. It also includes such uses as boating and fishing, where water is still available for other uses at the same site.

Nonpoint Source. A diffuse source of water pollution, such as general runoff over the land surface; a pollution source that does not meet the definition of a "point source."

Non-Tributary Ground Water. Ground water outside of the boundaries of any designated ground water basin, the withdrawal of which will not, within 100 years, deplete the flow of a natural stream at an annual rate greater than one-tenth of one percent of the annual rate of withdrawal.

Not Non-Tributary Ground Water. Denver Basin ground water, the withdrawal of which will deplete the flow of a natural stream at an annual rate of greater than one-tenth of one percent of the annual rate of withdrawal.

Outstanding Waters. Very high quality surface water that constitutes an outstanding natural resource and which is not allowed to be degraded.

Parshall flume. A specially shaped structure that can be installed in a channel to measure the water flow rate. The flume was developed by Ralph Parshall at Colorado State University early in the last century.

Point Source. A pipe, channel, conduit, or other discrete conveyance from which pollutants are discharged.

Pollutant. Any waste or other contaminant that adversely affects water quality.

Pollution. The man-made or man-induced alteration of the chemical, physical, biological, and radiological integrity of water.

Potable. Water that does not contain pollution, contamination, objectionable minerals, or infective agents and is considered safe for domestic consumption; drinkable.

Prior Appropriation. The water law doctrine that confers priority to use water from natural streams based upon when the water rights were acquired. Water rights in Colorado and other western states are confirmed by court decree; holders of senior rights have first claim to withdraw water over holders who have filed later claims.

Priority. The ranking of a water right vis-á-vis all other water rights drawing on the stream system.

Public Trust Doctrine. A doctrine of state ownership of stream and lake beds that has been applied, most notably in California, to cut back on historic diversions to sustain fish and wildlife habitat and recreation. It has not been recognized in Colorado.

Raw Water. Untreated water.

Reasonable Diligence. The efforts necessary to bring an intent to appropriate water to fruition; actions that demonstrate a good-faith intention to complete a diversion of water within reasonable time.

Reservoir. A structure used to collect and store water, or a tank or cistern used to store potable water.

Return Flow. Water that returns to streams and rivers after it has been applied to beneficial use. It may return as a surface flow, or as an inflow of tributary ground water.

Reuse. To use again, recycle; to intercept, either directly or by exchange, water that would otherwise return to the stream system, for subsequent beneficial use.

Reviewable Waters. Colorado surface waters that have not been designated "outstanding waters" or "use-protected," and which are subject to an antidegradation review before new or increased contamination is allowed.

Riparian. Referring to land or habitat immediately adjacent to the stream channel.

Riparian Rights. Water rights that are acquired based on ownership of the land bordering a source of surface water; the right to put to beneficial use surface water adjacent to one's land. Riparian rights are most common in states east of the Mississippi River and do not exist in Colorado.

Riparian Water Law. A legal system that permits water use only by those who own land along the banks of a stream or lake. The right is for reasonable use and is correlative with the right of every other property owner to prohibit unreasonable use that diminishes the instream quantity or quality of water. Colorado law does not recognize riparian rights.

Run-off. Water that flows on the surface of the Earth into streams, rivers, lakes, and oceans.

State Engineer's Office or SEO. Agency that administers water rights within the Division of Water Resources, Colorado Department of Natural Resources

Spill Water. Water released from a reservoir because the reservoir lacks sufficient storage capacity.

Statute. A law enacted by a legislative body such as the U.S. Congress or the Colorado General Assembly.

Statutory Inch. See Miner's Inch.

Storage. Water held in a reservoir for later use.

Stormwater Runoff. Rainfall or snowmelt that runs off over the land surface, potentially carrying pollutants to streams, lakes, or reservoirs.

Substitute Supply Plan. A State Engineer-approved temporary plan of replacement supply allowing an out-of-priority diversion. The State Engineer may approve substitute water supply plans while a plan for augmentation is pending in water court, for water exchanges, water uses that will not exceed five years, and in limited emergency situations affecting public health or safety.

Surface Water. Water located on the Earth's surface.

Temporary Modification. A temporary relaxation of numerical water quality standards, allowing time for actions to improve water quality and achieve a long-term standard.

Total Maximum Daily Load or TMDL. A calculation of the total amount of pollutants that can be added to a water body from all sources while still meeting water quality standards.

Transbasin Diversion. The conveyance of water from its natural basin into another basin.

Transmountain Diversion. The conveyance of water from one watershed to another, usually from the Western Slope to the Front Range.

Treated Water. Water that has been filtered and disinfected. This term is sometimes used interchangeably with potable water.

Tributary. A stream or river that flows into a larger one.

Tributary Drainage. The area from which water drains by gravity into a water course.

Tributary Ground Water. All subsurface water hydraulically connected to a surface stream, the pumping of which would have a measurable effect on the surface stream within 100 years.

Use Attainability Analysis or (UAA). A structured, scientific assessment of factors that may affect the ability to achieve a particular use of water. The analysis may consider physical, chemical, biological, and economic factors that affect whether a use can be attained.

Use Classification. A formal designation of the uses (aquatic life, recreation, water supply, and agriculture) for which the water quality in a stream, lake, or reservoir will be protected.

Use-Protected Waters. Water bodies that are not subject to antidegradation review, but rather are protected only for their classified uses.

Water Bank. A pilot program operating under rules of the State Engineer in the Arkansas River Basin to facilitate the lease, exchange, or loan of legally stored water as an alternative to sale of water rights, while protecting against injury to other water rights.

Water Commissioner. Official appointed by the Division Engineer to administer water rights in a water district, which generally coincides with a significant watershed, sub-basin, or tributary.

Water Quality Control Commission or WQCC. Appointed board within the Colorado Department of Public Health and Environment that establishes rules and regulations for the protection of water quality within the state.

Water Quality Control Division or WQCD. State agency within the Colorado Department of Public Health and Environment that administers the state's water quality and drinking water programs.

Water Quality Standards. Numerical or narrative criteria that specify allowable water quality conditions in a water body.

Water Right. A right to use, in accordance with its priority, a portion of the waters of the state by reason of the appropriation of the same.

Waters of the State. All surface and underground water in or tributary to all natural streams within the state of Colorado, except for designated ground water.

Watershed. An area from which water drains and contributes to a given point on a stream or river.

Well. Any structure or device used for the purpose or with the effect of obtaining ground water for beneficial use from an aquifer. Every well requires a State Engineer-issued permit.

Wetlands. Areas near the margin between water and land (such as swamps and marshes) that are wet enough to support plant growth typically found in saturated soil conditions.

WATER VOLUME AND
FLOW RATE CONVERSION TABLES

Volume		
Multiply	**By**	**To Obtain**
Acre-Feet (af)	325,850	Gallons, U.S. (gal)
	1,233	Cubic Meters (m3)
Cubic Feet (h3)	7.48	Gallons, U.S. (gal)
	28.3	Liters (l)
Cubic Meters (m3)	35.3	Cubic Feet (h3)
	264	Gallons, U.S. (gal)
	1,000	Liters (l)
Gallons, U.S. (gal)	3.79	Liters (l)
Liters (l)	0.264	Gallons, U.S. (gal)
	1.057	Liquid Quarts (qt)
Million Gallons (mg)	3.07	Acre-Feet (af)

Flow Rate		
Multiply	**By**	**To Obtain**
Acre-Feet (af)	.0362	Million Gallons/Day (mgf)
Cubic Feet/Second (cfs)	1.983	Acre-Feet/Day (akf)
	449	Gallons, U.S./Minute (gpm)
	28.3	Liter/Second (l/s)
	0.645	Million Gallons/Day (mgd)
Cubic Meters/Second (m3/sec)	22.8	Million Gallons/Day (mgd)
	15,800	Gallons/Minute (gpm)
	35.3	Cubic Feet/Seconds (cfs)
Gallons, U.S./Minute (gpm)	1,440	Gallons, U.S./Day (gpd)
	1.61	Acre-Feet/Year (af/yr)
Liters/Second (l/s)	15.8	Gallons, U.S./Minute (gpm)
	0.0353	Cubic Feet/Second (cfs)
Million Gallons/Day (mgd)	694	Gallons, U.S./Minute (gpm)
	1.55	Cubic Feet/Second (cfs)
	0.044	Cubic Meters/Second (m3/sec)

Index